CASE OF

THE POISONED
PARTRIDGE

THE
CASE OF
THE POISONED
PARTRIDGE

THE STRANGE DEATH OF LIEUTENANT CHEVIS

DIANE JANES

For Tim.

First published 2013

The History Press
The Mill, Brimscombe Port
Stroud, Gloucestershire, GL5 2QG
www.thehistorypress.co.uk

British Library Cataloguing in Publication Data.
A catalogue record for this book is available from the British Library.

ISBN 978 0 7524 7946 0

Typesetting and origination by The History Press
Printed in Great Britain

CONTENTS

ACKNOWLEDGEMENTS

This book would not have been possible without the generous co-operation of Surrey Police in allowing me access to their files on the case. I am also grateful for access to material at Surrey History Centre, the National Archives, the British Library both at St Pancras and Colindale, Bournemouth Library Local Studies, Eastbourne Library Local Studies, Poole History Centre, the Wellcome Collection, the Royal College of Veterinary Surgeons Library, where staff were particularly helpful and welcoming, and to Sandi at Aldershot Garrison for providing information from their records.

I would like to record my thanks to relatives and descendants of those involved in the case for talking with me, including David Braham, Patricia Beamish, and members of the Keating family, but principally Charles Jackson and Major Bill Chevis, who gave generously of their time and without whom the book would have been the poorer.

This brings me to the 'usual suspects' whose input, interest, enthusiasm and encouragement is beyond price: Jane Conway-Gordon, Matilda Richards, Erica and Peter Woolley, and of course my husband, Bill.

Diane Janes, 2013

CHAPTER ONE

'THE DOG IT WAS THAT DIED'

Oliver Goldsmith, 1766

In common with many of the officers stationed at Blackdown Camp in the 1930s, Lieutenant Elwin Evered and his wife Margaret were in the habit of keeping a pet at their bungalow. When their spaniel bitch came into season on 2 June 1931, Lieutenant Evered put her into kennels at the Farnborough Dogs' Home for three weeks, returning to collect her at noon on Saturday, 20 June. The dog appeared to be in perfect health and was allowed in and out of the bungalow as usual, but later that evening when she failed to return home, the Lieutenant's batman was despatched in search of her. He returned a few minutes later, carrying the dog in his arms. She was in a distressed state, unable to stand, and within fifteen to thirty minutes the unfortunate animal had died.[1]

The Evereds immediately suspected that their pet might have consumed some sort of poison – suspicions which would have been significantly reinforced had they been aware of an unfolding tragedy taking place a matter of a few dozen yards away – for while they mourned their dog, frantic attempts were being made to save the life of Elwin Evered's brother officer and close neighbour, Lieutenant Hugh Chevis, whose agonies lasted rather longer than the spaniel's, although the outcome was the same. At 9.45 the next morning Lieutenant Chevis was pronounced dead at Frimley Cottage Hospital, with the cause of death stated as strychnine poisoning. The police were summoned soon afterwards and so began the investigation into what has become known as 'The Case of the Poisoned Partridge'.

It was not until 1946 that George Orwell penned his famous and oft quoted essay, *The Decline of the English Murder*,[2] in which he wrote of the fascination which murder had once exercised over the British public and the enormous pleasure they took in reading of famous *cause célèbres*. Orwell proposed that the greatest period for these 'classic' murders occurred between 1850 and 1925, but the true connoisseur of 'classic' English murders would probably beg to differ, for it was not until 1931 that perhaps the most intriguing case of all would unfold – the murder of Julia Wallace in Anfield, Liverpool, for which her husband, Herbert Wallace, was arrested, tried, found guilty and then had his conviction overturned on appeal. It was also the year of the Evelyn Foster case, which brought the little

Northumberland village of Otterburn to the forefront of national consciousness for perhaps the first time since a battle had been fought there in 1388. The Foster case (which also remains unsolved) ceased to dominate the headlines within a few weeks of Evelyn's death on 6 January, but the Wallace case would feature in the news over a much longer period, starting with Julia's brutal murder on 19 January, continuing as her husband was arrested at the beginning of February and committal proceedings were heard in the magistrates' court later the same month. The trial itself took place in Liverpool towards the end of April and the case came before the Court of Appeal on 18 May. It is possible that in the wake of this five-month drama, the prospect of another domestic murder mystery failed to excite the public's palate in quite the same way as it might normally have done, or perhaps the appetite for sensational poisoning dramas had diminished after the long running Croydon arsenic saga, which had dominated the headlines for most of 1929, but ended unsatisfactorily (from the public perspective at least) inasmuch that no one had been arrested or charged.[3] It is more likely, however, that the public already had a sensational poisoning case to enjoy in the shape of Annie Hearn, whose trial for the murder of Alice Thomas was in full swing when news of Lieutenant Chevis's death broke. (Mrs Hearn was on trial for poisoning her friend with arsenic, using the unlikely medium of salmon sandwiches as her weapon.) In addition to the distraction provided by Mrs Hearn, several other headline-grabbing murders took place in the summer of 1931, including that of Mrs Annie Kempson in Oxford on 3 August – a brutal attack which sparked a nationwide manhunt and culminated in the apprehension of the killer in Brighton twelve days later.

Whatever the reason, 'The Case of the Poisoned Partridge' – although essentially the third in a hat-trick of classic unsolved cases in 1931 – never quite captured the public imagination in the same way that its Croydon, Liverpool and Otterburn counterparts did. Yet the case had many of the crucial factors which Orwell would go on to identify as 'from a *News of the World* reader's point of view, the "perfect" murder'. According to the premise set out in *The Decline of the English Murder*, the setting should be a domestic one and the main protagonists belong to the respectable middle classes. For preference the means should be poison and if at all possible the motive should involve guilty passions, or the damaging possibility of scandal and divorce. The murder itself should appear to display a high level of detailed planning and the utmost cunning in its execution. Not only did the Chevis case have all of these, but there was another facet which Orwell failed to mention in his list – one which was a virtual prerequisite of the fictional murders which formed an equally significant part of the nation's reading matter at the time – the hint of a mysterious outsider, bent on some kind of terrible revenge. No standard detective novel published during the period now categorised as the Golden Age of crime fiction would have been complete without at least one such character among its circle of suspects – but in spite of possessing all of these promising components, the 'Poisoned Partridge' story was slow to take off and after a brief flurry of excitement it vanished from the national dailies and was all but forgotten, save for the occasional anodyne chapter in one of the true-crime compendiums which appeared from the 1930s onwards.

Since the compilers of each successive murder compendia were apparently content to derive their information from one of their predecessors, unsubstantiated assumptions about the case were repeated, while key facts often went unchecked. The focus of these retellings was invariably a mysterious telegram received on the day of Lieutenant Chevis's funeral, which bore the message 'Hooray Hooray Hooray'. The 'Hooray' telegram and the identity of its untraced author provided such a rich source of speculation, that in several accounts the known participants in the drama are almost overlooked, with Lieutenant and Mrs Chevis dismissed as an ordinary army officer and his wife of six months, happily married, with no obvious enemies – such a commonplace couple – what could there possibly be to say about them? Mrs Chevis (who demonstrably could not have sent the telegram) is accorded such a minor role in events that some accounts do not even bother to provide her first name, still less the information that she was an immensely wealthy woman and (as in all domestic murders) the most obvious suspect. In all but ignoring Lieutenant and Mrs Chevis, however, these authors have done their readers a grave disservice – for Hugh and Frances Chevis were very far from being 'an ordinary couple' and 'The Case of the Poisoned Partridge' is worth far more than a routine regurgitation of half-known facts.

CHAPTER TWO

'ONE OUGHT NOT TO GIVE STRYCHNINE TO A RAT!'

Frances Chevis, 1931

Arsenic has sometimes been called 'The King of Poisons' and while cases of murder by arsenical poisoning have never been commonplace, they occurred with reasonable frequency throughout the Victorian period and well into the twentieth century. One of the supposed attractions of arsenic as a weapon was the possibility that the fatal symptoms might be confused with some naturally occurring gastric illness. Indeed it was the belief of several leading forensic experts, including Sir William Wilcox, that numerous cases of arsenic poisoning were going undetected in the first decades of the twentieth century, and a significant proportion of those tried for murdering their relatives with arsenic only appeared before the courts in the wake of an exhumation – their assumed victim having originally been buried following certification of death by natural cause.

Suspicious deaths by strychnine were far less common – not only was strychnine less abundantly available (by contrast there appears to have been scarcely a patent weedkiller sold in Britain during the 1920s and '30s which did not contain arsenic), but the symptoms of strychnine poisoning were sufficiently distinctive that even doctors who had never previously encountered a case were likely to recognise them.

A strychnine death was a particularly cruel and painful one.[1] Initial symptoms, which generally commenced within fifteen to thirty minutes of ingestion, included increased sensitivity, particularly to light, but also of hearing, taste and smell, together with restlessness, agitation or apprehension. To these unsettling sensations were soon added the commencement of cramps and muscle spasms, followed by violent painful seizures, or convulsions, some so dramatic that the sufferer's entire body stiffened and arched so that only the heels and skull remained touching the bed (a state known as *opisthotonic convulsions*) and drawing the face into a forced smile (*risus sardonicus*). As well as occurring spontaneously, convulsions could be provoked by any external stimuli, such as an alteration in light levels, movement nearby or physical contact. Although death could occur with relative rapidity, the symptoms might equally continue for several hours, until the patient expired of heart or respiratory failure. A particularly dreadful aspect lay in the fact that the patient was likely to remain conscious and in full possession of their mental faculties throughout.

The only condition presenting similar signs was Tetanus, but there were clear distinguishing features between the two, with the onset of symptoms occurring suddenly in a case of strychnine poisoning, but only gradually in a case of Tetanus. In Tetanus, the seizures usually commenced in the jaw (hence the common name 'lock-jaw') and there was some residual stiffness present in the muscles between convulsions, whereas in instances of strychnine poisoning, the symptoms were more likely to start in the legs, and the body became completely relaxed between seizures.

To further discourage any would-be assassin, whereas some debate existed about the ease with which a fatal dose of arsenic could be disguised in a victim's food or drink, and how swiftly thereafter the poison would take effect, strychnine had a strong, bitter taste and its dramatic effects were liable to manifest themselves within a few minutes of the poison being consumed. By way of a final disincentive, even had the symptoms been successfully hidden from public view, any attempt to pass off the death as a normal one was liable to be foiled by post-mortem analysis, which could identify strychnine via a chemical colour test, a physiological test, or just by taste alone, since strychnine's distinctive bitterness remained detectable even in dilutions of 1 in 70,000.

Presented with such a high chance of detection, it is hardly surprising that few people attempted to dispose of their nearest and dearest using this particular agent – but there were occasional exceptions. During the course of the 1930s, both Ethel Major of Kirkby-on-Bain in Lincolnshire and Rose Sandford of West Dereham in Norfolk came before the courts charged with murdering their respective husbands by placing strychnine in their food. (The former was found guilty, the latter acquitted.) A similar case came before the Irish courts in 1926 and resulted in the acquittal of Elizabeth Reilly.[2] All three deaths had occurred in poor rural households, into which strychnine had been introduced to control vermin. In the Sandford case the court accepted that there was no evidence as to how the poison had found its way into Lewis Sandford's system and nothing to suggest that his wife Rose had wished him dead, while in Reilly's the evidence was at best circumstantial and witnesses testified that her late husband had been 'a very peculiar and eccentric man' not thought capable of handling poisons safely. Ethel Major's guilt was supported by a variety of evidence, and underpinned by her own eccentric behaviour and self-incriminating statements. In giving their verdict, the jury made a recommendation to mercy, perhaps prompted by Ethel's obvious inadequacy and low intelligence. A perusal of the case papers leaves the modern reader questioning whether Ethel was entirely sane – though her mental state does not appear to have been called into question at the time.[3]

A similar whiff of insanity hangs over the strychnine-related trial of the Wheeldon family in 1917[4] – though here perhaps it was the blindness of collective fanaticism, rather than mental illness, which led the family into court.

The Wheeldons: mother Alice age fifty-one, daughters Harriett age twenty-seven and Winifred age twenty-three, together with Winifred's husband, Alfred George Mason, age twenty-four, were would-be terrorists, whose plot to poison the Prime Minister and various other senior government figures using strychnine was foiled by a 'secret government agent', known to them as 'Comrade Bert', who infiltrated their 'terrorist cell' by posing as a sympathiser and fellow traveller. During their trial at Derby Guildhall in February and March 1917, the public seems to have been more shocked by Alice Wheeldon's persistent use of bad language and the anti-religious sentiments she expressed, than by any actual threat posed by this middle-aged schoolmarm and her family. (So shocking to general sensibilities was the conduct of Mrs Wheeldon, that Mrs Pankhurst was allowed to make a public statement in court, disassociating herself and the Women's Social and Political Union with statement's made by the professed suffragette, Mrs Wheeldon.) Whether or not the quartet represented a real danger to anyone, the country was at war and a family said to be 'bitterly hostile to this country and [to] shelter fugitives from the army' was unlikely to be viewed with leniency – Alice Wheeldon was sentenced to ten years' penal servitude, Alfred Mason to seven years and his wife Winnie to five – the jury recommending mercy on account of their youth. Harriett Wheeldon was found not guilty.

Apart from this eccentric episode there had also been various instances of strychnine-laced confectionary turning up in the post (although arsenic was generally the preferred substance for such purposes), one of which ended in Annie Davenport facing charges of 'sending poison with intent to anger, grieve and annoy' at Gloucester Assizes in 1925,[5] and the other, in 1920, saw Thomas Liddle, a fifty-nine-year-old farmer from Shipton Thorpe in Yorkshire, accused of sending strychnine-laced chocolates to five witnesses who were due to appear against him in court over a disputed will.[6]

Between the end of the Great War and 1931, however, there had only been one instance of a strychnine murder coming before the British courts: the affair took place in 1924 and involved the death of a married man in Surrey, barely a dozen miles from the barracks where Lieutenant Hugh Chevis would be poisoned not quite seven years later. The victim was Alfred George Jones, the landlord of the Blue Anchor Hotel in Byfleet, a thirty-eight-year-old father of two children who had been married to his wife, Mabel, for nearly twenty years.[7] Evidence given during the trial suggests that the Jones' marriage had not been without its problems. Mabel was an argumentative woman who spent freely and had previously been declared bankrupt, while Alfred may have enjoyed the beverages served in his bar rather more than was good for him. While holidaying without her husband in France, Mabel had begun an affair with a Frenchman called Jean Pierre Vaquier and, when she returned to England, Vaquier followed her, initially continuing their liaison in London, then moving down to the Blue Anchor Hotel at an opportune moment, when Alfred was away in Margate, convalescing from a bout of influenza.

Vaquier, who spoke virtually no English (Mabel similarly had no French), appeared to become part of the household, taking his meals with the Jones' and making no secret of his infatuation with Mabel. Alfred Jones' view of this is unclear, although regular customers assumed that he resented it.

Alfred hosted a party in the hotel on the night of 28 March 1924 and took a dose of 'Health Salts' the following morning, as was his habit after an evening of heavy drinking. After taking the salts, Alfred immediately cried out that they tasted bitter. His wife took a taste and agreed. She administered salt water to make him vomit and openly accused her lover of attempting to murder her husband. In fact the attempt proved successful – Alfred died and Vaquier was arrested.

At his trial in July 1924, Vaquier (who needed an interpreter to understand and participate in the proceedings) could offer little in the way of a defence save increasingly fanciful stories about other members of staff at the hotel and various other people associated with the case, even claiming that he had purchased strychnine from a London chemist (who had identified him) at the behest of one of the solicitors acting for Mrs Jones, who, according to Vaquier, was also numbered among her paramours. The solicitor in question, Bruce Miller, came to court and denied these allegations on oath. Not surprisingly the jury found Vaquier guilty and his appeal was unsuccessful. Mabel Jones denied in court that she had been in love with Vaquier, insisting that she had merely been 'sorry for him'.

If Vaquier too seems at least a tad unbalanced, there still exists a faint chance that it was possible for a wholly rational person to employ strychnine as a murder weapon and get away with it. The majority of strychnine deaths which resulted in a coroner's inquest in the decade or so following the 1914-18 war were self evidently instances of accident or suicide, but a whiff of doubt exists in at least two strychnine-related deaths of married men in a domestic setting.

The cause of Kusel Behr's death in 1926 was a complete mystery until strychnine was identified in his remains at the post-mortem analysis.[8] Originally from Lithuania, Behr was a leading light in a family business concerned with the importation of luxury food items from the Far East, which had branches in London, Berlin, Paris and Hamburg. He had first visited Britain back in 1909, the same year he married his wife, Linda, but the couple only settled permanently in Hampstead in 1923. The marriage was stormy, with evidence of violent quarrels, and in the course of one such episode a few days prior to his death, Kusel Behr had grabbed his wife's throat and bitten her face, which certainly appears to offer a possible motive for her wishing him dead. On 18 March Behr had suffered what with hindsight appeared to be the symptoms of strychnine poisoning, although it was not immediately diagnosed as such. He recovered after a week to ten days in bed, but less than a fortnight after the first attack he suffered a second. Behr recognised the same symptoms of bitterness in his mouth and stiffness in his legs, followed by the onset of agonising spasms which left him screaming in pain. A doctor was summoned, but Behr was already dead by the time he arrived.

This second attack had taken place early in the morning, when the head of the household had apparently consumed nothing more than his usual cup of black tea. The tea had been carried up to him in bed by one of the maids, and tea from the same pot had been drunk by other members of the household without ill effect. However, Behr was also in the habit of dosing himself with various medicines which he obtained while on his frequent travels abroad, some of which were thought to have contained strychnine, and it was not known whether he had taken anything that morning. The inquest was adjourned several times, perhaps to afford the police a better chance of investigating the matter, though the efficiency of their application to the task is surely called into question by the fact that they only discovered the presence of strychnine in a bottle of gin in the sideboard – when they were offered a drink while eating lunch at the Behr household – and noticed that the gin tasted bitter!

The doctor initially called in to treat Kusel Behr, a Dr Jacob Gavronsky, appears to have been equally dilatory in his approach, attributing the symptoms of his patient's first illness to 'an irritation of the nervous system' and initially believing death was due to that 1920s medical catch-all 'influenza'. The coroner's jury decided that death was due to 'strychnine administered by person or persons unknown' – and there the matter rested.

Perhaps more astonishing was officialdom's take on the death of Sir Alfred Newton, who expired in June 1921 after taking a dose of his usual indigestion mixture, which was found to be laced with strychnine.[9] The mixture was prepared by no less an establishment than Harrods Dispensary and they proved to the court's satisfaction that there was no possibility of contamination up to the point when the bottle left their premises. The coroner summed up the affair as 'a strange case. As to how the strychnine got in the bottle, all the evidence called would not help answer that question. The bottle had passed through many hands before it came into the hands of Sir Alfred. Was it an accident? It probably was...' It is not easy to guess how a lethal substance such as strychnine can accidentally find its way into a gentleman's indigestion mixture without anyone noticing and raising the alarm before he drinks it, but the inquest jury followed the coroner's lead and their verdict stated that death was '...due to syncope, due to fatty degeneration of the heart, accelerated by strychnine poisoning. There was no evidence to show how the poison came to be in the bottle of medicine, some of which was swallowed.' A verdict which seems consciously obscure and long winded, presumably to avoid the point that whatever the state of Sir Alfred's general health, his death was the direct result of ingesting strychnine, which had been introduced into his medicine by either his own hand or the hand of another. The grieving widow was said to be too unwell to attend – a situation which would be repeated at the initial inquest into the death of Hugh Chevis.

CHAPTER THREE

'HE ORDERED THAT THE PARTRIDGE BE BURNED'

Nicholas Bolger, 1931

On Saturday, 20 June 1931, Hugh and Frances Chevis sat down to dinner at 7.30 in the evening.[1] All witnesses appear to agree on this point, though their accounts of subsequent events are at variance. The couple dined alone, although earlier in the evening they had entertained friends to cocktails. Their guests were Captain Philip Randolph Bowser and his wife, who had arrived at around 6.20 that evening and stayed for about an hour. In a statement made later, Captain Bowser, a thirty-four-year-old then serving in the Royal Artillery, told the police that when they arrived at the bungalow (by prior invitation) Lieutenant Chevis was in the sitting room and Mrs Chevis in the garden. The couple had both appeared perfectly normal, in no way worried or depressed, and the visit had passed off pleasantly. According to Captain Bowser, his host was away for part of the time, as he had to mount guard at the barracks, and although the others had cocktails immediately, Bowser recalled that Lieutenant Chevis had abstained until he returned from duty.[2]

Very soon after the Bowsers departed, the Chevises sat down to dinner, (they were eating slightly earlier than usual as they planned to attend a Military Tattoo later in the evening). The meal was served by Lieutenant Chevis's batman, Nicholas Bolger, and had been cooked and prepared by Mrs Ellen Yeomans, the only other servant at the bungalow. The first course was slip soles with anchovy sauce and when this had been eaten and cleared away, Bolger brought in the main dish: a pair of partridges, presented with new potatoes, peas, bread sauce and gravy. Mrs Chevis served a partridge onto each plate, after which she and her husband helped themselves to vegetables and sauce from the accompanying dishes, and they began to eat.

It was at this point that things began to go awry. After eating some of his bird, Hugh Chevis complained that it 'tasted horrible'. According to Frances, he asked her to taste a piece of his bird in order to ascertain whether there was something wrong with it, and he passed a small portion onto her plate. She tasted it and 'found it filthy. It seemed to burn.' Having confirmed that there was a problem with the partridge, Hugh Chevis rang the bell which summoned Bolger and ordered the batman to take the bird away and see that it was burned, so that the family dog (an Alsatian) would not get hold of it.

From this point both events and their timings become a little less clear. There is no doubt that Hugh Chevis instructed that the bird be burned. Bolger has him saying, 'Remove this bird, it's the most awful thing I have ever tasted. Have it destroyed. Don't even let the dog get it.' It is also undisputed that at some point Frances Chevis instructed Bolger to bring in some cheese and salad by way of an alternative, and it seems reasonable to assume that this instruction was issued when the Lieutenant's partridge was removed.

Bolger returned to the kitchen with the offending item and relayed these instructions to Ellen Yeomans, who obediently scraped the entire contents of Lieutenant Chevis's plate into the kitchen furnace, and set about preparing the cheese and salad. Meanwhile in the dining room, according to Frances's recollections at the inquest, the diners attempted to eat some vegetables but were unable to do so – neither of them ate any more of the meat, as even if the taste of her husband's partridge had not been enough to put her off, Frances had by now decided that her bird also tasted 'musty'. Hugh Chevis poured out a glass of sherry for each of them, which they drank in an endeavour to take the taste away, but it persisted even after they had both taken a second glass.

The amount of partridge actually consumed by anyone that evening is another source of dispute. According to Frances, neither she nor Hugh had more than a couple of mouthfuls each of their respective birds, whereas Bolger says that when he collected the second partridge from the table 'the bird was practically eaten, practically all the flesh off it...', while 'a good portion of the breast [had been] eaten off Mr Chevis's bird.' Ellen Yeomans recalled that 'a fair bit' of Mrs Chevis's bird had been eaten, although 'there was still plenty of meat left on it' and noted that 'only portions of the breast' had gone from Hugh's. Whatever amount of meat remained on the second partridge (about which there had been no complaint to the servants) when Bolger brought it into the kitchen it followed the first into the furnace. Mrs Yeomans subsequently agreed that no one had instructed her to burn it, but told the police that she often disposed of bones and carcasses in this way – a point confirmed by Bolger.[3]

The amount of cheese and salad consumed is similarly unclear. Bolger states that he delivered this to the dining room 'and they finished their meal', which tends to imply that some more food was eaten. Mrs Yeomans does not seem to have been questioned on the point. Frances said that she managed a little cheese, while her husband only ate some radishes (presumably hoping that their strong flavour would allay the bitter taste still lingering in his mouth). Certainly no subsequent interest was taken in the substitute dish by any of those investigating the case, and the constituents of the salad are not recorded anywhere.

After this, according to Bolger, both Lieutenant and Mrs Chevis went into the drawing room, where he served their coffee and left them, while he cleared away in the dining room, but, according to Frances, while her husband went into the drawing room she went into the bedroom to telephone her London flat and enquire after her children, who were there with their nurse. On her return to the drawing room, Hugh told her that he felt very unwell, saying that his legs hurt and he could not use them. It is evident that Frances had become somewhat confused about the order of events by the time she was questioned. In her original statement to the police – which was not made until ten days after her husband's death – Frances claimed that after making her phone call she met Bolger bringing the coffee, took it from him and carried it into the drawing room herself, but at the resumed inquest in August, she testified that Bolger brought the coffee in himself, shortly after she had returned to the drawing room, where Hugh had already told her that he was feeling unwell. She said that she drank her coffee, but her husband was unable to take any, and immediately after she had finished, her husband suffered 'some sort of spasm', after which she then telephoned for a doctor – a call she estimated to have taken place at 8 p.m.

There is something distinctly odd about this account and a dispassionate observer cannot help wondering whether a loving wife would sit casually sipping coffee after her husband informed her that he felt unwell and could not use his legs. Bolger's order of events, given in a statement to the police the next day, is somewhat different and certainly appears more logical. According to the batman, he served coffee in the drawing room and then returned to the dining room to clear away while they were drinking it. He had just about finished and was putting away the last of the silver when Mrs Chevis came into the dining room and said: 'Don't go away, Bolger, Mr Chevis has been taken suddenly ill and I may want you.' (Bolger did not live in at the bungalow and would normally have left for home after finishing his evening duties in the dining room.)

Bolger went immediately to the kitchen to acquaint Mrs Yeomans with the situation, but moments later he was summoned to the drawing room, where he found Hugh Chevis in dreadful pain. He stayed with the sick man while Frances telephoned for the doctor. In a much later statement at the August inquest, rather than being summoned to the drawing room by Frances, Bolger said he had just gone into the kitchen to relay the news of the sudden illness to Mrs Yeomans when he heard Lieutenant Chevis shout 'as though in great pain', and he and Mrs Chevis (who had apparently followed him into the kitchen) rushed back to the drawing room and found Hugh Chevis in agony there. In fact it is obvious when piecing together the various statements of Bolger, Frances Chevis and Mrs Yeomans, that during those first moments when Hugh Chevis suffered an initial spasm, there was an entirely understandable degree of confusion and anxiety: Frances is clear that she asked for Bolger's assistance at some point prior to calling the doctor, though the location of this conversation is uncertain; Ellen Yeomans states that she 'heard a noise' (Hugh Chevis crying out) which was immediately followed by Bolger entering the kitchen and summoning her to assist in the drawing room, as 'Mr Chevis is taken ill'; while

Bolger originally said that he went to the drawing room when called in by Mrs Chevis, but later said he went of his own accord after hearing Hugh Chevis cry out. This slight divergence of accounts and confusion about precisely what happened is only to be expected in the face of the distressing events which followed. There was universal agreement on one point at least – that it was Mrs Chevis who immediately telephoned the doctor.

Frances stated that she made the call at about 8 o'clock and that Dr Bindloss arrived within fifteen to twenty minutes. Dr Bindloss himself agreed with this, saying that he was called at 8 p.m. and arrived at the bungalow at 8.15 p.m. In his original statement to the police, Bolger's account differed slightly. He estimated that the call had been made after 8.15, which was the time he estimated that Mrs Chevis had come into the dining room, requesting him not to leave as her husband had been taken ill.

At this point it is worth recapping on the events of the evening. Not only did all three surviving occupants of the house agree that Lieutenant and Mrs Chevis sat down to dinner at 7.30, but this is also what Hugh Chevis told Dr Bindloss, who naturally asked for a full account of what his patient had eaten and when he had eaten it, when he attended that evening. In the version of events obtained from Hugh Chevis and relayed on via Dr Bindloss, the soles were served at 7.30 and the partridges brought in seven or eight minutes later. The stricken man claimed that within ten to fifteen minutes of tasting his bird, he felt ill and had a shivering attack. At face value this would appear to fit with the doctor being summoned at 8 o'clock, but when set against the evidence provided by the servants and applying practical considerations as to how long various things would be likely to take, these timings are almost certainly wrong.

Bolger stated that he served the slip soles at 7.35 and the partridge at around 7.45: recollections supported by Mrs Yeomans, who said she 'gave the birds forty-five minutes', timing them to be served at 7.45. This has a ring of accuracy about it. According to Ellen Yeomans, partridge was a regular dish at the bungalow, served on a weekly basis, so common sense suggests that she would have had a routine for cooking it, in which timing the main course to be ready about fifteen minutes after the commencement of the meal would make perfect sense. From the arrival of the main course we need to allow at least a couple of minutes for food to be transferred from serving dishes to plates and then tasted, for Hugh and Frances to agree that the bird tasted off and the bell then rung for Bolger. Bolger had then to return to the dining room and remove the suspect partridge, before Mrs Yeomans could possibly receive any instructions to replace the offending dish with some cheese and salad.

In the context of 1930s British cuisine, it is unlikely that the salad consisted of anything much more complicated than lettuce, tomatoes, radishes and cucumber, and since the Chevis's had lunched at home on cold lamb and salad that day,[4] it is possible that Mrs Yeomans had to do nothing more than fetch a dish of leftover salad from the pantry. Even so, minutes must have been ticking by and it is difficult to believe that the cheese and salad could have arrived on the table much before 7.50 at the very earliest. (Additional support for a longer delay lies in the account provided by Frances, in which she and Hugh found time to consume two glasses of sherry apiece between the departure of the partridge and arrival of the salad.)

An attempt was then made to eat the salad, before someone presumably rang the bell, alerting Bolger of the need to clear the table and serve coffee in the drawing room. By now it is reasonable to assume that a few more minutes had passed, placing Bolger's arrival in the drawing room with the coffee no earlier than 7.55, but probably somewhat later. The fact that Bolger had time to have 'almost finished' clearing up, before Mrs Chevis came to tell him that her husband was unwell adds further delay. While it is just about possible to accept that all these events had been compressed into a mere thirty minutes, it does not seem altogether likely, and if Dr Bindloss really was summoned at 8 p.m., rather than 8.15, it is particularly difficult to see when Frances could have fitted in a telephone call to the children's nurse in London – a point which seems to have escaped the investigating team entirely, since very little significance appears to have been attached to the timing of this call during the original inquiry.

The arrival of Dr Bindloss provides us with a new witness on the scene. When he reached the bungalow the doctor found his patient reclining on a couch in the drawing room, in a stiff, unnatural position, with his body fully extended and his heels touching the floor. The lieutenant was bathed in perspiration but otherwise seemed 'quite natural and cheerful' according to Bindloss. At this stage Hugh Chevis was evidently experiencing a lull in the seizures and in response to the doctor's enquiries, he gave a full account of the recent meal, saying that his partridge had tasted 'horribly bitter and sour, like quinine' and explaining that he had asked his wife to taste a portion of his bird, and she had also found it nauseating. When Bindloss – who initially suspected food poisoning – said the remains of the bird should be preserved for analysis, Hugh at once said that he had ordered it to be destroyed, so that the dog did not get any of it. The doctor claimed that he administered an injection and then sat conversing with the patient 'in an ordinary way on several subjects' until about 8.40, when Hugh had a sudden violent convulsion. Realising that he was confronted with something much more serious than had first appeared, Dr Bindloss telephoned his colleague Dr Murray, asking him to attend immediately with some chloroform. While they were awaiting the arrival of Dr Murray, Frances too began to suffer from convulsions.

Frances's own witness statements add some further detail, inasmuch that she recalled Dr Bindloss had also administered brandy (spirits were much favoured as a restorative when GPs had relatively few of the tools in their medical arsenal which would nowadays be taken for granted). As this had used the last of the brandy, Frances went to the kitchen and despatched Bolger for a replacement bottle. On her return she found her husband in the throes of another convulsion and went to help the doctor, only to find that her own legs were failing her. Frances places her first convulsion prior to Bindloss's telephone call for reinforcements, but again the seriousness of the situation and the speed at which events were unfolding may have created genuine confusion as to the exact order in which events occurred.

Bolger's statements make no mention of the bottle of brandy, but he does state that Frances informed him within about fifteen minutes of Dr Bindloss's arrival that Lieutenant Chevis was suffering from strychnine poisoning. Like Dr Bindloss, he also contends that Frances was not taken ill until after a second doctor had been summoned. Again Bolger's timing of events is out of step with those estimated by Bindloss – whereas Bindloss believes he placed his call to Murray shortly after 8.40 and has Murray arriving around twenty minutes later, Bolger reckons that Bindloss did not arrive himself until about 8.30, and that Mrs Chevis was not taken ill until around 9.30, by which time Dr Murray had been called, but had yet to arrive. (Dr Murray, who might have been considered a useful person to clarify these timings, was apparently never interviewed by the police and not required to attend the inquest.)

Ellen Yeomans offers nothing with regard to what time the various doctors were summoned and arrived, but did state that Mrs Chevis stayed in the drawing room with her husband practically the whole time after he was taken ill, though she thought Frances had entered the kitchen twice after the arrival of Dr Bindloss; once to check whether the partridges had indeed been burned, and once to fetch the fish paste which had been used in the sandwiches at tea time (in cases of food poisoning, fish paste was invariably one of the first commodities to come under suspicion). When specifically questioned on the point, Mrs Yeomans denied that Mrs Chevis had told her what was wrong with her husband, or mentioned strychnine poisoning during the course of the evening.

Dr Murray appears to have brought a new dynamic to the case, administering emetics to both patients which made them vomit. He had also brought chloroform with which to sedate them. At some point either Murray or Bindloss decided to call on the services of a third practitioner, Dr Cuthbert Hastings Attenborough, who arrived at 9.45 according to Dr Bindloss, at 10 o'clock according to Dr Attenborough and, by inference, at somewhat after 10 o'clock according to Nicholas Bolger.

By the time Attenborough arrived, both patients were exhibiting symptoms of strychnine poisoning, though Mrs Chevis to a lesser extent, while Hugh Chevis was having tonic convulsions.[5] It was now decided to convey both patients to the cottage hospital at Frimley; Lieutenant Chevis travelled in Dr Attenborough's car and Mrs Chevis in Dr Bindloss's, with Dr Murray continuing to administer chloroform to her throughout the journey. Frances described the scene in a statement to the police: 'The pains were ghastly. I screamed, I remember, starting for the hospital, and I remember before leaving "The Hut"[6] asking for some chloroform to stop me making such a ghastly row and not to disturb my husband.' Frances could not remember being carried from the car into the hospital and did not come round again until sometime during the night.

This removal to hospital took place some time after 10.30 – none of the doctors puts a specific time on it, but Nicholas Bolger told the police that he left the house at 10.30 in order to reassure his wife, who would be waiting at their home in Lightwater, wondering what was keeping him so late. When he set off for Lightwater the doctors were still at the house, but on his return at 11.40 he found the place deserted except for Ellen Yeomans. The servants dutifully stayed on until 4 a.m. in the morning, when, having received no further instructions or intimation as to what was going on, they both went home.

To the modern reader it may appear strange that no one had suggested taking the patients to hospital earlier, but this was still a period when the majority of conditions were treated at home. The Frimley District Cottage Hospital had been open since 1909[7] but it was a modest establishment, originally intended to bring skilled medical treatment and nursing care to the rural poor, rather than the upper and middle classes who could afford to pay for private nurses to attend on them in their own comfortable homes and would book into a private nursing home for any surgical procedure, confinement or major period of convalescence. Patients such as Lieutenant and Mrs Chevis were unlikely to be admitted to a local cottage hospital unless they required some sort of emergency surgical procedure for which equipment would not be available at home.

In fact both patients were rushed into the Frimley Cottage Hospital's single operating theatre and placed on tables side by side, where they were anaesthetised before having their stomachs washed out. After this procedure each of them was put to bed in one of the wards. By this time Mrs Chevis's condition was improving, but her husband's convulsions continued to be violent. At fifteen minutes past midnight he stopped breathing, but the team of doctors (by now increased to five) refused to give up and continued with artificial respiration for a further nine and a half hours, until 9.45 in the morning, when his heart ceased and he was declared dead.

It was only now that it appears to have occurred to anyone to involve the Surrey Police. Inspector Albert Pharo was informed of the suspicious death at around 10 o'clock on the morning of 21 June and he reached the hospital at 10.30, ascertaining some details from one of the doctors before supervising the removal of Lieutenant Chevis's body to the mortuary. After this he went to Aisne Bungalows at the Deepcut Barracks, erstwhile home of the deceased officer, and interviewed Mrs Yeomans and the batman, Bolger, who had both turned up for work as usual at D Hut. He was unable to interview the deceased's widow, however – for prior to his arrival at the hospital Frances Chevis had been transported away in a private ambulance, accompanied by her own general practitioner,

Dr Gibson, and her own nurse, Miss Ivy Thorne, the same woman with whom she had spoken on the phone the previous evening. It was Miss Thorne who had subsequently arranged a night nurse to remain with the children, the attendance of Dr Gibson and the private ambulance, which ensured the immediate removal of Mrs Chevis back to her London flat in Basil Mansions, Knightsbridge.[8]

CHAPTER FOUR

THE PRODUCT OF
AN ALLIANCE

Though some authors appear to have regarded Frances Chevis as no more than a minor character in the 'Poison Partridge' drama, in reality she had a rich enough life to inspire half a dozen novels. Heiress, tragic widow, glamorous divorcee, gorgeous socialite, Frances Howard Rollason, (who would go on to become Mrs Jackson, Mrs Chevis, Mrs Braham, Mrs Bickett and finally Mrs Rayson) not only had a life straight out of a Hollywood movie, but included movie stars among her numerous acquaintance.[1]

Frances was the product of an alliance between two industrial dynasties – the Howards of Bedford and the Rollasons of Birmingham. Her mother's family, the Howards, had in the course of just over half a century transformed themselves from modest beginnings into one of Bedford's premier families, listed in such august publications as *Walford's County Families of the United Kingdom*, their comings and goings of interest to the local newspapers, and their numbers deemed suitable to serve the area not only as Lord Mayors, but also on the wider political stage at Westminster.[2]

Frances's great-grandfather, John Howard, originally opened a small business manufacturing agricultural implements in Bedford High Street in 1813. The enterprise prospered, particularly after his son James joined the business in around 1837 and indeed by 1839 James had taken overall charge of production, leaving his father to concentrate on the commercial side of the business. Howard & Son developed and pioneered new types of plough, leading to a rapid expansion in their trade, so that by 1850 only two other firms in the country (Ransome & May, and Richard Hornsby & Son) could match them in production or sales. The second half of the 1850s saw the construction of the firm's new premises, the 16-acre Brittania Works, which dominated the town and became its largest employer (by 1881 the firm was employing in excess of 650 men and boys). By now John Howard had long since retired and James had taken his younger brother Frederick into partnership. Together the brothers continued to steadily expand their interests, not only dominating the market at home, but also exporting vast quantities of agricultural implements and machinery to Europe, India, Africa and Australia.

As befitted increasingly affluent industrialists, the family had also begun to play a larger role in civic life. James became Lord Mayor of Bedford in 1863 and was elected to parliament as the town's MP in 1868 and again in 1880. In 1872, he commissioned a country house for himself, Clapham Park – a far cry from the premises which he and the rest of the family had shared with a couple of apprentices a mere twenty years earlier. When James Howard died in 1889, his brother Frederick was left in charge of the business, which continued to go from strength to strength. Frederick received a knighthood in 1895, and like brother James enjoyed an active socio-political life. In addition to all this, following his marriage to Elizabeth Street in 1851, Frederick had found time to sire a large family: one son and seven daughters, the penultimate child being Kate Alexandra Howard, born in 1863, who would eventually become Frances's mother.

Frances's father, Frank Rollason, emanated from a very similar background, for the Rollasons were also a wealthy industrial dynasty whose fortunes extended back no more than two generations.[3] Frank's grandfather, Abel Rollason, was born towards the end of the eighteenth century in Birmingham and went into business as a metal roller – a promising trade for an opportunistic businessman, since Birmingham, the fastest growing British city in the nineteenth century,[4] was evolving into a centre which specialised in metal-based industries. Abel based his business in the area north-east of the city centre, where both industrial and suburban development was pressing out towards Sutton Coldfield, taking the lease on Bromford Mill Forge, which would continue to be the main works for Abel Rollason & Sons for several decades.[5] His growing family followed him into the enterprise (which later expanded to encompass other metal-related industry, including wire drawing) and like the Howards, as the family's wealth and status grew, they increasingly took a place on the civic stage, with Abel's son, Thomas, becoming Lord Mayor of West Bromwich, and a grandson, James, rising to be High Sherriff of Warwickshire in 1920.

Frank Rollason grew up within less than a mile of these industrial operations, in a house called Alton Lodge on Gravelly Hill, with his father (another Abel), mother and two older brothers. (Gravelly Hill is now synonymous with the motorway interchange known as Spaghetti Junction, but in the nineteenth century it was noted for the mini-mansions of *nouveau-riche* employers, many of which sat in generous gardens and grounds.)

In 1895, Frank's older brother, James Rollason, married Grace Evelyn Howard, the youngest daughter of Sir Frederick Howard. It is no longer possible to establish how the Rollason family came into the orbit of the Howards. They lived in completely different parts of the country and there are no obvious social or direct political links, so it may have been business interests which first drew them together. James Rollason and his bride set up home at Walmley House, near the then rural village of the same name and it would be romantic to surmise that James's brother, Frank, met and fell in love with his future wife,

Kate Howard, when she came to visit her sister there, but family legend tells a very different story.[6]

It is said that Kate Howard had once been in love with a young man in Bedford, but he was considered unsuitable by her parents and she was forbidden to marry him. Still a spinster at thirty-eight, Kate was instructed by her parents to marry Frank Rollason, the thirty-seven-year-old bachelor brother-in-law of her younger sister Grace; a dynastic marriage of convenience to a man she did not love and who did not particularly care for her either.

When the census was taken on 31 March 1901, Kate Howard was still living in Bedford: the only 'child' still left at home with her seventy-three-year-old father and seventy-seven-year-old mother (there were also six live-in servants) and Frank Rollason was domiciled in his home on Gravelly Hill, complete with a cook and a housemaid. Within a matter of weeks they were married and very soon afterwards Kate became pregnant – a situation she did not relish in an age when a first pregnancy at twenty-nine was considered somewhat risky and a pregnancy at thirty-nine positively dangerous.

In the event both mother and baby came through the ordeal safely. Frances Howard Rollason was born at Alton Lodge, Gravelly Hill, Birmingham on 10 March 1902. It was probably assumed (by Frank at least) that there would be other children in the years which followed. The child's name was clearly chosen with dynastic thoughts to the fore – the feminine derivative of her father's name, coupled with Howard. (The inclusion of the name Howard had become such an obsession within the Howard family that Kate's brother was named John Howard Howard.)

The sense of Frank and Kate's union being arranged and overseen by her family is underlined by the making of Frank's will. The document was drawn up on 25 May 1901, when the couple had been married for less than a month and was witnessed by Kate's brother, John Howard Howard, and William George Lovell, who was married to her sister, Mary. Both men lived in Bedford, implying that the will had been drawn up there, under the watchful eye of the Howard clan, rather than dealt with by a Birmingham solicitor, as might have been expected since this was where Frank normally lived and conducted his business, and where the newlyweds intended to make their home in the future. The trustees appointed under the terms of the will were also evidently chosen on the basis of blood and matrimonial ties. Frank named three trustees: his brother James (who was of course married to Kate's sister, Grace), his 'friend' Thomas Howard Rylands – who as his name suggests was yet another member of the Howard dynasty, the son of Kate's much older sister Agnes, and finally his bride, Kate herself, although Frank's view of the abilities of the fairer sex are betrayed by the clause requiring that there should always be two male trustees – in the event of one male trustee dying, he was to be replaced with another man.

Frank's will, although straightforward in its provisions, was a lengthy document, carefully worded and allowing for the assumed long life of the testator. It provided not only for any theoretical child or children, but also for any grandchildren born during his lifetime. It is unlikely that the prospect of Frank's imminent death crossed the mind of anyone who discussed the contents, or appended their signatures on 25 May 1901, that the document would come into operation before a year had passed.

On 16 April 1902, Frank began to complain of what transpired to be appendicitis. An operation on 19 April was unsuccessful and he died three days later. Death was registered by James Rollason (who had been at his brother's bedside) and together with his fellow trustees, he swiftly set about carrying out his duties under the terms of Frank's will, obtaining probate on 24 May 1902, just one day short of the anniversary of its signing. Kate Rollason was well provided for, receiving all the household effects and an immediate legacy amounting to around £6,000, plus a guaranteed income of £2,000 a year, topped up by an escalating sum, starting at £300 a year for the maintenance of her daughter.

The lion's share of Frank's wealth, however, was to be held in trust for his offspring. Frank Rollason's net estate amounted to £198,336 15s 5d. Calculating the true value of 'historical' money is fraught with difficulties. There are at least five different recognised methods,[7] which provide widely differing results. It has been suggested that the best indicator is a comparison with average incomes, and the fact that a domestic servant or labourer earned less than £50 per annum in 1902, while even the managing director of the Midland Bank, Sir Edward Holden (one of the highest salaried men in the country), received only £5,000 a year puts Frank's bequest into perspective. At the most conservative estimate, the six-week-old baby in the nursery at Alton Lodge had become heiress to a fortune which would today be worth at least £16 million.[8]

Under the terms of Frank Rollason's will, Frances would not inherit until she either attained the age of twenty-five or was married. In the meantime, Frank had left his widow and child financially well provided for – it was a childhood which probably lacked for nothing – except love. If the stories which have come down the generations are to be believed, Frances did not enjoy a close relationship with her mother, or a particularly happy childhood. Kate Rollason is recalled as a cold, distant woman, whose residual bitterness from an arranged marriage spilled over into her relationship (or lack of one) with her daughter.[9] One member of the family remarked that 'ice ran through her veins'. Children were to be seen and not heard, Sundays were strictly observed, with no toys allowed and the garden swing immobilised. Frances was left almost entirely in the charge of a succession of maids and nursery governesses.

Initially Kate and Frances continued to live in Birmingham, first at Alton Lodge and then at a house called Redcroft on Chester Road, which had twenty rooms, not including such offices as the scullery, pantry etc., but as Kate approached her sixtieth birthday she decided the time had come to retire to the south coast and by 1918 she and her daughter were installed in another Redcroft – this time in Gaudick Road, Eastbourne.

By now Frances was growing into a beautiful young woman, the absolute antithesis of her mother – lively and outgoing, remembered as someone who 'lit up a room' even in her later years, when she remained 'sparkling and vivacious', 'glamorous', and a woman 'with a very quick brain… and a devastating repartee'. It is difficult to establish what kind of social life Frances enjoyed as she approached her twenty-first birthday. Family connections alone should have guaranteed invitations to country house weekends and London parties, if Kate permitted it. By 1922 her uncle, James Rollason, had moved out to Hampton Manor in Warwickshire, obtained a coat or arms and served a term as High Sherriff of the county. His children, Melvyn, Neville and Mildred, were much of an age with Frances. The Ryland family (Thomas Howard Ryland, Frances's cousin, had been appointed one of her trustees in her father's will) was similarly well connected. Another cousin, Douglas Frederick Howard, after distinguished service in the Great War, was carving out a prestigious career in the Diplomatic Service. It was the kind of background which could have fostered multiple social opportunities and numerous introductions to eligible young men, inevitably followed by the kind of glamorous wedding which appeared in the society pages – but when Frances married for the first time on 19 November 1923, the event took place in a London Register Office, with little attendant publicity, and the groom, far from being an eligible young bachelor, was a divorced veterinary surgeon, who was old enough to have been her father.

CHAPTER FIVE

A SPORTING MAN

Of all those directly involved in the 'Poison Partridge Mystery', the character of George Thompson Trevelyan Jackson is among the hardest to fathom. In some ways his background mirrored that of the Howards and the Rollasons, albeit on a much smaller scale, for the Jackson family too had grown wealthy in trade – if not to the degree of the aforementioned dynasties, at least sufficiently to elevate their standing and expectations.

George Thompson Jackson (the Trevelyan came later) was born on 2 May 1877 at 4 Elizabeth Street, Horton near Bradford.[1] His father, Frederick Jackson, registered the birth, giving his occupation as a commercial traveller. George was the youngest of eight children and at the time of his birth the family fortunes appear to have been modest, but father Frederick was clearly something of an entrepreneur, because before too long the family was not only inhabiting a larger house in Grove Terrace, but had also acquired a four storey seaside residence in Bold Street, Poulton Barre – which would become better known to the world as Morecambe – one of the North of England's premier Victorian resorts, particularly popular with residents of the West Riding of Yorkshire, thanks to the direct rail link which opened in 1850.

Morecambe was an exciting place to be in the final decades of the nineteenth century.[2] The first of its piers opened in 1869 and the long promenade, just yards from the Jacksons's doorstep, became a place to stroll and be seen, bustling with open carriages, horse-drawn trams and charabancs. Trippers could enjoy the views across the bay to the Lake District hills, or watch the numerous sailboats and steamers, some carrying trippers from further down the coast. There were public gardens to stroll in (everyone naturally wearing their best clothes) and multiple amusements and entertainments to be had for those who could afford them.

It is possible that George Jackson was a sickly child, for whom sea air was deemed beneficial, for the 1881 census finds him lodging in the house at Morecambe with only his older sister, Maria, and a female servant for company, while the rest of the family were at their Horton residence – or perhaps this was merely a coincidental disposition of various members of the family which happened to occur on census night. Whatever the case, it is likely that these early experiences of Morecambe fostered a desire to live near the coast, because George Jackson gravitated towards seaside towns until the end of his life.

George's father Frederick appears to have been a self-made man. The son of Jonathan Jackson, a carrier's clerk, Frederick became a commercial traveller in provisions and eventually set up in business on his own account, so that by 1891 he was able to describe himself as a provision merchant. In due course his eldest sons, Frederick and John, followed him into the family concern, but as is often the case in an upwardly mobile family, it was the younger children who saw the greatest benefits from an improvement in family fortunes. Whereas his brother John had been apprenticed to a draper at the age of fourteen, George, who was a full ten years younger, had the opportunity of staying on at school and then studying at university.

George chose to read Veterinary Medicine in London.[3] This was a particularly expensive option as the veterinary course lasted for four years rather than three – always assuming that a student passed his examinations at a first attempt and did not have to repeat any years. George appears to have been a good student. He passed his first year exams in 1896, his second in 1897 and was awarded 2nd class honours (the only student to be distinguished with any honours at those exams) in 1898. In December 1899, George Thompson Jackson is one of the fifteen students recorded as passing their final exams and being admitted as members of the Royal College of Veterinary Surgeons.

Frederick Jackson had died in January 1896, just a few months after the commencement of George's university career, but he had left an estate worth in excess of £17,000 (at minimum estimates the equivalent of well over £1m today), so there would have been no problem paying George's tuition expenses out of his portion. As George was still a minor in 1896, his share of the money (which, after annuities had been provided for Frederick's widow, a niece, and one of the servants, had to be split equally between all his children) would have been held on trust by his older brothers, Frederick and John, until he came of age in 1898, following which he evidently invested at least some of it, as he continued to enjoy a private income to the end of his life.

After qualifying as a vet George Jackson did not return to Bradford (although this was initially listed as his home address in the Register of Veterinary Surgeons). War had broken out in October 1899 and on completing his training, George immediately volunteered to serve as a civilian veterinary surgeon with the British Army in South Africa. He was engaged in December and sailed out of the Royal Albert Docks aboard the SS *Andrew* on 25 January, with the 13th Brigade Royal Field Artillery.

The importance of qualified vets to an army in which the horse and the oxen were still the main means of transport cannot be overstated. In spite of attracting an influx of civilian volunteers at the outbreak of the war, articles in *The Veterinary Record* during 1900 continued to bemoan the fact that the Army

Veterinary Corps remained desperately short staffed, while the Army itself suffered huge losses among its livestock due to the lack of vets available to treat sick and wounded animals.

The life of the army vet was tough. In August 1900, one serving vet, H.C. Welsh, described how he had to examine every horse before it left for duty, then deal with the horses which arrived back from the front lines by the trainload for treatment. He calculated that he had examined or treated in excess of 6,000 horses in the space of two months.[4] Some of the vets were shocked at the way the troopers treated their animals and found themselves fighting an internal war within the army against cruelty and neglect. Even without this source of potential friction, their relationship with serving soldiers was not an easy one. Those vets who were officers in the Army Veterinary Corps (AVC) had their rank prefixed with the word Veterinary, which implied to some fighting men that they were not proper soldiers, and therefore enjoyed a lesser degree of authority, while the position of civilian vets like George Jackson was even more invidious, and many of them had great difficulty in exercising their authority over the men with whom they had to deal and sometimes command. Yet while the vets were not 'proper soldiers', they nonetheless suffered the same privations as their comrades who took up arms. By the spring and summer of 1900, a growing number of veterinary surgeons were being invalided home – some sick and some wounded. Illnesses, food shortages and unsanitary conditions took their toll on combatants and non-combatants alike. During 1900, *The Veterinary Record* includes accounts of army vets being taken prisoner by the Boers, shot at and even shipwrecked en route to the theatre of war.

Partly in order to mitigate the anomalous position in which the civilian vets found themselves and partly in order to strengthen the numbers of qualified men in the AVC, it was decided in 1901 to offer commissions to a number of civilian vets serving with the army in South Africa, and one of those recommended was George Jackson, who became a Lieutenant in His Majesty's armed forces in November 1901. It is unlikely that George had originally contemplated a military career, but from the age of twenty-four he acquired a military rank and his rank and association with the army stayed with him to the end of his life. In 1903, the army dropped the 'Veterinary' prefix for officers in the AVC and thus George Jackson became in due course plain Captain Jackson and later Major Jackson, the title by which he was known when he met Frances Rollason.

Well before achieving a military rank, he had already acquired a third initial. In what circumstances George Thompson Jackson came to be called in addition 'Trevelyan' is unknown – and somewhat confusingly the Register of Veterinary Surgeons originally lists him not as G.T.T. Jackson, but as G.T.C. Jackson – a state of affairs which persisted until well into the First World War, when the entry was finally corrected to G.T.T. Jackson. It may be that the young man simply did not like the names George or Thompson, and on the death of the parents who had chosen them, elected to be known instead as Trevelyan – shortened to Trev – which was how he was known to family and friends in later life, and how he signed himself in correspondence. Conversely, perhaps 'Trevelyan' had been with him since childhood and he had eventually incorporated it into his name to regularise matters and avoid confusion. Whatever the truth of the matter, George Thompson Jackson at some stage became known as George Thompson Trevelyan Jackson – a nicely aristocratic touch for the son of a provision merchant.

George Jackson's detailed army service records have not survived, so it is impossible to reconstruct his postings in any detail; however, surviving records show that he served in South Africa throughout the Boer War, after which he was posted for at least one spell of duty in India, from whence he returned at the end of 1907. In 1909, while still in England, he married his first wife, Mabel Palmer, and the couple's daughter, Audrey Trevelyan Jackson, was born in Kent the following year.[5] In January 1912 Captain Jackson, as he now was, sailed for India again, returning to England in April 1913, from whence he was posted to Glasgow.

At the outbreak of the First World War, Jackson was immediately sent to France. The campaign in South Africa had been a particularly difficult one, but even the hard fought war against the Boers had not prepared anyone for the horrors to come. Although non-combatants, veterinary officers advanced with the rest of their brigades, setting up points close to the front line, where they attended the horses injured on the field of battle, dressing wounds and assisting with their evacuation, often while under enemy fire. One of the numerous AVC officers to receive a gallantry award was a Captain Thomas Walsh McMahon, who received the Military Cross for conspicuous gallantry. 'By fine example and encouragement to his men, he was able to evacuate some 250 horses which would otherwise have been lost' – this in the face of 'machine-gun fire, intense shell fire and bombing from enemy planes'.[6] Others received gallantry awards not only for evacuating horses, but for rescuing the human wounded from the field of battle, regardless of their own safety.

Not surprisingly, the rate of casualties among these officers was high. From autumn 1914 to the conclusion of the war, *The Veterinary Record* carried lists of AVC officers who had been wounded or killed and in October 1914 came the first list of AVC officers mentioned in Despatches (as Captain George T. T. Jackson would be in 1916). In November 1918, a Royal Warrant decreed that henceforth the Army Veterinary Corps would be known as the Royal Army Veterinary Corps (RAVC) in recognition of the work it had done in the conflict. Even when the hostilities were over, the 'demob' of veterinarians was slower than that of ordinary combatants, since they were still needed to supervise the demobilisation of vast numbers of horses, mules and other animals previously involved in the war effort.

In 1921, George Jackson, by now a Major, left the army after more than twenty years service and looked for somewhere to establish a civilian practice. For reasons no longer known he settled on Eastbourne, where he set up a practice opposite the railway station in premises at 24 Terminus Road, in partnership with Captain

Jack Sergeant, a fellow ex-army vet, who had originally qualified in 1902.[7] By 1924 the practice was also advertising the boarding kennels at Langney, in which Major Jackson would retain a controlling interest until his death.[8]

By the time they settled in Eastbourne, George and Mabel had been married for more than ten years, but in common with all service families in time of war, there had been long periods when they were necessarily apart and this may have put a strain on their relationship. Even so, the speed with which the Jackson marriage broke down after their arrival in Eastbourne is remarkable, because by 4 February 1922, Mabel was writing to her husband from a London hotel, asking him to give their marriage another try.[9]

Mabel's handwritten appeal on the notepaper of The Hotel Rembrandt, Thurloe Square, London, is worth reproducing in full, as an intriguing reflection of the web of relationships and counterfeit relationships which were central to the lives of George Jackson, Frances Rollason and their immediate circle, and would become an important element in the subsequent police enquiries.

My Dear Trev,

I feel I must write and make one last appeal. It is over a week since we arrived here and I have been hoping against hope that you would write, asking me to return to Eastbourne – you know I would gladly do that, also take a house and do my best to make a comfortable and happy home for you and Audrey. I don't think you can realise what a terrible misfortune this is for all of us, especially perhaps for our sweet kiddie whom I know you love. I do beg of you dear to think the matter over very very carefully before deciding upon a course which would probably spell tragedy for us both. I am feeling the strain of things and the humiliation very acutely and am in fact far from well. It is difficult to express all that I feel for us. You know that I am very proud but I feel the time has come to put aside mere pride and think only of our future and I want to say in all sincerity that I will do all that a woman can do to further your interest and make you happy. Don't you think we might give and take a little more and even now make something of our lives? Take time to think over your answer, which I shall await with greatest anxiety.

Your wife

Mabs

This was, on the surface at least, a sincere and touching letter – but like so much in this story, the contents of the letter and the circumstances under which it was produced are open to more than one interpretation.

CHAPTER SIX

HOLY DEADLOCK

When the major protagonists are no longer available to offer us an explanation, it is generally the case that more than one construction can be placed upon events. It is therefore possible to believe that Frances Rollason did not meet her first husband, Major Jackson, until 1923 – well after his marriage to Mabel had broken down; that George and Frances then enjoyed a whirlwind courtship and were married in November of that year. One factor in particular, however, argues against this interpretation. At some point during 1922, Frances left Eastbourne to stay at Stagsden in West Cliff Road, Bournemouth. Stagsden was a private nursing home and it was here, on 4 June 1922, that Frances gave birth to a daughter, Elizabeth Boden Rollason.[1]

In an era when bearing a child out of wedlock no longer carries a stigma and couples often marry well after their offspring are born, it can be difficult for the modern reader to grasp the level of scandal which such an event would have generated in 1922, had it been widely known among Kate Rollason's social circle in Eastbourne. (The particular gentility of Eastbourne can be gauged by the fact that its street directories not only separated private citizens from tradesmen, but that a much smaller number of socially superior residents – including Kate Rollason – were listed in a 'Court Section'.)

There is a suggestion within the family[2] that baby Elizabeth did not initially live with her mother, with whom she was only reunited after George and Frances were married, and that some people may have been given the impression that Libby, as she came to be known, joined the family because Frances had adopted her. Certainly the choice of a nursing home the best part of a hundred miles from Gaudick Road, where Frances still shared a home with her mother, does tend to suggest an attempt to keep the birth from the eyes and ears of Eastbourne's respectable matrons.

The question inevitably arises as to whether Major Jackson was in fact Libby's father. No father's name is provided on the child's birth certificate and during her divorce proceedings from Jackson, when required to give details of their children together, Frances omitted Libby from the petition.[3] It is difficult to attach much significance to this, however, because at the time of her divorce Frances needed to appear as squeaky clean as possible, and since she had to give both the date on which she had married George Jackson and the ages of the children, basic arithmetic would have thrown up the fact that her eldest daughter had been born almost eighteen months before the wedding. This also meant that Libby was not technically a child 'of the marriage' and she may have been left out of the petition for this reason. Certainly Major Jackson acknowledged Libby as his daughter, referring in press interviews given during the 1931 inquiry to himself and Frances as having had three children together, which figure incontrovertibly included Frances's eldest daughter, and when Libby was married in 1949 *The Times'* announcement described her as 'daughter of the late Major G.T.T. Jackson'[4] – though a cynic might point out that Frances (by now married for a third time) would by then have counted on being able to pass her eldest daughter off as the legitimate child of her first marriage, since sufficient time and water had passed under the bridge for most people to have forgotten the exact chronology involved.

There is, however, an even stronger clue to Libby's parentage and it comes in the timing of the letter which constituted part of the evidence in Mabel Jackson's petition to the court. Frances's first child must have been conceived in the autumn of 1921. There were no pregnancy tests at the time[5] and while a woman might suspect (or in the case of an experienced mother even feel confident) that she was carrying a child, a medical practitioner was unlikely to provide firm confirmation until around the twelfth week of pregnancy – which would have fallen some time in December 1921.

Mabel's letter is dated 4 February 1922 and was therefore written within a relatively short time of Frances receiving confirmation that she was pregnant. There is one element in particular about this letter which makes it difficult to accept at face value. The letter which survives in Mabel Jackson's divorce papers is not the original – which would have gone to her husband – but a copy, carefully penned by Mabel, for production in court. It seems unlikely in the extreme that a woman would make and retain a handwritten copy of such a heartfelt letter unless it was with the intention of producing it to prove that the letter had been sent – a necessary last appeal prior to instigating proceedings against a wayward husband, on the advice of her solicitors. By the time it was written, Mabel was lodging in the Hotel Rembrandt and her husband was living at The Imperial Hotel, Eastbourne. The wording of the letter, their separate addresses, and Mabel's suggestion that she would be willing to take a house and by implication set up an already dismantled family home again, all imply that the separation has been ongoing for some time, but in Mabel's petition to the court, formally lodged on 3 April, it is stated that George Thompson Trevelyan Jackson 'has withdrawn from cohabitation since about 8 February'. Apart from the impression of the petition's being somewhat sloppily drawn up, this glaring discrepancy does suggest that the whole business may have been something of a put up job – a mutually connived divorce, which suited both parties.[6]

At this point it is crucial to understand the legal position with regard to divorce in 1922. Until the Matrimonial Causes Act of 1923 came onto the statute books, English law did not allow a wife to divorce her husband on grounds of adultery alone. Faced with her husband's assumed affair with Frances Rollason, Mabel had two choices – she could do nothing, which meant that Jackson remained legally tied to her, whether they continued under the same roof together or not – or she could separate from him, apparently unwillingly, and petition for restitution of her conjugal rights. If Jackson refused to return to her, the court would in due course dissolve the marriage. There was no such thing as divorce by mutual consent. The court took the view that it was there to uphold the sanctity of marriage and that having vowed to remain together until death (even if in fact they had been married in a register office and vowed no such thing) a couple should not part. Divorce was not granted on grounds of mutual incompatibility, but only where one party had clearly suffered such a grievous wrong at the hand of the other that they should be accorded legal release. In a cruel and bizarre twist, the law particularly frowned on the idea that a couple were merely colluding in order to gain a divorce, because both were equally keen to sever the tie – couples suspected of collusion would not be granted a divorce and in cases where collusion was suspected or became evident after a divorce was granted, either or both parties could find themselves back before the courts, facing charges of perjury.

Where the position was reversed, a man could of course divorce his wife on grounds of *her* adultery, but the position was further complicated by the fact that it was considered ungentlemanly to blacken the name of a lady in this fashion, unless she had cuckolded you so publically that she was already disgraced. The only semi-respectable way out for the Jacksons in 1922 (divorce could never have been seen as entirely respectable) was to follow the line they took – for Mabel to appear to want their physical relationship restored to its former footing and for her husband to ignore these entreaties. When the petition was heard before Lord Buckmaster on 21 July 1922, he issued a court order instructing Major Jackson to 'return to his wife within fourteen days and render her conjugal rights'. This, of course, Major Jackson did not do and so the proceedings ground slowly onward until both parties got their freedom.

No record survives explaining how Major Jackson and Frances Rollason originally met. It may have been at some social event, with the Jacksons introduced as newcomers to Eastbourne, but it is equally possible that Frances first encountered him in a professional capacity, since she was a great animal lover, who kept dogs all her life.[7] It would be all too easy to attribute cynical motives to either party. Frances may have been desperate to get free of an overbearing mother. She would not be the first young woman who had ever rushed into matrimony in order to gain some independence (to which, in her case, could be added the unusual fillip of gaining access to a large fortune for which she would otherwise have had to wait until she attained the age of twenty-five). Jackson may have been attracted by the prospect of a younger woman, an extremely wealthy wife, or a combination of the two: but it is equally easy to see this first marriage in the light of a passionate love match, between two people who were deeply attracted to one another.

Viewing the matter retrospectively Major Jackson inevitably appears in a bad light – he was a married man with an eleven-year-old daughter, who, on the face of it, appears to have cheated on his wife and seduced an innocent young woman, not yet twenty-one – but we do not know how things really stood within the Jackson marriage by this time. He had been apart from his wife and child for most of their married life, and confronted with the awful truth that with retirement from the army, an endless married life together now stretched before them, the Jacksons may have found it difficult to adjust. There is no actual evidence that Mabel had ever embarked upon a love affair during her marriage to Trev, but nor is it absolutely certain that she had led an entirely blameless life, or at the very least not wished herself free to make a life with someone else – and just as Major Jackson remarried as soon as he was able to at the end of 1923, so too did Mabel.[8] There is just a faint hint that after a mutually amicable divorce, Mabel may have remained on cordial terms with her first husband – she certainly maintained a friendly relationship with his family, choosing to appoint one of Trev's nephews as an executor when she rewrote her will, following her second marriage.[9]

It is also possible that Jackson did not initially realise how young Frances was before becoming romantically involved with her and nor is there any reason to believe that he was aware of her financial prospects, because in 1921 Frances still lived in a relatively modest house with her mother, and was not constantly referenced as an eligible heiress in the society pages.

Perhaps most importantly, it cannot be construed that Frances was in any way coerced or cornered into marrying him. Even with a baby imminent there could be no question of a shotgun wedding, since Jackson was a married man, whose divorce and remarriage could not possibly take place soon enough to provide a veneer of respectability when the baby was born, and nor was such a step needed to ensure financial security for the child and its mother, as would have been the case for many young women. It would have been perfectly feasible for Frances and her mother to have concealed the truth about the baby and for her to *not* have married Jackson, even when he was free to marry her. The evidence that Frances actively wished to marry 'Trev' thus appears to be incontrovertible.

The couple were married on 19 November 1923 and stayed at the Hotel Cecil in London, before honeymooning in Monte Carlo.[10] On returning to England they stayed for a while at the Bath Hotel in Bournemouth (it was then customary for those who could afford to do so to live in hotels for several weeks or months at a time, while seeking more suitable permanent lodgings) before moving into their married home, Rothwell Dene (though now converted into flats, Rothwell Dene was then a very spacious individual residence). Bournemouth was one of the most fashionable – some would have argued *the* most fashionable – resorts in the country. In order to tempt the best possible elements of society to sample its delights, the City Fathers advertised its virtues in *The Tatler*, where Bournemouth was described as 'a Mediterranean lounging place on the English Channel', which boasted two golf courses, together with good hunting and fishing in the neighbourhood.

Little wonder perhaps that after marrying Frances, Major Jackson gave up his veterinary practice and concentrated on his sporting activities. A regular polo player, huntsman and golfer (and reckoned to be extremely good at all three) the Major also took a keen interest in numerous other sporting activities and was an ardent follower of the turf – a pleasure which Frances also seems to have shared. It would later be suggested that Jackson was a womaniser, but whatever the truth of this he appears to have been a very popular man, among both men and women. He made friends easily, was good company and well regarded for his sportsmanship. His obituary in *The Journal of the Royal Army Veterinary Corps* records that he was 'held in high esteem by his brother officers'[11] and this appears to be borne out by the fact that he was elected Club Captain of the RAVC Golfing Society six years in succession.

Now that they were married, Frances and 'Trev' wasted no time in having another baby. Their daughter, Pauline Frances Jackson, was born on 15 September 1924 and a son, Peter Hubert Howard Jackson, followed on 22 May 1927. Well before this, however, another important character in the drama had made his entry, because at some point in 1926, Frances and 'Trev' were introduced to a young army officer whose own family connections had brought him on a visit to Bournemouth – Lieutenant Hubert George Chevis – known to his family as Hugh.[12]

CHAPTER SEVEN

'CHEVIS WAS A FASCINATING MAN'

George T. Trevelyan Jackson, 1931

Hugh Chevis was born on 21 September 1902 in Rawalpindi, which is now in Pakistan, but was then part of British India.[1] In 1902, his father, William Chevis, was a Divisional Judge – a career civil servant whose successive promotions culminated in his appointment as one of the High Court Judges in the Punjab and a knighthood, while his mother, Amy Chevis (*née* Dannenberg), was the daughter of John Christian Augustus Dannenberg, a 'gentleman missionary' of German origins, long established in India and almost certainly the J.C.A. Dannenberg who produced a volume called *Mutiny Memoirs* about the Indian Mutiny of 1857.

Though his mother was born in India, Hugh's father had his roots firmly in English soil and this probably influenced the decision to send Hugh and his older brother William back to England for their education. The boys initially attended Suagen School in Boscombe, then Stirling House Prep School in Bournemouth, before going on to Charterhouse. Hugh completed his education at the Royal Military Academy in Woolwich, before taking up a commission in the Royal Artillery in 1922. (His older brother William was already a serving army officer – one of the generation of men who saw active service in both world wars.)

Hugh appears to have been universally popular both with his men and his fellow officers.[2] He was a strikingly handsome young man and extremely fit, who played hockey at club and county level, and rugby for Woolwich Garrison. He was also a good horseman and it was this which would bring him into the orbit of Trev and Frances Jackson.

Sir William Chevis had retired from the Indian Civil Service in 1922, sailing back with Lady Chevis from the heat of Bombay to a retirement on the south coast. They chose a house in Argyll Road, Boscombe, which was comfortable but not particularly large or ostentatious, as befitted a couple who had a good pension, but relatively little personal wealth. Sir William had risen by his abilities rather than his connections and there is no evidence that he or his sons enjoyed a personal income over and above their government and army salaries.

Now that Sir William and his wife were domiciled near Bournemouth, it was only natural that their sons would come and visit when stationed in England, and it is almost certain that Hugh was down on a visit to his parents when his first meeting with Frances took place.

The introduction was brought about via mutual friends, Captain George Heap and his wife Dorothy. Captain Heap, formerly of the 20th Hussars, had served for a time with Trev Jackson during the 1914-18 war, when Jackson had been Staff Captain in the same brigade, but after the war the men had not seen each other again until George Heap chanced to bump into his ex-comrade when George and Frances were staying in the Bath Hotel in 1924. After this the Heaps became regular visitors when the Jacksons took up residence at Rothwell Dene.

The Heaps' first encounter with Hugh Chevis occurred at roughly the same time; the initial meeting taking place at a dance in 1923 or 1924 – when interviewed by the police, some seven or eight years later, Captain Heap could not recall the precise location, which, given the number of dances he and his wife seem to have attended, is hardly surprising. The couple became friendly with the young officer and, knowing that Major Jackson kept a number of horses and that Hugh Chevis would enjoy the opportunity to go riding while in Bournemouth, Dorothy Heap suggested that the Lieutenant call on the Jacksons.[3] (In the etiquette of the time, calling on complete strangers because you shared a mutual friend with them was a perfectly normal, acceptable means of introduction.)

Lieutenant Chevis went to tea at Rothwell Dene and was accordingly invited to ride out with Major Jackson when staying in Bournemouth. The arrangement was initially successful – Major Jackson and Lieutenant Chevis went riding together on a number of occasions[4] – but the unforeseen consequence of this introduction was that at some point Frances and Hugh fell head over heels in love with one another: whether it was a gradually deepening affection, or love at first sight, the ultimate consequence was that Frances decided she wanted to free herself of Trev Jackson, in order to marry the man she would subsequently refer to as the 'love of her life'.

On 11 June 1928, Frances filed for a divorce on the grounds of her husband's adultery. Parliament was still decades away from accepting that men and women who had freely entered into matrimony, similarly had every right to conclude that they no longer wished to be married to one another and sever the bond. However, things had moved on since the first Jackson divorce in 1922, so that it was now legally possible for a wife to divorce a husband for his adultery alone, and this had led to a new ritual being adopted to get round England's farcical divorce laws. Since it was not considered gentlemanly for a man to divorce his wife (and perhaps because it was embarrassing to admit that a woman had made a fool of you) in order to allow their wives to divorce them, husbands now embarked on an elaborate pantomime, booking into a hotel with a woman hired to pose as a girlfriend or mistress, with the express purpose of being seen with the woman when the chambermaid arrived to make up the room or deliver breakfast in bed the next morning. The assumption (not necessarily correct) that the male party in the case had enjoyed sexual relations with this unnamed woman was sufficient evidence for a wife to obtain her divorce, provided the court was unable to detect a whiff of collusion between the two spouses. One downside of this was that both parties in the divorce had to commit perjury, but at least these arrangements satisfied the expectation in polite society that a gentleman would not accuse his wife and her lover, or a wife besmirch the name of another member of their social circle with whom her husband was having an affair, or even intended to marry. It was at one time suggested that some hotels were specialising in 'divorce tourism' and the whole ludicrous system became the subject of a satirical novel *Holy Deadlock* by A.P. Herbert, published in 1934.[5]

Clearly not everyone was willing to play the game by the accepted rules of polite society. A partner who wished to be vindictive could resort to naming and shaming guilty parties, while one who wished to prevent their spouse from gaining their freedom and marrying a new love could simply refuse to co-operate – either by failing to petition for divorce, failing to oblige by providing evidence of their own 'wrongdoing', or by exposing the other party as equally guilty – because where both parties were found to have committed adultery, the court was liable to refuse the divorce on the grounds that instead of being asked to protect an innocent party from a guilty one, they were now being asked to assist two equally guilty parties by providing them with the freedom they craved – and the court's position as some sort of arbiter of the nation's morals was not consistent with 'rewarding sin'.

Like so many facets of this story, the 1928 Jackson divorce is anything but straightforward and the circumstances are open to a variety of interpretations. On the one hand it is clear that Major Jackson, although he moved out of the family home and took up residence again at the Imperial Hotel, Eastbourne (Frances had also decamped to her London flat in Stafford Mansions), was not prepared to oblige with 'hotel evidence'. Moreover, on being required to give formal answer to the petition, he stated that he was not guilty of adultery.

Further indication that this was not a run of the mill, undefended divorce (and thus one which in all probability was being connived by both partners) lay in the identities of the parties cited. At a time when evidence of congress with one unnamed woman would often suffice, providing the other party played ball, Frances had chosen to name two respectably married Bournemouth women, one of them the wife of a prominent local doctor. It must have been a scandal par excellence and under the circumstances it is small wonder that both Major and Mrs Jackson decided to leave town.

Irrespective of the truth or otherwise of the allegations, it was simply not done to drag another woman of one's own class through the dirt, and the situation may have been all the more distasteful to certain citizens of Bournemouth for the fact that rumours had already been circulating about Frances's own relationship with

Hugh Chevis – so much so that as Major Jackson later told the police, he had received anonymous letters while still living with Frances which made allegations about his wife's relationship with Lieutenant Chevis.[7]

The original petition presented to the court alleged that George Jackson had committed adultery with Beatrice Mary Granger, Dorothy Tomlins, a Miss Bradley and a fourth, unnamed woman. All parties (except necessarily the woman whose name was unknown) were served with notice of the petition and given eight days in which to respond. Both Mrs Granger and Mrs Tomlins immediately responded, denying adultery and requesting that the court dismiss their names from the suit. The fact that there was no word from Miss Bradley cannot necessarily be taken to indicate that she accepted the allegations as the truth. Divorce cases were then heard in the High Court in London, where legal representation was hugely expensive, and whereas Mrs Granger and Mrs Tomlins had good addresses and were by inference women of some means, Miss Bradley's address appears to have been a flat above commercial premises on Christchurch Road, which she shared with her parents.[8]

On receipt of denials from Major Jackson and two of the three named parties, the court contacted Frances, requiring her to provide further details of the allegations in the petition. Her solicitor came back with an extensive list of dates and circumstances for which the court would be 'asked to infer that they [Major Jackson and whichever woman was in question] committed adultery together'.

On the face of it a great deal of inference was required. It sounded from the information provided by her lawyers rather as if Frances had had her husband followed, but even this had not really thrown up much in the way of hard evidence of actual adultery. The sum total of the allegations against Major Jackson and the unidentified woman were that he had taken her out for a drive in his motorcar on four separate occasions in April 1928, and that during these jaunts the car had paused for periods lasting from half an hour to an hour in 'secluded places'. A 'secluded place' in this context may have amounted to little more than a spot in a country lane or at a viewpoint where the 'tail' could not get close enough to observe exactly what was going on. At a time when motoring was still the preserve of the upper and upper-middle classes, it was an exciting novelty to be taken for a drive in the country, if you belonged to one of the numerous families who did not own a car. Driving was considered a fashionable recreation in itself and while it is entirely possible that Major Jackson's intentions were less than noble, it is also feasible that he and his friend no more than paused to share a packet of sandwiches, or admire the view.

The evidence regarding Miss Bradley was somewhat stronger, for in addition to half a dozen motoring trips was added the allegation that she and Major Jackson booked into adjoining rooms at the Metropole Hotel in Brighton at the end of May 1928 – an episode which, were it to be substantiated, was far less open to innocent explanation.

Only one adulterous episode was alleged with Dorothy Tomlins, and this too was said to have taken place when Major Jackson took adjoining rooms with a woman at the Metropole in Brighton, this time at the beginning of May 1928 – though the petition refers to this episode involving 'a woman called Tomlin' – which seems to indicate a degree of uncertainty as to whether or not this woman really was Dorothy *Tomlins*, against whom no other allegations were made.

The longest list of guilty assignations was levelled against Beatrice Granger. It was alleged that Major Jackson and Mrs Granger had spent a night together at the Bridge Hotel in Staines in June 1927 (not quite three weeks after Frances had given birth to her son Peter), that the couple had spent more than a fortnight together at a hotel in Minehead during August 1927, and that they had enjoyed numerous nights of passion between February and May 1928. In the light of such apparently damning and extensive evidence it is interesting to consider not only that Mrs Granger believed she could successfully deny that there had been any wrongdoing, but also that the court accepted her position and dismissed the case against her.

Again there is just a chance that things were not quite as they seemed. Trev Jackson allegedly visited Beatrice Granger's home on more than a dozen occasions between 21 February and 9 May 1928, and all but one of these visits took place during the evening, with Major Jackson sometimes staying for three or four hours at a stretch, but always leaving before 11.45 at the latest. While it is possible that Beatrice's husband (a doctor) was always out on call, this still left the Granger's young children on hand in the early part of the evening (the Granger's eldest son, Norman, was eight years old in 1928) and there were three resident domestic staff on the premises too, which was hardly propitious for the conduct of a covert affair.[9]

Beatrice's husband, Henry Granger, was a virtual contemporary of Major Jackson and had served in the Royal Army Medical Corps during the war, which may have created an initial bond between the two men, leading to the Grangers becoming his close friends. By the beginning of 1928, Jackson can have been in no doubt that his marriage was in trouble and that his wife wanted a divorce. Is it possible that he was merely seeking the company and counsel of close friends during this period? He would not be the first man to have spent hours and hours chewing over his marital dilemma with a sympathetic audience and, on the face of it, this is almost as likely as the idea that Beatrice was inviting him round for an illicit half hour every time her husband was called out to attend a patient.

What of the time spent together in hotels? With all due respect to Staines, it hardly sounds like a location for a romantic tryst and the couple's simultaneous presence in the hotel may have been down to coincidence, to some entirely legitimate shared enterprise, or was perhaps even a case of mistaken identity, given that the names Jackson and Granger are not particularly unusual.

The sojourn in Minehead certainly sounds more suspicious, for though it is possible for two adult friends of the opposite gender to spend a fortnight or so at the same hotel, enjoying each other's company during the daytime while keeping to their separate bedrooms at night in an entirely platonic and proper manner, it sounds odd that Beatrice Granger – or for that matter Trev Jackson – would be holidaying separately from their respective families, he driving her about in his motorcar, showing her the polo ground at Dunster and taking her out riding on his horses, but this notwithstanding, had both parties continued to strenuously deny that anything inappropriate had taken place, there was no real evidence to prove otherwise. The polo grounds at Dunster were among the most important in the country and the fixtures there drew large crowds – particularly the season finale in August. Judging from photographs which appeared in *The Tatler*, The Metropole Hotel appears to have been the choice of the visiting players and thus perhaps a slightly odd one for an adulterous assignation.

However, the fact that Major Jackson spent almost a month at the Metropole Hotel in Minehead (Mrs Granger's stay was much shorter) during the summer of 1927 and that he seems to have scarcely spent an evening at home during the spring of the following year, if nothing else indicates that there was a great deal wrong with the Jackson marriage at that time. The list of dates provided to the court gives considerable support to the theory that he was a philanderer, because if the petition is to be believed he spent ten out of fourteen consecutive nights in April 1928 committing adultery with three different women – and on 12 April he was reckoned to be simultaneously committing adultery with two different women in two different locations – but was everything quite as clear cut as the litigant in the case would have the court believe?

The fact that Jackson refused to provide 'hotel evidence' so that Frances could easily obtain her divorce might be taken to imply that he initially had no intention of letting her go – yet had that been the case, the Major had a card at his disposal which he never attempted to play. Rumours had circulated about Frances's relationship with Hugh Chevis and if adultery could be inferred from some of his own conduct, then why not from hers? While there is no way of telling from the contemporary documentation whether Frances and Hugh began an adulterous love affair when she was still legally married to Trev Jackson, the decision to name her son Peter Hubert Howard Jackson rather than including the names George, Thompson, or more likely Trevelyan, is undoubtedly suggestive. (For what it is worth, Frances's second son, David Gerald, born in 1934, was named after his father Gerald Montague Braham.)

It is not difficult to find motives behind Major Jackson's reluctance to give Frances her freedom. He and Mabel had been financially comfortable before Frances appeared in their lives,[10] but marriage to Frances had brought strings of polo ponies, regular trips to the South of France, and a huge house on the south coast – he had given up his veterinary practice and become accustomed to the lifestyle of a gentleman of means. There is also the fact that Frances was an extremely attractive woman and in spite of his conduct, his long absences from home and sojourns at the Metropole Hotels in Minehead and Brighton (he appears to have enjoyed a penchant for Metropole Hotels) Trev Jackson may still have been in love with her.

The divorce was heard at the Royal Courts of Justice on 15 November 1928. Separate counsel intervened on behalf of Beatrice Granger and Dorothy Tomlins to contest the allegations made against them and these were not proceeded with. This left the evidence regarding Miss Bradley and the unnamed passenger who had been taken on expeditions in Major Jackson's motorcar – evidence which might have appeared somewhat flimsy if the respondent had chosen to fight it – but he did not. At some point since his initial response to the petition, Major Jackson had changed his mind and Mr Bayford KC announced that his client would not after all be defending the suit. (Frances was represented in court by Norman Birkett KC, one of the foremost – and therefore most expensive – advocates of the day.)

Witnesses were called on Frances's behalf and Sir Maurice Hill, the presiding High Court Justice, pronounced that the petitioner had sufficiently proved the contents of the petition – though once the respondent had declined to defend himself against the allegations, the matter was a virtual foregone conclusion. The marriage was dissolved on grounds of adultery and a decree nisi issued. Custody of the children was granted to Frances and costs of £1,666 6s 10d[11] were awarded against Major Jackson (a sum which remained unpaid at the time of his death in 1934).

What had brought about Major Jackson's change of heart? Was the evidence against him too strong to contest? Had the intervening months given him time to accept that the marriage was over? Or was it simply the impossibility of fighting a case through the High Court against a petitioner buttressed by virtually unlimited funds? This was certainly the view expressed to the police by Mrs Dorothy Heap,[12] who assumed that Jackson's finances did not allow him to fight on – the law was a rich man's game and Trev Jackson was no longer a rich man. It is interesting to note that Mrs Heap also expressed surprise at the allegations made against Major Jackson – informing Inspector Pharo in an off the record chat that she had no idea Major Jackson was 'carrying on' with any other women and that she had always looked on him as 'quite a decent gentleman' – she had thought the Jacksons 'very happy' – but to this must be added the fact that by then she had not seen Major Jackson for more than three years.

What of the other women caught up in the divorce? While it is difficult to read anything into outward appearances, Beatrice and Henry Granger remained married until his death in 1960,[13] while Dorothy and Herbert Tomlins continued to reside together at their house in Queens Park Avenue for a couple of years, but had parted by 1935.[14] The fate of Miss Bradley and the unnamed woman remain necessarily unknown.

Whatever the rights and wrongs of the case, Frances got her decree absolute in June 1929, but by then Hugh Chevis had been posted to India.[15] When he returned to England in November 1930, the couple wasted no time in arranging a wedding – they were married at Chelsea Register Office on 20 December 1930.

CHAPTER EIGHT

'PRINCIPAL EVIDENCE DESTROYED BY THE VICTIM'

Mr W.J. Francis, 1931

On the morning of Hugh Chevis's death the due processes of law swung into motion. Sudden deaths were automatically reported to the police and the coroner, though at this stage there was no reason to lean towards a theory of foul play. The vast majority of deaths involving poison turned out to be accidental. Medicinal use of strychnine was still widespread in the 1930s, with small doses often used as a stimulant or restorative. Indeed, strychnine was frequently mentioned in contemporary inquest reports as one of the drugs administered (by injection) in an attempt to revive a patient who was dying,[1] and it was also present in a variety of medicines – particularly tonics – many of which could be purchased without prescription over the counter of a chemist's shop. Such was the ubiquitous nature of strychnine that newspaper advertisements for Phyllosan pointed out that it did *not* contain 'deleterious chemicals' such as strychnine, quinine and a whole list of other substances which we would now regard with considerable suspicion.[2] Easton's Syrup, a particularly popular patent medicine, contained sufficient strychnine that, in 1923, theatrical agent Meyer Goodman was able to commit suicide by taking a large quantity of Easton Syrup tablets.[3]

In fatalities involving patent medicines the victims were often children, like eighteen-month-old Sadie Gilbert, who found and consumed tablets containing strychnine in her own home in February 1918. Eleven-month-old Stanley Brett died in similar circumstances later the same year.[4] However, adults appear to have been equally liable to death by accidental ingestion. Sometimes this was the fault of the dispenser: in March 1916, Maud Coveney, age twenty-eight, and Beatrice Stockwell, age thirty-four, both died when their local chemist made up their medicine using strychnine in error for another drug. At the inquest the man admitted his error, explaining that when he made up the prescription he had been tired and distressed, owing to the illness of his wife. It was a less litigious age, in which mistakes of this nature were often accepted as no more than bad luck. The inquest jury brought in verdicts of death by misadventure.[5] This was not an isolated case – three children from the same family[6] died as the result of a similar error in 1901 – but for the most part there were no prosecutions and only sporadic attempts to make dispensing safer.

Occasionally a victim of error attempted to fight back. In 1922, a Mr and Mrs Holt brought a claim for damages and were awarded £150. They had taken medicine dispensed by a chemist, Mr Northen, only to become ill about thirty minutes later with symptoms their GP at once recognised as strychnine poisoning. Though the couple survived the overdose, they had both been very ill and Mr Holt had been off work for six weeks afterwards.[7]

Medical men had ready access to the drugs they required for house calls, and though one might have hoped for vigilance on the part of those qualified to deal with dangerous substances, an appropriate degree of care was not always in evidence. In November 1909, Dr Thomas Alexander drank some strychnine in mistake for gin, while working in his surgery. He immediately realised his error and injected himself with morphine as an antidote, before informing his wife and daughter of his fatal blunder. As morphine is not an antidote to strychnine (for which there is no known antidote) this intervention was ineffective and he died later the same evening.[8] Dr Charles McDonnell suffered a similar fate in 1928, when making up medicines in his Dundalk surgery. He explained to the doctor called to attend him as he lay dying, that he had had two glasses on the bench, one containing water and one containing strychnine, and, feeling thirsty, he had taken a drink out of the wrong one. He too died within a relatively short time of ingesting the poison.[9] In 1921, Ada Lister, the wife of Dr Walter Lister of Leeds, took a fatal dose of strychnine in mistake for morphine, when apparently helping herself from her husband's supplies because she was tired after a long journey.[10]

There was a strong culture of dosing oneself throughout the first half of the twentieth century, not just among doctors' wives but throughout the population at large. It was expensive to consult a doctor, but relatively cheap to buy preparations at the local chemist shop. Not only was it possible to buy a great many potentially dangerous preparations over the counter, but there was also a considerable trade in illicit drugs, with numerous drug dealers being brought before the courts – and strychnine was usually listed as among the substances discovered in the haul when their premises were the subject of a police raid.[11] At least some of these black market supplies derived from doctors' bags, which appear to have been the subject of regular thefts, while left unattended in cars parked outside patients' houses. It was such a frequent occurrence that Agatha Christie referenced it in her 1936 novel *Cards on the Table*,[12] in which one of her characters explains that a murderer probably obtained some stolen poison thanks to doctors 'always leaving cases of dangerous drugs in cars all over London and getting them stolen' – an impression which contemporary newspaper reports do nothing to dispel.[13]

Strychnine was in demand for a variety of uses which would not have been accepted as a legitimate reason for purchase from a chemist's shop.[14] As well as doping racehorses, strychnine was in use to improve the sporting performance of some human athletes. In 1953, *The Times* published a letter from Dr Woodward of Harley Street,[15] alleging that track cyclists were taking strychnine to enhance their performance, and the debate was still rumbling on more than thirty years later, with articles in the mid-1980s claiming that cycling was 'awash' with performance enhancing substances, including strychnine.[16] Its supposed efficacy for this purpose no doubt encouraged some gentlemen to assume that a small dose would enhance their performance – or that of their partner – in bed. This too could occasionally have tragic consequences, as when the ironically named Mrs Cynthia Valentine took a 'love potion' in the form of an overdose of Easton's Syrup and died of strychnine poisoning in 1968.[17]

The officer who first made enquiries into the death of Lieutenant Chevis would have been well aware of all these possibilities. This was Inspector Albert Pharo, a forty-three-year-old Surrey native, married with a teenage daughter – an experienced officer who had been with the Surrey Police for more than twenty years.[18]

When Pharo arrived at the Cottage Hospital on 21 Jume 1931, he initially interviewed the doctor who had certified death, taking charge of the samples of vomit from both patients which had been secured by Dr Bindloss the previous evening.[19] He then visited the bungalow lately occupied by the couple, where he took statements from Nicholas Bolger and Mrs Yeomans. He also performed a routine search of the premises and secured various items which he considered to be relevant to the inquiry. These included a jar of water taken from the drain of the kitchen sink, and all the items which remained from the preparation of the previous night's dinner: a basin containing dripping, a vegetable dish containing peas and potatoes, a bottle of anchovy sauce, an empty Smedley's pea tin, packets of Bisto and Bovril, a bag of flour and a bottle of Harrod's Orijny coffee. To this haul he added a tin of carbolic – the only obviously poisonous substance he could find on the premises – and a bottle of 'granules' supplied to Mrs Chevis from Heppells of Knightsbridge. The 'granules' were 'health salts' or a 'stomach wash' – Pharo no doubt had in mind the method used to despatch Alfred Jones seven years before and was taking no chances. (During the period in question a tin or jar of 'health salts', for the treatment of indigestion, constipation, or just about any other stomach upset, was routinely kept in the majority of households throughout the land.)

Pharo prepared his report for the coroner the same day, outlining the basic facts and including the information that Mr Chevis had ordered his batman to see to it that the remnants of the partridge were destroyed. The coroner, Mr Francis, subsequently noted in the margin 'Principal evidence thus destroyed by the victim'. Pharo had also heard about the death of the Evered's dog, and noted in his report that the dog had apparently been in the habit of lapping water from the sink drain of Lieutenant Chevis's bungalow.

The inquest into Hugh Chevis's death opened in Camberley on 23 June. By now the police enquiries had extended to the suspect partridge itself and the firm who had provided it, Messrs Colebrooks, took the precaution of having a solicitor present to guard their interests,[20] though no Colebrooks employee was to be called as a witness that day.

The first witness was Captain William Chevis of the Royal Engineers, the older brother of the deceased, who was by then a married man with two young sons, three-year-old William and one-year-old Hugh.[21] Captain Chevis and his family were stationed nearby at Aldershot, which enabled him to take on the legal duties which generally fell to the next of kin – formally identifying his brother at the mortuary and going on to make all the funeral arrangements.

In answer to the coroner's questions, William Chevis confirmed that his brother had been a very healthy man, happily married to Mrs Chevis for just over six months. The coroner wanted to know more about Mrs Chevis and was told that she was a divorcee, with three children from her first marriage, which had been to Major G.T.T. Jackson, a retired RAVC officer. Asked about financial matters, Captain Chevis said that his brother and sister-in-law had had no money worries, or indeed any other worries that he was aware of. Asked about enemies, he told the coroner that Hugh had been a popular man since school and had no enemies. So far as he knew, his brother's life had not been insured and nor had he made a will. He confirmed that he and his brother had been in the habit of seeing a good deal of one another – although not over the past three weeks, as Hugh had been at a training camp out of the area.

Nicholas Bolger was called next. He said that he had been employed as Lieutenant Chevis's batman since March – his duties involved serving at the table, cleaning the silver and acting as valet to Lieutenant Chevis. Prompted by the coroner, he went through the events of Saturday evening, explaining what food he had taken into the dining room and in what order. According to Bolger, the Chevises had nothing to drink with their meal and he served them coffee in the drawing room after it. The only food which had been the subject of complaint was the partridge. In answer to further questions he said that he had not tasted any of the food himself, as the only meal he ever ate at the bungalow was his breakfast.

After this Bolger was asked about the arrival and cooking of the partridges, but he had not seen them arrive and had had nothing to do with cooking them. It had just been a normal routine day, he said. He had arrived at the bungalow in time to have his breakfast as usual, did his work there until lunchtime, when he went home for his meal. He returned at six in the evening and would normally have left as soon as his duties were finished after dinner. He agreed that the couple always seemed very happy and had a lot of visitors, although there had been no visitors that day apart from Captain and Mrs Bowser, who came for drinks before dinner. Asked why he had not called the police when Lieutenant Chevis was taken ill, he said that no one had instructed him to do so, and asked whether he had reported the occurrence to a senior officer, he said that it was not his job to report things unless so instructed.

Dr Bindloss and Dr Attenborough were called in turn and described the circumstances of their involvement, the symptoms of the deceased and those of his wife, and confirmed that their diagnosis was strychnine poisoning.

They were followed into the witness's chair by Ellen Yeomans, who, like Bolger, had not been employed at the bungalow very long, having been with Mrs Chevis for less than six months. Mrs Yeomans, who was in her early fifties, had been a widow for nearly twenty years.[22] Her husband, Albert, had been the innkeeper at The Fox in Farnborough until he died from a brain haemorrhage at the age of just thirty-three in 1913, leaving her with two young sons, Leslie and Ernest (who were grown up by 1931). Mrs Yeomans told the coroner that her hours of work were generally from 7.30 in the morning until between 8 p.m. and 8.30 p.m. at night. She and Bolger were the only servants, so she did most of the cleaning and all the cooking. The partridges were part of an order which Mrs Chevis had telephoned to Colebrooks and the order had been delivered by one of their drivers. The birds were already prepared for the oven and Mrs Yeomans therefore had only to cook them, which she had done by putting them in a tin with some dripping and giving them forty-five minutes in the gas stove, basting them with the dripping while they cooked. The birds were ready at about 7.45 and she had noticed nothing unusual about them at all. For the benefit of coroner and jury she went through the entire menu again: slip soles, anchovy sauce, partridges, tinned peas, new potatoes, bread sauce and gravy. There had been nothing else served except coffee, she said (thereby completely forgetting about the cheese and salad).

She too confirmed the sequence of events, explaining how Bolger had answered the bell, returning almost immediately with Lieutenant Chevis's partridge and passing on his message ordering its destruction, and how she had subsequently consigned first one bird and then the other to the furnace. After Bolger cleared the table, she had washed everything up. There had been no leftover bread sauce, as she had only made a small quantity, and all that remained was washed out of the sauce boat, but there had been some leftover peas and potatoes and she had put these in the pantry, for future use.

The coroner returned to the actual arrival of the birds, and Mrs Yeomans confirmed that she had placed them both onto a plate, then put the plate in the meat safe outside the bungalow. (Before most households had a refrigerator, uncooked meat was often kept in a 'meat safe' – at its simplest, this was a pyramid-shaped object with sides of finely woven mesh which completely covered a large plate containing the meat, thereby keeping it safe from flies, marauding cats, visiting mice and so on. In larger or more affluent households, where several pieces of meat or fish might need to be stored at once, the meat safe was likely to be a larger, static construction, sometimes fixed to the north wall, to keep the contents as cool as possible.)

The jury wanted to know more about the process of cooking – where had the dripping used to cook the birds come from, and had she herself not tasted the birds before sending them in? The cook said that the dripping derived from the joint of lamb which she had cooked for Lieutenant and Mrs Chevis the day before. She had not tasted the birds before sending them in – both on the same serving dish. No – she had not washed the birds prior to cooking, because they were delivered ready for the oven – she had, however, washed the fish and the potatoes using ordinary tap water and had also rinsed the tinned peas. The peas had been warmed in a saucepan on top of the stove, with a little butter. The gravy had been made from flour, butter, Bisto, Bovril and water. The gas supply was directly metered, rather than being paid by the slot. No – she had never seen any poison in the house or bought any poison in herself, and no – she had never seen the neighbours' dog lapping out of the drain.

Finally, she was asked by the coroner whether Mr and Mrs Chevis had appeared happy, and she said that they had.

Mr Francis now announced that he would be adjourning the inquest until 21 July, by which time the analysis of various samples would have been completed and he hoped that Mrs Chevis would be well enough to give evidence.

Hugh Chevis was buried the next day, his funeral having been arranged by his brother William. As befitted an officer, it was a military affair, the coffin resting on a gun carriage drawn by greys, his body laid to rest in the Military Cemetery at Aldershot.[23] His widow was in London, too ill to attend, and his mother, Lady Amy Chevis, was also absent – whether she would have found the strain too much, or perhaps because she belonged to that generation who believed that women should not go to funerals[24] is not recorded. Whatever the reasoning, Lady Chevis was still awaiting the return of her husband from the funeral when a telegram arrived at around 5 o'clock in the afternoon.[25] It was addressed to Chevis, 14 Argyle Road, Boscombe, Hants and the message was short and sweet: 'HOORAY HOORAY HOORAY'.

CHAPTER NINE

DOGS, PARTRIDGES AND IRISHMEN

Sir William and Lady Chevis were naturally shocked and distressed by the telegram and on the morning after its arrival Captain William Chevis took it to the Post Office in Boscombe, both to verify that the message had been transmitted correctly and in the hope of tracing the sender. Here he learned that the telegram had been sent from Dublin at 4.30 on the afternoon of the funeral and that no name had been provided within the message. In order to investigate further, Post Office procedure required that the telegram be handed back to them and an enquiry form submitted. Captain Chevis completed the form on behalf of his parents, handed back the telegram as required and, whilst awaiting further elucidation from the Post Office, he also reported the matter to the Bournemouth Police, who unfortunately do not appear to have appraised their colleagues in the next county of the telegram's existence for several days, perhaps because they were unaware that this was potentially rather more than a complaint about a malicious telegram.[1]

In the meantime the investigation in Surrey was proceeding at a steady pace. Inspector Pharo had been to Deepcut Barracks and made enquiries about the training camp at Okehampton, where Lieutenant Chevis had been in the weeks preceding his death. Nothing untoward had occurred during his time there, although the Lieutenant had been engaged in the court-martial of a Gunner Selby, who had been sentenced to fifty-six days' detention for losing part of his kit; but Selby was ruled out as a suspect since he was still serving his sentence in a military jail. Pharo had also established that there was no strychnine kept at Deepcut Barracks apart from some tablets in the medical kit, and that these were in sealed packets which had not been tampered with. He learned that Lieutenant Chevis had been stationed at Deepcut since February, was an extremely popular officer, and had no troubles that anyone was aware of.[2]

Pharo had also been to Colebrooks and interviewed the manager, Charles Tyler, who was able to give him chapter and verse regarding the partridges sold to Mrs Chevis. Tyler explained that he had received two separate consignments of Manchurian partridges from A.S. Juniper & Co. in Smithfield market – twelve on 8 June and another half dozen on 13 June. The partridges had all been placed in the cold store on arrival, and nothing added to them by way of preservative. Nor was there any possibility of accidental contamination, as the only poisonous substance kept on the premises was carbolic. Fifteen out of the eighteen partridges had been sold (including the pair sold to Mrs Chevis) and three remained in the cold store. Tyler was able to provide the names of the customers in only three cases other than the Chevises, as the remaining birds had been sold for cash (as opposed to on account, which necessitated recording the transactions for billing later), but there had been no complaints about any of the other birds and in due course the Medical Officer of Health for Camberley tested the three remaining birds and found no evidence of poison in any of them.[3]

Pharo went on to interview the Colebrook roundsman who had delivered the birds to the bungalow. This was William Noyes, who said that he had picked out the birds himself and watched the butchery assistant prepare and truss them. He had left the shop at around 9 o'clock in the morning and made deliveries in Ash Vale, Mytchett, Frimley and Blackdown, not arriving at Aisne Bungalows until about 1.30 p.m., when he had handed the order – which comprised three parcels wrapped in white paper, overwrapped in brown – to Mrs Yeomans. As well as the brace of partridge, there had been a pair of slip soles and a piece of beef, which Mrs Chevis had intended to have for Sunday lunch. He had noticed nothing wrong with any of these items and while out delivering he invariably locked the van and kept the key with him to avoid the possibility of theft, which coincidentally ruled out the chance of anyone tampering with the birds en route.[4]

It did not fall to Pharo, however, to interview the most important witness in the case. That task came within the remit of his superior, Superintendent James Stovell, who travelled to London on 1 July, in order to question Frances Chevis at her London flat. Stovell was one of the county's most experienced officers – another family man with a wife and teenage children at home, who had less than three years to complete before retiring after forty years' service.[5]

It might appear a little surprising that it had taken almost ten days for the police to schedule an interview with Frances, who was, after all, the person who had actually seen her husband ingest poison and whose testimony might have been thought every bit as pertinent as that of her servants, her husband's fellow officers, a delivery roundsman or the manager of the store which had supplied the suspect partridges – and while due allowance had to be made for her illness, it may have crossed the mind of more than one person that someone who was well enough to be driven back to London was also well enough to cope with some gentle questioning about such a serious situation. The truth of the matter may well lie in sentiments expressed by a fictional detective, Inspector Grant, the creation of Josephine Tey, who, when questioning a suspect in a murder inquiry, soliloquised, 'Oh well, there was no getting away from the fact; one didn't demand information from the son of a ducal house as one demanded it from a coster. A rotten world no doubt, but one must conform.'[6]

The novel in question, *A Shilling for Candles*, was published in 1936 and the duke's son with whom Inspector Grant was required to tread so carefully, was the spouse of a murder victim and thereby high on the list of suspects. It would be easy to dismiss the ruminations of Inspector Grant as no more than the imaginings of just another author, but Tey had essentially hit the nail on the head. In the class-ridden 1930s, policemen did tread softly when it came to dealing with members of the upper and upper-middle classes, and numerous examples of this can be uncovered from surviving records. Louis Heren, who rose from a poor working-class background in London's East End, later wrote of the '30s, 'In those days the police... dealt firmly with the lower orders,' going on to contrast this with the treatment of Oswald Mosley, who, 'whatever [he] stood for and whatever rabble were at his heels, he was an obvious gentleman'.[7] Similarly in the weeks following her husband's demise, Frances Chevis would repeatedly be treated with kid gloves by the Surrey Police – at one stage even being afforded a tête-à-tête with the Chief Constable. (By contrast, in 1938, Rose Sandford, the wife of an agricultural labourer, would be arrested and charged on the slenderest of suspicions.)

Quite aside from the point that in any case of domestic poisoning it would be normal to place the surviving spouse at the head of the suspect list, it was and remains a well-established fact that the longer the delay between the interview and the event, the less likelihood exists of obtaining a completely accurate recollection from a witness.

When eventually interviewed by Superintendent Stovell, Frances began her statement by responding to the usual routine questions about how long she and her second husband had been married, where they had resided and so on. She told Superintendent Stovell that they had gone from the Chelsea Register Office to her flat, 14 Basil Mansions and from there to the Queens Hotel in Farnborough, where they had stayed for a while until their bungalow was ready. On 16 March they had moved into 'D Hut', Aisne Bungalows. 'We were perfectly happy,' she said.

While her husband had been away for three weeks at the Devon training camp in Okehampton, she had returned to stay at her flat in London, but when he came back to Deepcut Barracks on 19 June, she had immediately travelled down to rejoin him at the bungalow. On Saturday 20 June, she had telephoned Colebrooks to order the soles, partridge and beef, asking for them to be delivered, and that day they had lunched on cold lamb, mint sauce, salad, custard tarts and junket – all of which had tasted fine. She then described the meal on Saturday evening and the events which had followed, ending by explaining that she could not recall actually arriving at the hospital in Frimley – however, she had come round during the night to find that her nurse had arrived. 'I was removed from Frimley next day by ambulance to Basil Mansions, where I have been ever since.'[8]

Stovell completed his questions by asking whether Frances was aware of any poison being kept in the bungalow, but she could not think of anything except disinfectant.

When the coroner received his copy of this interview, he was evidently unimpressed and the margins are full of scribbled queries – all the questions which he presumably felt that Stovell should have asked: 'Did she swallow the partridge given to her by her husband? How did her bird taste? How much did she eat of it? Has she seen Jackson since the divorce? Where does he live? Has he remarried?' and so on and so forth, culminating in a question which was to develop increasing significance during the following days: 'Any friends of self or Jackson in Ireland?'[9]

It is unclear from the surviving documents at precisely what point the Surrey Police first heard about the 'Hooray' telegram. Captain Chevis submitted his enquiry form to the Post Office on 25 June, and Superintendent Stovell and his officers were definitely aware of the telegram's existence by 29 June, but Frances Chevis was not questioned about a possible Irish connection on 1 July and it appears that the Post Office's internal inquiry took some time – in his statement to the police on 29 June, Captain Chevis still knew no more than that the message had originated in Dublin. However, the suggestion of an Irish connection quickly gained prominence in the inquiry, with Inspector Pharo noting in his report that Nicholas Bolger was an Irishman, who had originally joined the British Army in Dublin on 10 January 1920. It was a connection the police (and others) considered suggestive, but in a further interview with Mrs Yeomans, Pharo ascertained that the batman would have had no opportunity to tamper with the partridges before they were cooked, since he had gone home to Lightwater immediately after serving lunch, only returning in time to clean Lieutenant Chevis's kit and serve the dinner. Mrs Yeomans assured the Inspector that she had had sole control of the cooking and that it would have been equally impossible for Bolger to have put anything down the sink unnoticed, as he was busy in and about the dining room while she did the washing up. Mrs Yeomans was also asked if she knew any other Irish people apart from Bolger himself, but said she did not.[10]

At this stage Pharo and Stovell were still working on the assumption that the Evereds' dog had died of strychnine poisoning after lapping contaminated drain water from outside 'D Hut'. Not only did this appear to make perfect sense, but there was almost a folk history of canine involvement in strychnine cases. An English Terrier had died after licking the floor in the Reilly case in 1925,[11] and in the Major case too a neighbour's dog would expire after gobbling up scraps of Arthur Major's last supper, thrown out for the birds by his wife, Ethel.[12]

On 12 July, the police took formal statements from Lieutenant Evered about the death of his spaniel, and another from Arthur Paling Slater, the veterinary surgeon attached to Farnborough Dog's Home, who confirmed that the dog had left the kennels in perfect health. He had performed a post-mortem on the unfortunate animal on 21 June and made the confident pronouncement that: 'There was every symptom of strychnine poisoning.'[13] He had extracted and sent the dog's intestines to a chemist in Fleet for analysis (and presumably confirmation of his own diagnosis) – but the results had come back in the negative.

One of the difficulties facing us at this length of time is the impossibility of establishing how thorough or experienced the chemist Slater had chosen for this experiment actually was. William Million, proprietor of Fleet Pharmacy in Hampshire, sent his findings back to Slater on headed notepaper, which announced himself as 'Chemist by appointment to Princess Charles of Bavaria, sole agent for Elizabeth Arden's Venetian Toilet Preparations, Chiozza & Turchi's Italian Castile Soap & Rexall Products. Also Kodak Supplies, Developing & Printing, Analysis of Every Description Undertaken.'[14] It therefore seems likely that Million was a general chemist who provided the public with a very wide range of services, of which the occasional analysis of substances was but one, and whose previous experience of post-mortem analysis was probably non-existent.

Mr Francis, the coroner, sent a copy of Million's report to the Home Office analyst John Ryffel – who had by then been appointed to handle the analysis of exhibits from the case on behalf of the police – asking if Ryffel felt that the tests used by Million had been the proper ones. Ryffel wrote back confirming that the tests employed should have shown up strychnine, but added that the situation was hardly satisfactory since Million had tested only for strychnine rather than attempting to determine what *had* caused the dog's death and adding that the post-mortem report on the dog was equally unsatisfactory, since Slater had not bothered to define what 'clear indicators' of strychnine poisoning had actually been present. With the verdict on the dog somewhat inconclusive, the coroner wrote back thanking Ryffel and saying: 'It is clear to me that no useful purpose will be served in pursuing the dog question any further.'[15]

The 'dog question', as Mr Francis described it, could never have been easily resolved. No vet managed to examine the afflicted animal in life and even had they done so, the symptoms associated with strychnine poisoning – seizures and stiffening of the limbs – are also associated with various other types of poisoning in canines. Death can occur within as little as ten minutes of a dog ingesting strychnine and there are no particular post-mortem signs specific to it.[16] When Arthur Paling Slater stated that there was every sign of strychnine poisoning, he did not add that such signs were common to poisoning by a variety of other substances too, some of which might easily have been picked up by the animal, from weedkillers, pest killers and even rotting vegetation.

The only sure fire way of establishing that strychnine caused the dog's death would have been the isolation of that specific substance in a chemical test, but even this could be difficult to achieve. Current authorities on the subject recommend that the dog's stomach contents be tested, as other organs are 'less likely to achieve positive confirmation'.[17]

Million's analysis and Slater's post-mortem can at best be described as inconclusive, but it would surely be a remarkable coincidence if both Lieutenant

Chevis and his next door neighbours' dog were poisoned within the space of half an hour of one another, after exposure to two different toxic substances? Had the spaniel been the only dog in the locality, its demise might have given weight to the theory of an outside assassin, craftily disposing of the dog to prevent it from alerting anyone to his own presence, but this does not work on any level, since there was more than one dog in the vicinity and the crucial time for any external tampering with the partridges had occurred at least an hour earlier, when they were still in the meat safe. It remains far more likely that the dog had indeed taken a drink out of the Chevis's drain when Mrs Yeomans was washing up – attracted by the scent of meat juices which had been washed out of the dish used to cook the partridges – and thereby received a dose of strychnine in the process.

If the investigation had lost interest in the dog, it was becoming increasingly fixated on the Irish question, with all interviewees now routinely being asked whether they knew of any Irish persons associated with the Chevis household. Lieutenant Evered responded that his household servant, Margaret Casey, was originally from Ireland, but as she had only been with them for three days and came with a very good character (she had previously been with a Major Wilcox) he would prefer it if the police did not interview her, as 'we do not want to lose her.'[18] Evidently sympathetic to the 'servant problem', which was becoming an almost constant topic among the middle classes, the police obligingly left Ms Casey alone.

Bolger was not so fortunate and had his antecedents closely investigated, but although an Irishman, links with the land of his birth had become tenuous. His parents were dead and he had not been back to Ireland for six or seven years, having apparently lost touch with most of his relatives there. He told the police that he had once had an aunt in Dublin, but believed that she now resided somewhere in Kildare. Connections to England had been further strengthened in 1931, when he married a local girl, Amy Parker, who at the time of the police investigation was already expecting their first child. Far from being a disgruntled servant with a grudge, the batman spoke warmly of the late Lieutenant, saying that Mr Chevis was the best officer he had known in his twelve years service, and pointing out that he was financially worse off by his death.[19]

Police interest had also begun to focus on Frances's first husband, Major Jackson. Captain William Chevis was asked about Jackson, and told them what he knew (there is no particular inference that the two men were acquainted), which was relatively little. Major Jackson had served in the war with the RAVC, he said, but was now retired. He assumed that the Major had not suffered any war wounds or injuries since he was 'a great polo player, racing man and huntsman' – and agreed that it was entirely possible that Jackson had friends in Ireland, since 'it is such great hunting country'. He understood that Mrs Chevis had divorced Jackson 'about three years ago' on account of his association with other women. Apart from this he could add nothing except that Mrs Chevis's nurse told him that Major Jackson had been in Northamptonshire three days after Lieutenant Chevis's death, as Mrs Chevis had received a letter of condolence written from him there.

It is clear from this interview that Captain Chevis was also being quizzed about his sister-in-law. He agreed that it was possible Frances had friends in Ireland, but said that she would be better able to answer that than he would. He was also asked about Frances's relationship, if any, with Lieutenant Jack Gwynn-Jones, a friend of his brother Hugh, who was also serving in the Royal Artillery. Captain Chevis said that Gwynn-Jones was 'a nice young man', who had been a friend of his brother's for several years, and that he did not think Gwynn-Jones had met Frances until after she and Hugh were married. He thought that the last occasion on which Jack Gwynn-Jones had called on Hugh, coincided with Frances being away in London.[20] The cook and the batman had also been asked about Lieutenant Gwynn-Jones, but they only confirmed what Captain Chevis had already told the police. Bolger described the young man as 'a very great friend of the deceased', who had frequently visited the bungalow, with and without his fiancée, though never in the absence of Mr Chevis. Mrs Yeomans added for good measure that so far as she knew, there had never been any male visitors at the bungalow when Mr Chevis was not there.[21]

In the meantime, the Home Office analyst had communicated his preliminary results to Mr Francis, writing that he had found a fairly small amount of strychnine in Lieutenant Chevis's organs, but 'a considerable amount' in the vomit of both Mr and Mrs Chevis. There had been a very small amount of strychnine in the dripping, but none in the sample of water from the sink drain, the vegetables, or anything else taken from the bungalow. He therefore concluded that the strychnine poisoning must have been associated with the partridges.[22]

Mr Francis responded on 9 July, thanking Ryffel for his preliminary results and writing: 'It seems clear that death was caused by strychnine poisoning through eating the partridges.' He went on to tell Ryffel about the 'Hooray' telegram, which he noted 'sounds like the act of a madman' but adding that 'it seems curious that the sender should know the exact address, the day after the inquest. I did not know it until yesterday and I do not think it has appeared in any of the newspapers. The police are investigating, but so far have not found out who sent the telegram.'

Mr Francis followed this up by sending Ryffel a copy of a letter which had been forwarded to him by the editor of the *Daily Express*. The letter had been written on 25 June and sent to the newspaper specifying that it was not for publication, but instead requesting that it be passed on to the appropriate authorities. It had come from a man called Cullen Mather, who, although staying in Hove, normally lived in the Far East, where he was a manufacturing agent. Mather explained that strychnine was used by Chinese and Manchurian fur trappers to kill foxes and other animals without spoiling their pelts. He pointed out that it would be very easy for birds to take the bait instead and for one of these birds to then be exported for consumption in Britain. Did Ryffel think this a possibility, the coroner wanted to know? Could the bird have picked up as much strychnine as had been identified in this particular case, and what would the effects of the strychnine have been on the bird? Would there have been any outward sign that it had been poisoned? Would the strychnine have acted as a preservative, or the reverse?[23]

Forensic science was still in its infancy in the 1930s and a certain degree of exaggeration coupled with self-aggrandisement on the part of some of the men who appeared regularly as expert witnesses had led many coroners, judges and policemen – to say nothing of the general public – to believe that the regular team who worked on behalf of the Home Office possessed a far greater level of knowledge and expertise in all manner of areas than was actually the case.[24] Ryffel's experience of poultry and game birds was probably limited to eating them when they appeared on restaurant menus or his dinner table at home, but Home Office 'experts' in the 1920s and '30 were not in the habit of conceding a lack of knowledge on any subject, so Ryffel's response followed his time-honoured tactic of appearing to offer informed comment on the original question while actually diverting the interrogator towards a preferred theory of his own, which was not infrequently based less on scientific fact than on unsubstantiated speculation.

Thus Ryffel informed the coroner that he did not believe there would be any outward signs of poisoning to the bird and that a 'sufficient quantity' of strychnine would act as a preservative, rather than the reverse. However, he considered that the quantity of strychnine identified in the samples of vomit (he estimated ⅓ grain) indicated a total amount of at least 2 grains[25] and if a bird took a very large dose of strychnine 'it would presumably die before most of it was absorbed, so that a considerable quantity would remain in the crop and gizzard...' These would have been removed before the bird was exported, Ryffel explained, and therefore, 'I fail to see how a poisoned bird can possibly contain in its tissues enough to kill a human being.' It would, Ryffel added, be possible to make experiments to assess the effect of keeping a poisoned bird in cold storage, but he would rather leave that to someone else.

Having thrown cold water on Mather's theory, he proceeded to propound one of his own, suggesting that if strychnine-based vermin killer was mixed with the butter that was placed inside the birds before cooking, the blue dye in the vermin killer would escape notice, and this 'would fit the facts as I have them'.[26] The notion that a bright blue dye would escape notice if present in a lump of butter placed in the body cavity of a small game bird which was then subjected to the heat of an oven tends to suggest that matters culinary were not Ryffel's strong suit – nor had Ryffel ever been told that anyone had placed a lump of butter inside one of the birds – so the statement that this theory in any way fitted the facts was optimistic, to put it mildly.

Coroner Francis must have been reasonably impressed by the authoritative tone of Ryffels's letter, however, because he replied with thanks on 16 July, enclosing

Million's report regarding the analysis on the dog's intestines and the vet's post-mortem opinion,[27] again inviting Ryffel to comment, though his knowledge of veterinary matters was unlikely to be much greater than his experience of cooking partridge. It is somewhat ironic that while Ryffel's reply included the information that he had found 'only a trace of alkaloid, presumably strychnine' in Hugh Chevis's stomach and 'only a minute trace' in his liver, it does not appear to have occurred to either man that the lack of strychnine found in samples from the human victim might have suggested an explanation for the absence of strychnine in the one portion of the dog's organs which had been sent to Million for analysis.[28]

The coroner finally received Ryffel's formal report on 21 July, the day of the resumed inquest. (It is difficult to see why it had taken Ryffel so long to produce this report, as he had received all the items for testing by 24 June and completed his analysis by 7 July.) The report essentially confirmed what he had already told the coroner. All items had been clear of strychnine except those numbered C1 and C2 on the exhibit list, which were bottles of vomit from Frances and Hugh Chevis respectively, exhibit C3, the stomach contents which had yielded only traces of an alkaloid which he had presumed to be strychnine, and exhibit C5, 'dripping with small amount of gravy', which had also contained a small amount of strychnine. From the amount found in C1 and C2, Ryffel concluded that the amount of strychnine in the partridges 'could not have been less than 2 grains' and added that the minimum fatal dose is accepted as 0.5 grain.[29]

Ryffel's description of exhibit C5 – 'dripping with small amount of gravy' – fostered confusion in 1931 and has been causing confusion ever since. Gravy had been served with the fatal meal, but when the meal was over any gravy that remained had gone down the sink when Mrs Yeomans washed up the gravy boat, so that none had been available to be sent to Ryffel for testing. It is perfectly clear, therefore, that wherever Ryffel did find traces of strychnine, it cannot possibly have been in the gravy served with Lieutenant Chevis's final meal, because none of it had ever come into his possession. Pharo's list of exhibits clearly described item C5 as 'One basin containing dripping',[30] but instead of sticking with this accurate and perfectly satisfactory form of words, Ryffel substituted a description of his own, introducing the word 'gravy'. It later transpired that what Ryffel meant by 'gravy' was the darker juices within the dripping – but this was far from obvious in his report and in deviating from the description on the exhibit list Ryffel showed typical disregard for the importance of maintaining an accurate, methodical and consistent approach when engaged in a serious criminal investigation. This would not be the only problem occasioned by Ryffel's slipshod methods, although that was not immediately apparent when the inquest resumed.

In the meantime, various other lines of enquiry were also being pursued. Inspector Pharo had returned to the bungalow for a closer look at the meat safe. Unlike the small, easily transportable boxes employed by some households, the meat safe at 'D Hut' was a fixture on the outside wall of the bungalow – a framework of deal, with the front and sides made from perforated zinc, the whole thing measuring 25 inches wide by 25 inches long by 15¾ inches deep. There were two moveable shelves inside, each measuring 22 inches long by 9 inches wide. The safe had a lock, and was in good order (although, strangely, the question of whether it *was* actually locked while the partridges were inside never appears to have been established). The base of the safe was 4 feet 7 inches from ground level, immediately above the roof of a low lean-to store, located on the rear wall of the bungalow. It was just over 4 feet away from the scullery window and a similar distance from the back door, which was round the corner of the building, so it was theoretically possible for a person to tamper with the contents of the meat safe without being seen from within the building, although the proximity of the other officers' bungalows added to the likelihood of observation, with only 21 feet separating 'D Hut' from its nearest neighbour.[31]

Pharo had also enquired after the beef, which had been delivered at the same time as the partridges, and discovered that this had been eaten by Mrs Yeomans and one of her neighbours with no ill effects whatsoever. He had instigated checks with all the chemists in the area, but none had recorded any sales of strychnine. He had found out that Major Jackson was currently residing at the Mostyn Hotel in Eastbourne. The most tantalising clue, however, was surely the telegram, over which the Post Office were dragging their heels. As late as 18 July, Inspector Pharo was informing the coroner that the police would pass on any information they received about the telegram as soon as it was to hand.[32]

On 17 July, the General Post Office (GPO) finally wrote to confirm that the telegram wording had been transmitted correctly, and added that the name and address on the form completed at the Dublin Post Office, where the message originated, was J. Hartigan, Hibernian. The Dublin Police had already been to question Miss Ruttledge, the assistant who had accepted the form, and she described the man who handed it to her as 'low sized, small grey moustache, dressed in a grey suit and aged about fifty years'. It was assumed that 'Hibernian' referred to the Hibernian Hotel in Dublin and the Irish Police had sent a communication there addressed to J. Hartigan, but it had not been claimed. Further enquiries confirmed that the name was not recognised at the hotel and no guest of that name had been recorded in the hotel register on 24 June. The report concluded with the information that the original telegram form had now been sent to South Farnborough Post Office, where it could be inspected on production of the GPO letter.[33]

The postmistress at Farnborough proved to be an infuriating jobsworth, who refused to part with the telegram when the police requested it, on the grounds that she was only authorised to allow them to *inspect* it. In exasperation, the coroner wrote to the GPO on 21 July, pointing out that he could simply subpoena the woman, ordering her to attend the inquest and produce the telegram, but since he and the police were endeavouring to make enquiries about the telegram without the press getting hold of the story, could he ask the GPO to please authorise the postmistress to give the telegram either to Inspector Pharo or Superintendent Stovell of Surrey Police without further delay?[34]

As the inquest resumed, the police were still awaiting the original telegram and this, together with various other outstanding aspects of the inquiry, made it apparent that the proceedings could not yet be brought to a conclusion.

CHAPTER TEN

TIME TO CALL IN THE YARD?

The hearing resumed on 21 July before Mr Francis and the ten-man jury which had been empanelled for the original sitting almost a month before. Mr Ricketts again attended in his capacity as solicitor for Messrs Colebrooks and Mr W.H. Rose, a partner with Ford, Lloyd, Bartlett & Mitchelmore, was present to watch over Mrs Chevis's interests.[1]

Frances Chevis was the only witness called and after being asked the inevitable questions which officially established how long she had been married to Lieutenant Chevis, the interrogation turned to her first husband, with the coroner wanting to know how often she had seen Major Jackson since she had remarried. (A question which had no obvious relevance to an inquiry into the death of her second husband, unless her first was assumed to have been implicated in some way.) Frances said there had been only two meetings, both of them accidental – once about three months after her marriage to Lieutenant Chevis, when the couple had bumped into Major Jackson on the doorstep of a hotel, and the other just over a week ago, when she had been out walking in Eastbourne and had again unexpectedly encountered her ex-husband.

The coroner returned to her second marriage and asked Frances where she and Lieutenant Chevis had lived. She said that since marrying again she had lived for a short time at Basil Mansions, then in a hotel in Farnborough and ultimately at Blackdown Camp, though she had returned to London while her husband was away at the training camp. He had returned to 'D Hut' from the Okehampton camp on Friday 19 June and she had left London to join him the same day. Asked about ordering the partridges, she said she could no longer recall whether she had telephoned Colebrooks on Friday or Saturday, but she knew that the order was delivered on Saturday, although she had not seen it arrive. Asked about the actual preparation of their dinner, she assured the coroner that she had had nothing whatever to do with the cooking – 'the first time I saw them [the partridges] was when they were served.'

Bolger had brought the partridges in on a dish, she said, and she had served as she always did, giving her husband the slightly larger bird. He had only eaten a couple of mouthfuls when he complained that he did not like the taste of it.

'I said I was sorry. He then asked me to taste a bit of it, to see whether it was the bird, or whether he had a bad taste in his mouth.'

Hugh had passed a piece of meat from his plate to hers, she said, and: 'I ate a portion and swallowed it. It had the most biting, bitter taste of anything I have ever had. It seemed to burn the back of my throat and the filthy taste seemed to be everywhere. We did not eat anymore.' Her husband had then poured some sherry, which they drank in an attempt to get rid of the taste. He rang the bell for Bolger, and when Bolger came 'my husband instructed him to take the bird away and burn it'.

Frances then went through the rest of the meal, the arrival of the cheese and salad, the clearing away of plates and then the moment when the couple left the dining room and Frances went into the bedroom to telephone her nurse in London and ask after her little boy, 'as he was being operated on next day'.[2] When she returned to the drawing room her husband complained of feeling unwell and in this latest retelling of events, Frances said that Bolger brought in the coffee and she drank hers before Hugh had a spasm, at which point she telephoned the doctor.

Once Frances's account of the evening was completed, the coroner, the jury and Mr Rose asked a series of supplementary questions (Mr Ricketts was invited to put questions but declined) which established that there had been no problems with the servants, who were both 'excellent', that Lieutenant Chevis had no regimental troubles, that there was no poison kept in the house apart from carbolic and Jeyes Fluid, and that Mrs Chevis had no friends in Ireland (a question which must have puzzled the jury, who had no knowledge of the telegram at that stage). The jury asked about the position of the meat safe, and it was also established that Mrs Chevis always served the meat at mealtimes and did the carving; and that she assumed her husband had asked Bolger to burn the partridges because he did not want their Alsatian dog or Mrs Yeomans' cat (for whom the cook sometimes took home leftovers) to get any part of the bad meat.

When there were no further questions for Mrs Chevis to answer, the inquest was adjourned until August. Up until this point the death of Hugh Chevis had not attracted a great deal of outside interest. This was somewhat surprising because sudden deaths and inquests were grist to the mill of local newspapers, with very few of them failing to merit a mention, under headlines such as 'Drowning Tragedy', 'Typist's Suicide' or 'Sudden Death of a Local Man'. On 27 June, the weekly *Surrey Advertiser & County Times* had included a short report of the Chevis inquest entitled 'Army Officer's Death After Meal', which opened with the words: 'The death apparently from food poisoning of a 28 year old...'[3] – evidently with the analyst's report still awaited at that stage, the reporter had assumed that this was merely another case of food poisoning and left it at that.

The story had also been picked up by the national dailies and a number of them had included a desultory paragraph about the tragedy on their front page, where it was somewhat lost among much bigger stories involving Hoover's proposals on War Debt Payments, the hopes of Bunny Austin and Fred Perry in the Wimbledon Tennis Championships, and the trial of Mrs Hearn, accused of murdering both her sister and a friend with arsenic.[4] The *Bournemouth Daily Echo* made more of it than most, thanks to Hugh Chevis's local connections, which were dwelt on at some length, but they too had ascribed his death to suspected food poisoning.[5] Essentially the story had been considered newsworthy only because it involved a serving army officer.[6]

It was customary at the time for the local paper to send at the very least a junior reporter to cover any local inquests, but the inquiry into Hugh Chevis's death appears to have been an exception – either that, or the reporter who had been detailed to attend must have left early or fallen asleep, because during his evidence at the first inquest, Dr Bindloss had not only described the distinctive symptoms of strychnine poisoning, but also stated without equivocation that in his opinion strychnine had been the cause of death. The papers normally loved a poisoning case and seized on the slightest possibility of foul play with relish, but in this instance they had inexplicably missed an opportunity.

Quite aside from the usual practice of sending someone to the inquest, many regional papers had a close relationship with their local police force, which ensured a tip off if anything suspicious was in the air.[7] However, relations between the Surrey Constabulary and the Press appear to have been somewhat frosty during this period and, as a consequence, the newspapers had remained in blissful, albeit temporary, ignorance of the unfolding drama.

Surrey Police's activities *were* making the newspapers at the end of June 1931, but not in connection with this particular case. On 27 June, the *Surrey Advertiser* reported a proposal to increase the strength of the county force from 356 men to 391, mentioning that it was more than twenty years since manpower had been increased. There had also been a proposal to recruit some women, but this had been turned down, as the Joint Standing Committee was 'convinced that neither the organisation nor the duties of the Surrey Constabulary lent themselves to the help of women police.' (At the time of writing, Surrey is being led by its first female Chief Constable – *plus ça change*.) It was also noted that Surrey had proportionately fewer inspectors than almost any other force in the country and some counsellors questioned whether it would not be a good idea to amalgamate the separate Guildford and Reigate police forces into the county force.[8]

In the meantime, other stories were presenting the local editors with much more exciting fodder than mere food poisoning. A 'love triangle' involving a New Malden man, his typist and his wife had ended in the latter attempting suicide and this story initially attracted much lengthier coverage than that devoted to the Chevis death.[9] The Lieutenant's death had been reported in the paper on 27 June, but by the following week's edition, with the inquest adjourned until 21 July and the cause of death wrongly ascribed to food poisoning, the

Chevis case disappeared from the Surrey press altogether. The 4 July edition of the *Surrey Advertiser* had Surrey Assizes to cover, which included a lively selection of cases incorporating bigamy, infanticide, and the death sentence being passed on William Baldwin for killing Sarah Isaacson. To this were added a Royal visit (Princess Mary inspecting a detachment of VAD and Red Cross volunteers at Dorking), and the usual mix of sudden deaths, fatal and non-fatal motor accidents, accidental drownings and Womens' Institute garden fêtes.

The resumption of the inquest on 21 July similarly attracted barely a ripple of interest in the press, with the *Surrey Advertiser* devoting the same amount of space to a complaint received by West Byfleet Council from Mr W.R. Evans, who objected to the fact that West Byfleet Tennis Club refused to include him in their matches played on the public tennis courts there. The council decided that the tennis club's refusal was eminently reasonable, given that Mr Evans had consistently refused to pay a membership fee and join the club, even when invited to do so.[10]

The national papers gave the renewed inquest similarly scanty coverage, devoting perhaps a couple of dozen lines to the story if that. Suspected poisoner Mrs Hearn had long since been acquitted, but there were fresh sensations to take over the front page, in particular the arrest of Arthur Salvage for the murder of twelve-year-old Ivy Godden in Kent. The child's body had been discovered on 5 July, two days after she had gone missing, and Sir Bernard Spilsbury had been called in to perform the post-mortem – the mere involvement of Sir Bernard always calculated to create a frisson of interest. Salvage lived in a bungalow just 600 yards from the Godden family home and less than 150 yards from where the child's body had been recovered from a shallow grave, and the notion of a murderer on the doorstep sent a shiver of horror down the spine of half the mothers in England.[11] If this was not enough to satiate the public's appetite for sensational murders, there was also news of renewed enquiries into the 'Blackheath Murder', with links being suggested to an attack on a Romford schoolgirl. (Though not explicitly stated in most of the papers, the renewed enquiries were directly linked to the arrest of Arthur Salvage.)[12]

If the Chevis case had not made much of a splash with the Press so far, it was about to generate a tidal wave of interest – for on Saturday 25 July the *Evening News* carried the story of the telegram. Under the headline 'Mystery of a Telegram and a Death', the paper recapped the story of Hugh Chevis's demise and broke the news of the telegram's arrival at Sir William's Bournemouth home on the day of the funeral. According to this initial report, the telegram had been handed over to Boscombe Police, who had forwarded it immediately to Inspector Stovell, who had in turn communicated at once with the Dublin Police (which was, of course, not the true sequence of events at all). The paper had also got hold of the description of the sender, which they sub-headlined as 'The Man in Grey'. There was even a lengthy reprise of Sir William's life history – 'an Oxford man with a brilliant career in the Indian Civil Service' and a variety of speculative comments about how the poison came to be in the partridges, though 'experts are convinced that poison [if eaten by the birds] could not reach the flesh'.

Surrey Police and the coroner, Mr Francis, were understandably appalled by this leak. In order not to compromise the hunt for the sender, they had gone to great lengths to keep the telegram a secret – even to the point of waiting a considerable time to get their hands on information concerning it – a delay created entirely as a result of the Chevis family having initiated their own enquiries with the Post Office rather than immediately handing the matter over to the Surrey Police, as had been wrongly implied in the newspaper account. To maintain confidentiality, the existence of the telegram had been a closely kept secret: apart from the coroner, the Home Office analyst and senior officers in the investigation, no one knew about the telegram except Sir William and Lady Chevis, their surviving son William, and their daughter-in-law Frances, who had all been sworn to secrecy:[13] but there was no mystery about the manner in which news of the telegram had found its way into the hands of the *Evening News* reporters. On the contrary, prior to publishing their scoop, the paper had approached Superintendent Stovell and invited him to comment, saying that they had been given the information by Sir William Chevis. Stovell had declined to co-operate and asked the paper not to publish news of the telegram as both the police and the coroner were most anxious that it should not be made public, but the *Evening News* response was to splash the story across its front page.[14]

The coroner was so incensed by the newspaper's disregard of the police request that he wrote to the Attorney General, explaining the situation and asking whether there was any 'machinery for dealing with the Editors of newspapers' and if so, what were the appropriate steps, adding that, 'In my view it is a very serious state of affairs if the Press can, just for stunt purposes, publish anything which the responsible authorities do not desire published.'[15]

Mr Francis received a response from the Director of Public Prosecutions (DPP) on 31 July, which, while sympathetic, said that action could only be taken in 'glaring cases' of contempt of court, and that in this case it would be difficult to prove that the publication of the information had specifically interfered with the due processes of law and justice.[16]

The obvious point which the DPP did not make was that any complaint would be compromised by the fact that the information had been freely volunteered to the Press by the recipient of the telegram, and while the coroner was careful to infer no direct criticism or comment regarding the actual leaking of the telegram in his letter – reserving his ire for the Pressmens' insistence on publishing it – he cannot have been at all pleased with those responsible. He was therefore probably not in the mood for a letter which arrived from Captain William Chevis on 5 August.

Captain Chevis wrote that he had been discussing the situation with his father and they both felt that such an important case required the full-time attention of a senior officer. He did not wish to imply that Superintendent Stovell had been in any way lacking in ability or diligence, but felt that it was time for Scotland Yard to be called in; 'this is the wish of myself and my family and also Mrs Chevis.' The letter was couched in extremely polite and reasonable language and asked the coroner to forgive the letter as 'of course I realise that the police know their job better than I do.'[17]

Mr Francis responded at length the same day, explaining that the question of whether or not to call in Scotland Yard rested with the Chief Constable of Surrey and was entirely outside his own jurisdiction. He assured Captain Chevis that he was personally aware that Superintendent Stovell was keeping the Chief Constable informed, that the Home Office was similarly fully appraised of the case and that he himself had seen Sir Ernley Blackwell[18] at the Home Office, and understood that the assistance of Scotland Yard would be placed at the disposal of the Chief Constable, should the need arise. Superintendent Stovell was 'practically exclusively engaged upon enquiries concerning your brother's death and has had the assistance of Scotland Yard Officers in the investigation, as well of course as the Dublin Police,' the coroner wrote, and in view of all this, was it still the case that Captain Chevis wished him to approach the Chief Constable – something about which he 'had a good deal of diffidence... as the matter is not one within my province' – though if Captain Chevis still wished him to pass the letter on to the Chief Constable, he would do so.

Having already mentioned that his visit to the Home Office had come about thanks to the publication of the 'Hooray' telegram, Mr Francis concluded by asking, 'I suppose you cannot tell me how the Press came to get hold of the "Hooray" telegram? After the promise you gave to the Police I thought the contents of the telegram were perfectly safe, but the Press got hold of it and said they got it from a most authentic source. If you could tell me definitely whether they obtained it from your parents, or any member of the family, it would influence me in the remarks I propose to make at the adjourned inquest.'[19]

The coroner had already embarked on a similar fishing expedition regarding the leaked telegram during the course of correspondence with Frances Chevis's solicitors, who, like Captain Chevis, had originally written to him on a different matter. As a result of the coroner's letter, Ford, Lloyd, Bartlett & Mitchelmore communicated with their client about the telegram and subsequently conveyed her assurance that she had no idea from whence the Press had obtained the information, and that she personally had been very careful not to mention it to anyone.[20]

The coroner's inquiry to Captain Chevis met with a similar result. William Chevis assured the coroner that 'neither I, my wife, nor any member of my family divulged it ... it is not likely that Mrs Chevis or Nurse Thorne did so; but of that I cannot be certain. As far as my own relations go, I personally warned them not to divulge it as soon as I was told...'[21]

Captain Chevis had begun this same letter by thanking the coroner for his reply, but explaining that in spite of the contents, he had 'heard this morning from my father, who wishes this matter pushed on as far as possible', adding that this was of course the wish of the entire family and that he understood Mrs Chevis (Frances) 'is instructing her solicitors to write accordingly'. He repeated that 'none of us wishes to in any way belittle the work of Superintendent Stovell, or anybody else, or to suggest that he is in the least lacking in efficiency or industry...' but all the same, the captain wrote, he could not help feeling that 'Scotland Yard officials might be able to produce some tangible results more quickly'. Pointed remarks had already appeared in the Press, Captain Chevis went on, to the effect that whereas in a recent murder investigation in Oxford, Scotland Yard had immediately been called in, Surrey were still working independently a full seven weeks after his brother's death. He therefore appealed to the coroner to use whatever influence he had as 'naturally your influence will be very much greater than anything I could say' and ended by apologising for giving any trouble and expressing deep gratitude for all the coroner had done so far.

A letter from Frances's solicitors arrived the same day, explaining that Mrs Chevis had been in communication with her father-in-law, Sir William Chevis, and that both were anxious that some explanation be found as to what had caused the death of Lieutenant Chevis. While recognising 'the very valuable efforts made by the detective in charge of the case' they nevertheless felt that 'in a case of this sort it is almost beyond the power of one detective officer, however efficient, to do full justice to the extraordinary circumstances surrounding the death of Lieutenant Chevis' and they were thus requesting on behalf of both Mrs Chevis and Sir William and Lady Chevis that the coroner use his influence to have Scotland Yard called in.[22]

Mr Francis forwarded the correspondence for the attention of the Chief Constable, and replied to Captain Chevis confirming that he had acted as requested, while again stressing that the matter was well outside his remit, and informing him that, 'I ascertained yesterday that Superintendent Stovell has for some time deputed an inspector to do all his routine work and that in addition to having the assistance of Scotland Yard, had a previously arranged appointment with Sergeant Brown – one of the Big Five[23] – for today.'[24]

It had probably not escaped the coroner that the moving force behind these petitions seemed to be Sir William Chevis, who was evidently urging both his son and his daughter-in-law to contact the coroner and request the involvement of Scotland Yard – indeed there was a positively apologetic note to Captain Chevis's missives, which may have indicated a reluctance on his part to become involved in petitioning the coroner. In the meantime, presumably believing that a two-pronged approach would serve him best, Sir William had himself entered into correspondence with the Deputy Chief Constable of Surrey. Whereas the letters from both Frances Chevis's solicitors and Captain William Chevis had been polite and respectful in tone, Sir William's letter was considerably less so. He acknowledged the Deputy Chief Constable's letter dated 4 August in response to his earlier one (unfortunately neither of these letters has survived) but said that he could not let the matter rest there. He was 'by no means satisfied that Superintendent Stovell is spending <u>practically</u> his whole time on the investigation. Such a case surely demands the <u>whole and undivided</u> attention of a skilled officer.'

Like his son and daughter-in-law, Sir William did not wish 'to cast doubts on Stovell's abilities or energy' but so far as he was aware the police had yet to make any discoveries which brought them nearer to a solution, and while Sir William admitted that he could not be sure Scotland Yard would have done any better, he was unhappy to read in the *Morning Post* that the Yard had been called straight in to assist over the murder of Mrs Kempson in Oxford. Among other complaints was the fact that Superintendent Stovell had not bothered to call on him until 31 July, when he had gone down to see the Chevises in Bournemouth in connection with an anonymous letter Sir William had been sent about the case. Sir William thought this an astonishing lapse on the part of the police, since he claimed that apart from his son's widow, 'I am probably the one person in the world who was best acquainted with my son,' (an opinion which seems at best misguided, given that Hugh Chevis had done most of his growing up on a different continent and then spent his adult life in the Army, rather than domiciled at home with his father).

The letter ended on a particularly unpleasant note: 'I do not wish at this stage to add to the distressing publicity attending this case by writing to the Press, but I request that you forward this letter to your superior officer for orders. I do not know at the present moment which authority is superior to the Chief Constable, but I assume there is some such authority.'[25]

In any circumstances such a letter, peremptorily ordering the Deputy Chief Constable to forward correspondence, attempting to blackmail the Surrey Police with thinly veiled threats of enlisting the Press and public opinion against them, to say nothing of implying that he would not hesitate to go over the Chief Constable's head, were unlikely to win Sir William many friends in the investigation, but given his earlier disclosure of the telegram, the reaction of Surrey's senior officers can be well imagined and probably turned the air blue.

The issue of the telegram was catching up with Sir William, however, for Captain Chevis had relayed the contents of the coroner's letters back to his father, and Sir William had presumably realised that it was perfectly obvious to the coroner and the police that the Press must have received their information from a member of his family, which in turn reflected badly on his son, who was entirely innocent in the matter. Perhaps sensing the potential for his son's embarrassment in the coroner's remarks when the inquest resumed, Sir William wrote direct to the coroner on 7 August, marking both envelope and letter <u>PRIVATE</u>. Having read the coroner's letter to his son, he wrote, he had decided it was 'my duty to inform you how the Press got to know about the telegram, though I beg that you will treat this letter as strictly confidential.' According to Sir William, a reporter from the *Evening News* had called at the house while he was out and 'managed to interview Lady Chevis' who had 'acted on the impulse of the moment' and told him about the telegram.[26]

This is certainly an interesting way of describing what appears to have been a lengthy interview, during which the reporter managed to draw out a considerable amount of information, including a protracted eulogy to Sir William's 'brilliant' career. Sir William excused his wife on the grounds that she was 'half distracted with grief and worry' and that the reporter had posed as 'having good detective abilities and being anxious to help'. He went on to say that neither she nor he had received any warning from anyone to keep the matter of the telegram secret, then launched into a litany of complaint about the way in which they had eventually learned more about the telegram – not from the police, but from the Post Office – conveniently ignoring the fact that as he himself had initiated an inquiry with the Post Office, rather than placing the matter directly in the hands of the police, the Post Office seem to have believed themselves duty bound to report back to him *before* they reported back to the police.

He further protested on Lady Chevis's behalf that by the time she spoke with the press, the police had had a month in which to investigate the telegram and if they had failed to do so then it seemed to him 'a most glaring case of red tape'. He concluded the letter by again begging that the coroner keep the matter confidential: 'Lady Chevis bitterly regrets that she ever mentioned the telegram to the reporter and we have not even informed our son or our daughter-in-law how the matter came to be published.'

Following hard on the heels of Sir William's bullying missive to the Deputy Chief Constable, an unpleasant whiff of hypocrisy lingers over this letter, in which the sender clearly intends to involve the coroner in a conspiracy of silence over Lady Chevis's conduct, while continuing to carp about the supposed shortcomings of the police officers involved in the case. Unfortunately for Sir William, both Captain Chevis and the police had separately recorded that Lady Chevis and her husband had been told not to divulge the contents of the telegram and Mr Francis was not going to let the retired judge get away with such a blatant fib.

Writing back on 8 August, the coroner opened by saying that he wished to offer his sincere sympathy to the couple on the loss of their son, since it was the first time he had had any direct communication with either of them. He felt for them very much, he wrote, and particularly for the sorrow and distress resultant from all that had been appearing in the Press. (Whether Sir William recognised that the Press frenzy to which the family was now being subjected had come about entirely as a result of the decision to reveal the existence of the telegram cannot be known – apparently ever swift to point the finger elsewhere, he may not have been so quick to attribute any of his problems closer to home.)

'With reference to the telegram,' Mr Francis wrote, 'it had already been established prior to the receipt of your letter that Lady Chevis gave the information, but I am glad of your confirmation. Your son does not know [that Lady Chevis provided the information] ...' Mr Francis then quoted the relevant section of Captain Chevis's letter, ending with the phrase, '"as far as my own relations go, I personally warned them not to divulge it" – I mention this as it does not agree with what you say.' The coroner went on to inform Sir William that he would not expose Lady Chevis as the originator of the information, unless it became necessary to do so in order to protect someone else from being blamed, and concluded by repeating that he could not interfere in the police investigation and that it would not be appropriate for him to comment on the methods adopted by the Chief Constable.[27]

Cornered by the plain dealing and honesty of his own son, Sir William wrote back – a much shorter letter this time, chilly in tone, but for once not containing a word of complaint against anyone. He thanked Mr Francis for his sympathy and his efforts to solve the mystery, saying that, 'I am well aware that you have nothing to do with the conduct of the police inquiry' (which rather begs the question why he had been encouraging his relatives to pester the coroner on this very matter less than a week earlier). With regard to the telegram, 'As my son tells you that he personally warned his relatives, I feel that I must have made a mistake in saying that he had not warned us ... I still do not remember him warning us, but considering the great trouble we have been through, perhaps it is not to be wondered at that my memory is at fault.'[28]

Sir William's protestations of a joint failure of memory in the face of a terrible bereavement might have elicited more sympathy had the police not by then suspected that he was behind the agitation now appearing in the Press for Surrey Police to call in Scotland Yard. The police were coming in for a great deal of criticism and harassment and it was known that Sir William was speaking with what Deputy Chief Constable Bird would describe in a report to his superior as 'innumerable' journalists.[29] It is not beyond the realms of possibility that far from the revelations regarding the telegram having escaped Lady Chevis's lips in a moment of distracted grief, when under pressure from a cunning reporter, the news was leaked to the Press on purpose, by a man dissatisfied with the police's handling of the case, who had decided to ignore their instructions and take matters into his own hands. It is certainly very odd that a reporter from a London newspaper should have suddenly turned up on Lady Chevis's doorstep in Bournemouth, at a point when the story had entirely ceased to be news.

The Chief Constable of Surrey, Major Nicholson, was on holiday, but he was in regular correspondence about the case with his deputy, William Bird (who had only taken over in the role on 1 August, following the retirement of the previous

Deputy Chief Constable).[30] Bird was apologetic for bothering his chief while on vacation, but explained that Sir William was 'creating a stir' in the Press regarding the 'non-appearance' of Scotland Yard, and since it had now been ascertained that the Press had obtained the telegram from Lady Chevis, 'it behoves one to exercise care, as no doubt the gist of any reply [made to Sir William's letters of complaint] will be published.'[31]

Major Nicholson penned a reply on the headed notepaper of The Solent Yacht Club, Yarmouth, Isle of Wight on 8 August (which was retyped and sent on to Sir William under an official Surrey Police letter heading), explaining that he saw no useful purpose in calling in Scotland Yard. He pointed out that his officers were able to call on the expertise of Scotland Yard at any time and had already sought their opinion on various points. He offered his sincere condolences and 'the assurance that we are doing everything in our power to clear the matter up.' In the meantime, he instructed the Deputy Chief Constable to meet with Sir William personally, in order to convey the results of the recent conference at Scotland Yard and to hopefully restore his confidence in the investigation.[32]

Deputy Chief Constable William Bird, together with Superintendent Stovell, travelled down to visit Sir William in an attempt to reassure him that they were doing all that could be done to solve the mystery, but the visit was not a success. Reporting back to Chief Constable Nicholson afterwards, Bird described how, in spite of the officers' 'conciliatory tone', Sir William 'kept repeating with parrot-like regularity' that he was not satisfied and nothing the officers could say would convince him that Scotland Yard should not be called in. Bird and Stovell had stayed for an hour, but irrespective of what they said, Sir William 'has it firmly embedded in his mind that Surrey Police would not be up to finding how the strychnine came to be in the partridge.'

According to Bird, their host became increasingly agitated during the interview, 'his features twitching' and at one point he tried to light an empty pipe. 'Sir William is an ex-Indian Judge,' Bird wrote, 'and when I tell you he is true to his kind, you will understand, I am sure, the type of man we have to deal with here.'[33]

Bird's comment may strike an odd note to the modern reader, but Major Nicholson would have understood what his deputy was getting at immediately. In the rigidly snobbish 1930s, everyone had their place – but that place was sometimes dependent on what part of the world you happened to find yourself in. Whereas on the British mainland only aristocratic lineage or extreme wealth opened the door to the upper echelons of society, the social structure in Anglo-Indian circles functioned rather differently. To be sure, wealth and breeding still guaranteed respect and status by the bucket load, but in India it was possible to live in considerable style on a much lower income than would have been the case in Britain, and the white minority was dominated by senior civil servants, who were considered superior to just about everyone else, with the social distinctions observed even more rigidly than they were in Britain. A Deputy District

Commissioner outranked a barrister or a doctor, but was of course outranked in turn by a District Commissioner or District Judge, while High Court Judges were at the very top of the tree. The Indian Civil Service recruited bright young men, often from lower middle-class backgrounds, who, by promotion through the Service, could end up at the top of Anglo-European Society in India, where cheap labour enabled them to live like demi-Gods. Years of excessive kowtowing and absolute authority over the natives encouraged many of them to acquire a sense of superiority and entitlement, affecting airs and graces which were thought 'jumped up' by those in Britain, for whom a 'gentleman' needed to have either a great deal of money or a great deal of breeding, or preferably both, before he could start throwing his weight about, expecting policemen to dance attendance on him, or grandly informing them that he 'was not satisfied'.[34] Snobbery was alive and well in every strata of English society and often particularly rampant among the British working classes, who were not prepared to be lauded over by anyone they suspected of not being 'a proper gentleman'.

Irrespective of precisely how news of the telegram had found its way into the Press, it created a storm of interest, elevating the death of Lieutenant Chevis from a minor curiosity into headline news, with reporters laying siege to Frances, her children, and, of course, Lord and Lady Chevis, whose ill-judged disclosure had provided their address to every hack and nosey parker in the land. Years later, Frances's daughters could still remember being followed on their daily walks by reporters shouting questions, and blinded by flash bulbs going off whenever they opened the front door.[35]

The *Evening News* had the benefit of their scoop on Saturday, 25 July, but by Monday every paper in the capital had a man on the story. The Press had also got hold of the fact that Frances had an ex-husband, and it did not take them twenty-four hours to track Major Jackson to his hotel in Eastbourne, where they succeeded in door-stepping him for comments about the case.[36] Nor was it only the newshounds from Fleet Street who were interested in Frances's former husband – for the Surrey Police too had been turning their attention in his direction.

CHAPTER ELEVEN

DISCREET ENQUIRIES AND ASSUMED INDISCRETIONS

The first intimation that police interest was focussing on Trev Jackson lies in the notes of an informal interview between Inspector Pharo and Captain William Chevis, which has already been mentioned. On learning that Major Jackson resided in Eastbourne, Superintendent Stovell contacted the Eastbourne Police (who were then a separate force in their own right) and asked that some discreet enquiries be put in hand regarding this particular resident of their borough. The job was given to Detective Inspector Ernest Sawkins, whose report was forwarded to Surrey by the Chief Constable of Eastbourne, Mr W.H. Smith.[1]

Jackson was said to be living at the Mostyn Hotel on the Grand Parade (a seafront location which no doubt appealed to the coast-loving Major), where 'he appears to keep himself very quiet and does not make many friends.' One particular friend these 'discreet enquiries' had thrown up was a Mrs Lawrence – an Eastbourne resident whose husband was said to be abroad. Sawkins wrote that while to all outward appearances the friendship was platonic, 'this is doubted.' (It is not explained why or by whom. The current author has established that Mrs Lawrence was a keen golfer, which may well have been the conduit by which she and Trev Jackson initially became friends.)[2]

The Eastbourne force had made enquiries into the Major's background and confirmed that he had served in the RAVC and, after retiring from the army, had set up a veterinary practice with Captain Sergeant, which had by now been dissolved for some years, though Jackson remained the proprietor of a canine boarding kennels at Langney, on the outskirts of the town.

Sawkins had also ascertained that Major Jackson had been out of town from the 19th to the 24th of June, but had not managed to establish whether he – or indeed Mrs Lawrence – had any friends in Ireland. The report concluded by stating that 'nothing is known to the police which is prejudicial to his character.'

As well as these various observations, Sawkins had also included the information that Jackson was 'still friendly with Mrs Jackson'. It must be assumed that the woman in question was Frances – who was actually Mrs Chevis – since the other Mrs Jackson, Trev's former wife Mabel who had gone on to become Mrs Anderson – had been dead since 1926.[3] Sawkins gave no indication as to whence these snippets of information regarding Major Jackson's relationships with members of the opposite sex derived, so their accuracy or otherwise is open to speculation. It can be construed with some certainty that they did not come direct from Trev Jackson himself, because when first approached directly by the police for personal information, he clearly regarded the process as a damnable cheek and offered them only limited assistance.

Inspector Sawkins was asked to follow up his initial sleuthing by having a chat with Major Jackson, the results of which were passed on to the Surrey Police and the coroner in due course.[4] Sawkins described Trev Jackson as 5 foot 8 inches tall, broad and well built, with a red face, blue eyes, greyish brown hair and a close-clipped moustache. He estimated his age at about fifty (the Major was actually fifty-four) and noted that he was wearing a check suit, striped collar and shirt, and used a monocle to read. The significance of asking Sawkins to provide a description of his man becomes apparent further down the page, where someone has noted that the man who handed in the telegram form in Dublin was aged about fifty, slightly below middle height, had close cropped grey hair, a moustache and was wearing a smart suit. The same hand also noted that Mrs Chevis had just returned from her London flat after spending the weekend at Eastbourne. The possibility that Frances Chevis had in some way colluded with her former husband to dispose of Hugh Chevis, or that Jackson had acted alone, were clearly under consideration, although it had apparently not occurred to the Major himself that he might be a suspect, for he was not particularly co-operative when Sawkins initially called on him, refusing to provide the name and address of the friends with whom he claimed to have stayed during the weekend of Lieutenant Chevis's death, and giving the officer short shrift when the conversation turned to his divorce from Frances.

While such an attitude might seem strange today, it was very typical of the time. Stories of policemen arriving to enquire into crimes and being told to go to the servants' entrance were not apocryphal. In 1932, when a policeman laid his hand on Elvira Barney's arm while attending the property where she had just shot her lover, she slapped his face. Mrs Barney was a wealthy socialite and did not expect to be 'manhandled' by the lower orders under any circumstances. She referred to the attending officers as 'foul swine' and threatened them with dire consequences for presuming to ask her to accompany them to the police station, informing them that she was the daughter of Sir John and Lady Mullens. As the author Andrew Rose wrote; 'It is a reflection on contemporary social attitudes that she was not charged with assaulting a police officer and that, after making a statement at the police station she was released unconditionally and remained at liberty until her arrest four days later'[5] – leniency which was unlikely to have been extended to a costermonger's daughter. Similarly Trev Jackson, as an officer and a gentleman, had no intention of discussing his personal business with the police or involving his friends in 'unpleasantness' if it could possibly be avoided.

In Jackson's world an officer's word was his bond – or at any rate should have been accepted as such by a mere policeman.

Not satisfied with the outcome of this informal approach, the Surrey force asked Sawkins to take a proper statement from the Major and the result of this was forwarded to Superintendent Stovell, accompanied by a letter from Sawkins, advising that 'Major Jackson is a rather difficult person to interview as he will say nothing with regard to the divorce proceedings taken by Mrs Chevis...' – and indeed this was not the only subject on which the Major was initially tight lipped.[6]

Taken at the Mostyn Hotel, Trev Jackson's statement began with the inevitable recital of his career to date, explaining that he had given up his vet's practice after his marriage to Frances, whom he said he had initially met in 1921 in Eastbourne, married in 1923 and with whom he had had three children. Once married they had lived together in Bournemouth until 1928, when she had divorced him. Since the divorce he had lived in four different hotels in Eastbourne: The Imperial, The Cavendish, The Queen's and The Mostyn.

He claimed to have seen his ex-wife only twice since the divorce: the first occasion had been on 5 November 1930, when she had been staying at the Grand Hotel in Eastbourne and had asked him to meet her there. The other occasion had been an accidental encounter on the Parade in Eastbourne, which had taken place after Lieutenant Chevis's death. He could not recall the exact date, but knew it was during the recent race meeting at Sandown. He could remember this because afterwards he had written to her, offering a couple of badges for the meeting, which he thought might cheer her up as she looked so ill. She had written to him in reply, but apart from this exchange they did not usually correspond.

In response to further questions, he explained how Mrs Heap had initially arranged an introduction for Hugh Chevis, who had then become his occasional riding companion ('I had a lot of ponies at that time'). 'He never stayed at my house,' Jackson said. 'I would not allow it – but I used to go down to the South of France with my wife's mother, to play polo at Cannes. What happened while I was away in Cannes I do not know. I received anonymous letters when I got back, but I tore them up.' He had encountered Hugh Chevis only once since he married Frances, the Major told Sawkins, and that had been in Bournemouth in January 1931. Pressed further on the question of his ex-wife's new husband, he suggested that Mr and Mrs Heap 'know all about the late Lieutenant Chevis and some information might be obtained from them,' adding that he believed the couple lived at Egham in Surrey.

It is noticeable that while still not entirely forthcoming, Trev Jackson was now prepared to give the police much more information than had formerly been the case, and this was undoubtedly due to the fact that by the time Sawkins approached him for a formal statement the story of the telegram had broken, he had himself been pursued by reporters, and had belatedly appreciated that he was a suspect in a possible murder inquiry. With this in mind, he now provided his alibi for the weekend of Hugh Chevis's death. According to the Major, he left Eastbourne at around 8.30 on the morning of 19 June with an unnamed friend, to whom he had promised to give a lift. (The police later established that this passenger had in fact been Mrs Lawrence.) He had dropped his friend as arranged at Ashford in Middlesex, then driven on to Heyford Hills in Northamptonshire, which was the home of his friend, Major Campbell. Here he had spent a long weekend, not returning to Eastbourne until 24 June. Aside from asking members of the Campbell household, he said, his whereabouts could also be corroborated by a policeman who had called on him during his weekend there, in connection with a minor motor accident in which he had been involved on his journey.[7]

Major Jackson's initial refusal to explain his whereabouts on 20 June together with his apparent resemblance to the man who sent the telegram, undoubtedly fuelled suspicion against him – and to this could be added several minor points which gradually emerged. To begin with, he and Frances did not agree on the number of times they had met since their divorce. Both said there had been two meetings, but between them they had described three. Frances said she had bumped into Trev twice by accident, once on the doorstep of a hotel with her new husband and once following his death, while out walking in Eastbourne. Jackson on the other hand, while confirming the circumstances of the latter meeting and mentioning that he had bumped into Hugh Chevis in January 1931, claimed that the other occasion on which he met Frances had been back in November 1930, when he had gone to meet her in Eastbourne at her specific request.

These chance meetings were easily forgettable and Frances may well have forgotten asking Major Jackson to meet her in Eastbourne the preceding Guy Fawkes night – but to the police, discrepancies of this nature may have seemed unduly suspicious, when coupled with Frances's decision to keep popping down to Eastbourne, the one place where she was particularly likely to 'bump into' Jackson, if the two of them had wished to contrive it. (By 1931 Frances's mother no longer lived in Eastbourne, so there was no particularly obvious, compelling reason for her to go there.[8])

In addition to this, intimations that all might not have been as it seemed in the Chevis marriage were starting to emerge. When asked if he had any Irish connections himself, Trev Jackson could only say that he had served for a time in Ireland before the war, but had not been there since. (RAVC officers were often despatched to Ireland to select and purchase horses for the army direct from breeders and it would appear that this had been Jackson's mission there.) Asked whether he knew of any other possible Irish connections to the case, however, the Major had speculated off the record that 'Chevis may have been philandering with an Irish woman'[9] which, set alongside Trev's witness statement, which contained clear implications that there might have been some 'philandering' with Frances while the Major had been away in Cannes, ensured that one way and another the inquiry was starting to take on dimensions and travel in directions of which Sir William Chevis would not have dreamed.

CHAPTER TWELVE

LEADS, BLIND ALLEYS AND A THICKENING PLOT

One noticeable oddity in the evidence lay in the fact that while both participants in the fatal dinner had apparently succumbed to strychnine poisoning,
the timing of their symptoms and the ultimate outcome had been different. In his
report, written on 21 June, Inspector Pharo noted that Mrs Chevis had become
ill about an hour after her husband.[1] It was very unusual for the symptoms of
strychnine poisoning to take more than an hour to manifest themselves – the
usual time lapse was not much greater than 15-30 minutes. Moreover, whereas
Lieutenant Chevis had collapsed and died, Mrs Chevis had recovered sufficiently
to be moved to London early the following morning. Of course, strychnine poisoning was not inevitably fatal and it was an established fact that the same dose
did not always prove fatal in two different individuals, though for obvious reasons
there was no hard and fast information on how much any individual could toler-
ate in comparison to any other. The delayed symptoms exhibited by Mrs Chevis,
however, undoubtedly prompted suspicion in some minds.

On 9 July the coroner had written to Ryffel, thanking him for his preliminary
analysis results and saying: 'It seems clear that death was caused by strychnine
poisoning through eating the partridges.'[2] (While this was a reasonable inference,
it was far from 'clear' since the destruction of the partridges had made it
impossible to confirm or deny whether either or both had actually contained
any strychnine.) He added, 'Whether there has been foul play or not, we may
know at the adjourned inquest.' Unfortunately, the resumption of the inquest
had provided no additional clues to settle the question and the arrival of the
telegram had caused further doubt and confusion. While waiting for the GPO
to report back on the telegram, Mr Francis evidently decided to pursue a line
of his own, and when writing to the Home Office analyst again on 4 August, to
notify him that he would be required to attend at the resumption of the inquest
which was scheduled for 2.30 p.m. on 11 August, he said, 'I would be obliged if
you would tell me for my own information whether there was any difference
between the quantities of strychnine in exhibits C1 and C2.' (This was the vomit
which had been preserved from Frances and Hugh Chevis respectively.) 'You say
in your report that you found the sum total of 0.3 grain, but do not say what each

contained individually...This information may be of no importance but I should like to have it, if you can give it to me.'[3]

Far from being of no importance, this information was absolutely vital if there was any question over the genuineness of Frances Chevis's symptoms. The presence of strychnine in exhibit C1 would prove without doubt that Frances had ingested strychnine and been suffering from its effects – its absence would of course have implied the opposite.

Alas John Ryffel's reply was unhelpful: 'I am afraid I cannot say anything definite as to the relative quantities of strychnine in C1 and C2. Both contained a considerable amount, as did C3. C2 and C3 contained more meat than did C1.' There is a distinct sense here that Ryffel is being a trifle disingenuous. He had not been asked about exhibit C3 (Lieutenant Chevis's stomach contents) or indeed about the amount of meat present in the exhibits, which was neither here nor there, since that presupposed that all the meat found was associated with the poison, which was not necessarily the case.

Although part of a highly respected team used regularly by the police in cases of criminal poisoning, the truth (not alas appreciated during his career) was that Dr John Ryffel could sometimes be slipshod and cavalier in his methods. During his involvement in the 'Croydon Arsenic Case' in 1929, he submitted as sworn testimony a report which contained basic mathematical errors and demonstrated ignorance of the appropriate way to test for the presence of arsenic in fingernails.[4] It was his habit to use an entire sample on a first test, leaving himself no opportunity to perform a second test in order to check his results – something which had created an element of doubt in the Croydon analysis. In the case of Lieutenant Chevis, the fact that Dr Ryffel could give a total quantity of strychnine found in respect of exhibits C1 and C2, but was unable to give the respective separate quantities can only mean one thing – the analyst had not tested each sample separately and then added his resulting totals together – he had tested the two samples together and thereby arrived at the joint total. This was an inexcusable shortcut in the context of the case, but ever the slippery witness, Ryffel now employed his usual distraction technique to drag the coroner off the scent, writing: 'As to the amount of strychnine absorbed, the medical evidence is the most important...' and following this up with a long excursion into a lot of irrelevant speculation as to why it took Lieutenant Chevis so long to die, concluding that 'so far as the information I have received goes, everything indicates that Lieutenant Chevis received a fully fatal dose and absorbed sufficient strychnine to cause death in a typical way.'[5]

If the best way to avoid answering an awkward question is to ramble on at sufficient length until your interrogator forgets what he asked in the first place, then the tactic worked perfectly with Coroner Francis – who, in fairness, was also in the midst of dealing with the fall-out from the release of the telegram and being hassled to throw his weight behind the idea that Scotland Yard should be called in. Faced with a lengthy piece of waffle from the Home Office analyst, he wrote back thanking Ryffel for his letter and saying that he much appreciated the very full information given therein[6] – apparently unaware that Ryffel had neither answered his question, nor provided any fresh information whatsoever.

In his long response, Ryffel had elected to introduce a discussion on the treatment provided by the doctors who had attended the bungalow that night and in particular he questioned the use of magnesium sulphate, which had been administered in the form of injections to both Hugh and Frances Chevis, referring to this as a 'drastic measure'. On consideration of the letter, the coroner, full of misplaced faith in a man who, having failed to do his own job properly, was now throwing up a smokescreen by casting doubt on the work done by others, wrote to Ryffel again, inviting him to comment on the treatment provided by Dr Bindloss.

Returning to the statement provided by Dr Bindloss, the coroner noted that he had arrived at 8.15, but no emetic[7] had been administered to Hugh Chevis until the arrival of Dr Murray at least forty-five minutes later. Should Bindloss not have done this sooner, the coroner wanted to know – and might this have improved the chances of saving Lieutenant Chevis's life?[8]

The coroner may have been under the impression that because Ryffel enjoyed the prefix 'Dr' before his name, he was a fount of medical knowledge, whereas in fact Ryffel was not a medical doctor, but an analytical chemist, who had graduated in chemistry in 1908. It was therefore inappropriate for Ryffel to hazard any opinions on medical matters and particularly inappropriate for him to be invited to pass comment on treatment provided by a man who *was* medically qualified. Lack of relevant qualifications or clinical experience was no deterrent to the Home Office analyst, however. He responded the following day, stating that having diagnosed strychnine poisoning, Dr Bindloss should have lost no time in removing the remaining food from the stomach, going on to say that he thought the injection of magnesium sulphate which Dr Bindloss had administered to Lieutenant Chevis may have been an element in his respiratory failure, because, according to Cushing in 1928,[9] injecting magnesium sulphate as an anaesthetic causes death from respiratory failure, though Ryffel was forced to add that he did not understand 'why Mrs Chevis's injection acted differently'.[10]

It may be that having received this question from the coroner, Ryffel was genuinely doing his best to answer it, but there is a lingering suspicion that he had originally introduced the question of Bindloss's competence in order to distract Mr Francis from his own blunder in failing to separately analyse samples which had come from two different people. Irrespective of Ryffel's motives, it was highly unprofessional to trespass into another man's speciality, particularly when it entailed implying that Bindloss had in some way been negligent, even to the point of hastening his patient's death. Ryffel's reliance on partial knowledge, backed up with whatever he had read in a recently published textbook, were in any case leading him astray, because magnesium sulphate injections were (and remain) an accepted method of controlling convulsions.

There was no sequel to these thinly veiled accusations of medical malpractice. Having made this enquiry of Ryffel, the coroner can hardly have been reassured by his answer, but there is no evidence that he attempted to look any further into the matter. It is of course possible that he undertook some discreet verbal enquiries of some other medical authority and was reassured on the question of the magnesium sulphate. Nor was Dr Bindloss's failure to administer an emetic likely to have been an issue, because strychnine is so rapidly absorbed from the gastrointestinal tract that its effects are not particularly influenced by vomiting up the medium in which it was consumed. (As illustrated in the case of Dr Charles McDonnell mentioned in Chapter 8, for although the doctor immediately realised his mistake and made himself vomit, the strychnine still proved fatal. The instruction to a First Responder in the twenty-first century is *not* to attempt to make the patient vomit in cases of strychnine ingestion.) There remains no known antidote to strychnine and the patient's best hope is in fact to have his/ her convulsions controlled with the use of sedatives and muscle relaxants, such as those employed by Bindloss.

Mr Francis had included another query in his letter which was at least somewhat closer to Ryffel's area of expertise, asking whether, if the poison had been present in the partridge when it was cooked, 'which it must have been as you found strychnine in the gravy under the fat', should it not also have got into the other partridge, which was basted using the same fat? If that was the case, the coroner wrote, then he could not understand why Mrs Chevis had not complained about the taste of her bird too.[11]

Ryffel's response to this question was a classic example of the muddle and confusion which he so often managed to introduce. He began by agreeing that as the partridges were cooked together, you would have expected both of them to taste bitter. He had re-examined the dripping, he wrote, and while the dripping tasted bitter, the gravy tasted *very* bitter, 'so my previous idea that most of the strychnine I found in the dripping was in the gravy was correct' (a phrase which again suggests that some of his conclusions appear to have been based on his own 'ideas', rather than actual scientific results).

Having said that he would have expected both partridges to taste bitter, Ryfell then performed an about face a few paragraphs later, saying that because basting sealed the birds, you might *not* expect too much strychnine to have transferred from one bird to the other, 'but some bitterness should have been noticeable' and 'the gravy served must have been very bitter, if what I received was a fair sample.'[12]

It is reasonable to assume that John Ryffel's culinary experience was in the range of limited to non-existent. Middle-class professional men of Ryffel's vintage did not involve themselves in cooking, living as they did either in a household which at the very least enjoyed the services of a 'cook-general' or else living and dining at their club or a hotel. Even so, Ryffel's persistent use of the term 'gravy' for the darker element within the dripping was inexcusable. Every household in which meat was cooked kept a dripping bowl in the pantry, into which the fat left over from roasting meat was tipped at the end of the cooking process. (In working-class households where, well into the 1960s, bread and dripping was a staple teatime and suppertime treat, the solidified dripping was often spread cold onto bread.) On cooling, the dripping inevitably separated into two distinct layers of off-white fat above a reddish brown jelly. If not consumed on bread, some of it would be used the next time meat was roasted, with the residue from the process again poured into the existing contents of the dripping bowl, so that fat and juices derived from several different sources could end up mixed together in one job lot.

While it is unlikely that bread and dripping formed a staple part of Dr Ryffel's diet, and fair to say that his direct encounters with dripping basins were presumably limited, Ryffel had been provided with copies of the witness depositions[13] and had he read these, or taken the trouble to check on the way dripping was normally constituted, rather than wasting his time in cross-checking his medical textbooks on the subject of magnesium sulphate, he would have been aware firstly that the dripping sent to him for analysis derived not only from the partridges, but also from the lamb cooked the day before; secondly that the presence of darker matter at the bottom of the dripping was perfectly normal and had nothing whatever to do with the gravy poured over the food at the table; and thirdly that the gravy served for Lieutenant and Mrs Chevis's dinner had not been made with fat from the roasting tin, as was the practice in many households, but from a concoction of water, flour, Bisto and Bovril. Clearly the residue of the gravy served at dinner had not magically transported itself into the bottom of the dripping basin, but had been washed down the sink, when the gravy boat was washed up, so for Ryffel to speak of the gravy served at dinner tasting bitter, based on the 'sample' of it he had received, was an absolute nonsense, while his use of the term 'gravy' at all in respect to the dripping could only serve to confuse the issue.

It is possible that the coroner had finally lost faith or patience in his favourite 'expert', because he seems to have turned next for advice to Dr Bindloss, by a strange twist asking of him one of the questions which Ryffel, the chemistry graduate, would have been better placed to answer. On 10 August, he telephoned Dr Bindloss and asked him about the solubility of strychnine in water. He also enquired about what Hugh Chevis had actually said regarding the taste in his mouth. It is most unlikely that Mr Francis was familiar with the earlier cases of poisoning mentioned in Chapter 8, which involved the accidental ingestion of strychnine which had been dissolved in glasses of water or gin, but it may well have occurred to him that like the majority of middle-class families, the Chevis household was likely to have had a jug of drinking water on the table at meal times, and that when everyone was asked what had been drunk with the meal and said 'nothing', what they meant was no wine, or beer, with water being as 'invisible' and unremarkable as the ubiquitous cruet set containing salt and pepper, which also graced every table, but was never mentioned in evidence about what had been eaten or drunk.

Bindloss evidently did not know the solubility of strychnine off the top of his head, but he looked it up and sent the information to the coroner on the same day, also recording that 'Mr Chevis spoke of the partridge being horrible – tasting sour and bitter, like quinine.'[14]

While the coroner was pursuing these lines of enquiry with the Home Office's junior analyst[15] and Dr Bindloss, Superintendent Stovell and his officers were busy with other matters. Inspector Pharo was despatched to the barracks yet again, this time to measure the distance between the nearest bungalow (Lieutenant Evered's) to the meat safe. (It was 30 feet 1 inch.)[16] Having initiated enquiries at all the chemists in the locality of the Blackdown Camp, he asked the Eastbourne Police to make enquiries about any strychnine purchases made in their area.

At this point Major Jackson was evidently still well up the list of suspects and Stovell had written to the Chief Constable of Northampton, requesting them to make 'discreet enquires' with the aim of establishing whether or not Jackson's claim to have been staying at Heyford Hills during the crucial weekend could be confirmed. Unfortunately, Northamptonshire (just like Surrey and Sussex) was not covered by a single police force[17] and the Chief Constable wrote back to Stovell, explaining that Heyford Hills fell within the jurisdiction of the county force, rather than the borough force, and that he had forwarded Stovell's request on to them.[18]

When Superintendent Brumby of Northamptonshire Police eventually called at Heyford Hills, the butler refused to admit him, stating that Major Campbell was not at home.[19] Untroubled by areas of jurisdiction or issues of discretion, the Press had preceded the police, so that by the time Brumby arrived the butler knew all about the reason for his visit and was happy to confirm that Major Jackson had stayed there between 19 and 24 June, never leaving the house except in the company of his host. Brumby left a message asking Major Campbell to contact him on his return, which Major Campbell duly did, stating that he was anxious to speak to the policeman and inviting him to call at his earliest convenience.

When Brumby arrived for the second time he was shown in and Campbell told him that he had received a letter from Major Jackson, which explained that he had been visited by the police in connection with the death of Lieutenant Chevis, and asked to account for his movements, making it likely that the police would be contacting Major Campbell for confirmation. At Brumby's request Campbell produced the Major's letter, which appeared to be no more than a courteous warning that the police were liable to call and explaining their reason for doing so.

Major Campbell was only too happy to confirm his friend's alibi, telling Brumby that Jackson had arrived at about tea time on 19 June and not left the house and grounds again until Saturday, when they had gone to Daventry, where both men played in a cricket match,[20] not returning home until after tea. On Sunday, while Major Campbell and his daughter went to church, Major Jackson had stayed at the house writing some letters, and in the afternoon the two men had gone to nearby Maidwell Hall, the home of Sir Reginald Loder, to play tennis. On Monday they had driven into Leamington and on Tuesday into Northampton, and during the remaining time they had played cricket and tennis at home.

Asked about his relationship with Major Jackson, Bruce Campbell said that he had originally met Jackson about two years previously in Eastbourne and since then had invited him to stay at Heyford Hills on two previous occasions, making June 1931 his third visit. As Major Campbell kept a diary, he was able to substantiate his account of their recent weekend together by showing it to Brumby, who recorded that the entries on 19, 20 and 21 June confirmed what he had been told, while the entries for 22 and 23 June related only to family matters. Major Campbell was 'a highly respected gentleman,' Brumby wrote, 'and his statements can be relied on.'

News of this cast-iron alibi did not reach Superintendent Stovell until 3 August, by which time he had already obtained a photograph of Major Jackson and forwarded it to the police in Dublin, to see whether the postmistress could recognise him as the man who had sent the telegram.[21]

Stovell initially placed enormous importance on the telegram and was sure that the sender must have had some knowledge of the crime, for though Lieutenant Chevis's death had been widely reported in the newspapers, there had been nothing in what was published to link him with Sir William and Lady Chevis, still less to offer a clue as to their address. Once he had been apprised of the telegram's existence and received notification of the sender's details, Stovell had wasted no time in contacting the Dublin Police to solicit their assistance, and they too were asked to check chemists' Poison Registers for any purchases of strychnine made in the name of Hartigan or Jackson.[22]

The Dublin Garda threw themselves enthusiastically into the investigation. Explaining to Superintendent Stovell that 'Hibernian' was probably the Royal Hibernian Hotel in Dawson Street (a well-known landmark in the city until it was demolished towards the end of the twentieth century), Inspector Kinsella, who was leading enquiries on that side of the Irish Sea, despatched an officer to check the hotel register. No guest by the name of Hartigan or Jackson had stayed there on the night of 24 June, but a C. Hartigan of Charleville had been there from 16-20 June, and so had a Ronald Jackson. Hotel workers were able to provide a description of Ronald Jackson, who was remembered as a regular visitor, as he always stayed at the Hibernian when making an annual trip to Dublin on behalf of his employers, Messrs Harvey & Clarke of London. At thirty-five years old, 5 feet 9 or 10 inches tall, and very slightly built with a dark moustache, Ronald Jackson was clearly not a match for the man described by Miss Ruttledge, the postmistress at Merrion Row Post Office, who had accepted the telegram. Unfortunately, no one at the hotel could recall anything at all about C. Hartigan and it was therefore decided to contact the Garda at Charleville, asking them to check up on the man calling himself C. Hartigan.[23]

Detective Sergeant Malachey Doddy and Detective Officer McEvoy had been to interview Miss Ruttledge at the Post Office and the description she had provided – a man of around fifty years old, with grey hair, a dark grey moustache, low size (by which she meant 'not tall'), wearing a grey suit and grey trilby hat, with small shapely hands – had been circulated to Dublin police stations and all hotel keepers, asking that they 'keep a sharp look out' for him – a request which must surely have provoked a certain amount of amusement, given that it was a description which fitted a significant proportion of Dublin's citizens. It might also be added that it was certainly not a description which fitted the photograph Stovell had provided of Trev Jackson, who, pipe in hand and wearing tweedy plus fours, looked every inch the retired English army officer that he was – and sure enough when Miss Ruttledge was shown the photograph she confirmed that this was not the man from whom she had accepted the telegram form.[24]

Accents are always an important clue and the Garda officers wanted to know how the man who sent the telegram had spoken, but Miss Ruttledge said the man had not spoken at all during the transaction. She had not thought there was anything unusual about him, or the message (though surely the man's complete silence might have been thought a little unusual, as in the normal course of a transaction one might have expected a customer to say something). He had not been in a rush, she told the policemen, in fact the transaction had been 'leisurely'.[25]

Results from the Poison Registers were similarly disappointing. The Garda interviewed every single person who had purchased strychnine in the Dublin area during the preceding three months, but produced no results which had any bearing on the investigation. (One sale was traced to a person called Jackson, but this turned out to be merely another coincidence of names.) By 5 August they had extended their enquiries to anyone who had purchased strychnine in County Dublin or County Wicklow.[26]

The Garda based in Charleville, County Cork, had by now called on Dr Cecil Hartigan and confirmed that not only had he not been in Dublin on 24 June when the telegram was sent, but also that he bore no resemblance whatsoever to the description of the man in question.[27] Indeed, Superintendent Brennan of the Dublin Garda had already sounded a somewhat gloomy note in his report to Stovell, mentioning that unlike England, 'Hartigan is a fairly common name here'.[28]

In the first days of August there seemed to be a breakthrough, when a Mr E.H. Milmoe of Belmont Avenue in the Donneybrook district of Dublin provided the police with a remarkable statement relating to an encounter he claimed to have had on 24 June.[29] According to Mr Milmoe he had been standing outside Gerrards, the stationers in Merrion Row, at about 3 p.m. in the afternoon, when he was approached by a stranger who asked him the way to the nearest telegraph office.

Mr Milmoe replied that he thought the nearest ones were College Green, or the General Post Office in O'Connell Street, but the man said surely there must be one closer, as they were in the vicinity of the Shelbourne Hotel and other important buildings. Milmoe said that there was a sub-post office nearby and as he was going that way, he would show him where it was. When they reached the building in question – the same office from which the Hooray telegram would be despatched – Milmoe observed that there was indeed a sign above the door, which read 'Telegraph Office'.

On the way the stranger had been remarkably talkative, remarking how quiet the city seemed to be, adding that there appeared to be a lot of money in the country and that it was great sporting country, where he had often 'in the old days' attended race meetings at the Curragh and Punchestown. He had then asked Milmoe where the B & I boats sailed from (B & I for many years ran a ferry service across the Irish Sea) and what time the boat left Dublin and arrived in Liverpool. Mr Milmoe told him that the boat left at about 9 p.m. each night and got into Liverpool between 7 a.m. and 8 a.m. in the morning, to which the stranger responded, 'And I presume you can still get a connection straight to London?' When Milmoe agreed that he thought this was so, his companion enquired what time he thought the train got into London. Milmoe said he thought it arrived at about noon. Having utilised Mr Milmoe as a walking travellers' timetable, the man then asked where he could buy a ticket in the Irish Hospital Sweepstake, and the ever-obliging Irishman told him.

By now they had arrived at the Post Office and Milmoe bid the stranger farewell and crossed the road. When he looked back the man had not gone inside the Post Office but was walking up and down the pavement. He was about forty-five to fifty years old, 5 feet 6 to 7 inches tall, well built, with hair turning grey; he had a brownish moustache and was wearing a grey double breasted suit with well creased trousers, a grey hat and a gold watch with an expanding bracelet. He wore a gold ring set with a bloodstone on a finger of his left hand and spoke with an English accent.

As if this were not enough, at about 7.30 that same evening, while on the top deck of a tram travelling along O'Connell Street, Mr Milmoe had spotted the same man, walking along the street.

On the face of it this was an exciting lead, but Mr Milmoe's testimony needs cautious scrutiny. The description of the man is similar to the one provided by Miss Ruttledge, but whether or not Mr Milmoe had genuinely encountered a man that day and shown him the way to the Post Office, his recollections could easily have been influenced by the postmistress's description, which had by then appeared in both the English and Irish newspapers.

The long and detailed conversation between the two men (which Milmoe had managed to remember in great detail, some six weeks after the event) has some distinct oddities and sounds suspiciously like the sort of conversation which might be invented for a visiting Englishman, by a native of Dublin who has not quite thought things through. On the one hand the stranger implied that he was a visitor to the city who had not visited Ireland for some years, but if that were the case he would surely have arrived recently enough to know where the ferry docked? Moreover, a traveller from England would have been likely to know better than a Dublin native whether there was a direct train linking Liverpool to London – and to have ascertained the return travel arrangements in advance, rather than seeking this information from a complete stranger, of whom he had originally asked only directions to the Post Office.

As well as the series of questions which established that this English traveller would shortly be returning home across the Irish Sea, the Englishman had casually dropped other clues to his identity into the lap of his new acquaintance, mentioning what 'great sporting country' Ireland was, and how he had been accustomed to attend race meetings there 'in the old days' – sentiments which sounded remarkably like the sort liable to be expressed by Major Jackson, who had spent time in Ireland 'in the old days' before the war, and was a keen racing man – information which had by then found its way into the press via interviews with Major Jackson himself.[30]

It may also be significant that having asked directions to the telegraph office, rather than going inside and sending his telegram, the stranger was observed to walk up and down outside – the classic behaviour of the fictional villain, who, having reached the brink of an action, paces to and fro (presumably while engaging in a fierce inner debate with his conscience about whether to proceed). By way of a further discrepancy, whereas Mr Milmoe placed these events on 24 June at 3 o'clock, the telegram was actually sent at around 4.30 – information which had not been revealed in the papers.

After showing the photograph of Trev Jackson to Miss Ruttledge the Dublin police had returned it to their English counterparts, but now they requested it again and Stovell concurred, even though he knew full well by then that whoever Milmoe had encountered in Merrion Row that afternoon, it could not possibly have been Frances Chevis's ex-husband.[31]

Detective Sergeant Doddy (whose reports were all written in a delightfully archaic police-ese, opening with phrases such as 'in consequence of pursuance of diligent enquiries') took the photographs to show Mr Milmoe, who said that the man he had met on 24 June had appeared a little younger, but the lower portion of his face, moustache, mouth and nose were identical to the man shown in the photograph. He further claimed that he would have no difficulty in picking out and identifying this man as the man he had encountered on 24 June, if he were paraded before him.[32] For this, as well as other reasons, it was extremely fortunate for Major Jackson that he had a good alibi.

While the Garda did their best over the telegram, the Surrey men were busily looking into other aspects of the case. Major Jackson had implied that the police would do well to interview Mr and Mrs Heap on the subject of Lieutenant Chevis, but the Heaps initially proved elusive. Trev Jackson had believed them to be living at Egham in Surrey, but from Egham Stovell's men were directed to try Buckinghamshire. The Buckinghamshire Police learned that the couple had been until recently at Rose Hatch, a cottage in Bisham, Berkshire, but had moved on again and were thought to be living at Flat 5, Hans Crescent, in London.[33] Inspector Pharo finally ran them to ground in Cookham, back in Surrey, where he called on 5 August and found Mrs Heap at home.

George Tweedale Heap was born in Birkenhead in 1890, the son of an East India Company merchant.[34] His wife, Dorothy Rose Felicia Heap (*née* Houghton), was two years younger and the daughter of a Birmingham doctor. The couple had married in 1914, by which time George was an officer in the 20th Hussars. After service in the Great War (during which he had served with Trev Jackson in France) George had retired in 1919 with the rank of Captain and joined his younger brother, Arthur, in a farming venture in Hampshire, which unfortunately went bankrupt in 1921. The partnership was dissolved and although George endeavoured to settle the debts and continue the business for a while, by 1931 he was a commercial traveller, and the couple appear to have been attempting to live slightly beyond their means.

Mrs Heap told Inspector Pharo that she and her husband had initially become acquainted with Hugh Chevis after meeting him at a dance, and had separately met Frances when her husband became reacquainted with Major Jackson after encountering him in a Bournemouth hotel. There had evidently been a time when the Heaps' social life coincided with Frances's to a significant degree – they had called on one another and attended some of the same dances and parties – but by July 1931 Felicia Heap said that she had not seen Frances, Hugh Chevis, or Major Jackson for over a year.[35]

When George Heap returned home three days later, he in turn was interviewed by Inspector Pharo and essentially confirmed what his wife had already said. It is apparent that after the Jacksons parted, while George and Dorothy no longer saw Trev Jackson, they continued to maintain friendly relations with his wife, who, as well as meeting them in other places, occasionally motored out to their house at Marlow, and it was there that they had seen her for the last time. She had driven out from London on her own, Mr Heap recalled, and that had been about eighteen months ago (around January 1930).

Asked about Mrs Chevis's friends, George Heap said somewhat cagily that, 'She has a number of male and female friends, but I know of no one in particular.'[36]

This was not the only subject on which the Heaps seem to have been somewhat circumspect in their answers. Both claimed to know nothing about the Jackson divorce except 'what they had read in the papers' but this seems a little unlikely, given that their friendship with Frances had continued right through this period and beyond, while on one subject in particular they were giving nothing away at all. Inspector Pharo noted in his report of the encounter that when asked if he was under any financial obligation to Mrs Chevis, 'Captain Heap appeared startled'.[37] Heap denied that this was the case, but in fact the police had reason to believe that both husband and wife were in debt to Frances, Dorothy owing between £20 and £25 and George to the tune of some £80 (the equivalent of several thousand pounds today).[38]

Finally Pharo wanted to know where Captain and Mrs Heap had been at the time of Lieutenant Chevis's death, but he found that, like Major Jackson, they had been many miles away from Surrey, staying with a Mr Norman Cappel at his home in Liverpool. They had driven up there on Thursday, 19 June and not returned to Surrey until six days later.

Though the Heaps had not been forthcoming about the identity of any of Frances's friends, it is evident that other people had spoken off the record, for the police soon found their way to John Milligan Blair, the son of Sir Robert Blair, and, like Captain Heap, an ex-army officer (given that Britain had just fought a major war, very few men of this age and class had not seen service as army officers).[39] John Blair had served firstly in the East Surrey Regiment and then with the Royal Corps of Signals, being posted to both the North West Frontier and Mesopotamia, and finally retiring from the army in 1920. Blair was forty-three in 1931 and had been divorced since 1927, after a brief marriage. In comparison with the rather abrupt responses provided by Captain and Mrs Heap, the statement he gave to the police was conversational to the point of being downright chatty.

He told Inspector Pharo that he had initially been introduced to Frances Jackson (as she then was) by a mutual acquaintance called Lieutenant Cran, who had subsequently been posted to Egypt.[40] This had been in July 1930, after which he had seen a good deal of her, 'in fact we stayed in the same hotel in Hove for a couple of weeks.'

In approximately November 1930, Frances had phoned him and said, 'I just got the shock of my life. Hugh walked in last night.' (Her surprise had been due to the fact that she thought him still in India.) Blair had subsequently been introduced to Hugh Chevis at a cocktail party given by Frances and another friend, Rita Thompson, at the flat Miss Thompson shared with Stella Charnaud (who had recently become Lady Reading, after marrying Lord Reading on 6 August 1931). Blair had next encountered Hugh in March 1931, when the latter came up to London from Deepcut Barracks to attend a regimental dinner. While her husband attended the dinner, Blair had taken Frances to the Savoy for dinner and dancing, going up to her flat for a drink afterwards. Hugh Chevis had joined them later, helpfully providing his wife's friend with some quinine tablets when he complained of having a cold.

After this John Blair said he had not seen Frances again until 17 June, when he took her to dinner at the Savoy Grill, while Hugh was away at the Okehampton Camp. He recalled that Frances had not been feeling well on that occasion – he did not know why. He did know, however, that Lieutenant and Mrs Chevis were very happy together. In answer to further questions, he assured the inspector that he had never been to Blackdown Camp, never met Major Jackson, and was under no financial obligation to Mrs Chevis.

Among the working and lower-middle classes (from whence the majority of serving policemen came until well after the 1930s) no married woman would be squired around town by another man in her husband's absence unless she wanted to attract 'talk' – indeed such behaviour would be generally perceived as indicative of 'something going on'. Moreover, while it is evident from the tone of Blair's statement that he did not intend the police to imagine that the unexpected arrival of Hugh Chevis, when Frances had thought him still with his regiment in India, was anything but a pleasant surprise, Stovell and his colleagues probably viewed it somewhat differently, for here was Frances, spending a good deal of her summer with another man – even staying at the same hotel as him for a fortnight – and then being 'surprised' when the man with whom she had an understanding and would shortly marry, turned up unexpectedly. Nor had the friendship with this other man ceased once she had married her handsome young Lieutenant – on the contrary, Blair had taken her dancing. Added to this, the police had presumably worked out by then that while Frances spent some of her time down at Blackdown Camp, she also returned regularly to her London flat, which, quite aside from being far more comfortable and spacious than the officers' accommodation at Deepcut Barracks, was home to her three children, for whom there was insufficient room at the bungalow – and these sojourns in London would obviously have provided an opportunity for infidelity had she been so inclined.

Moreover, if the police initially imagined that any unexpected entanglements were confined to Frances's life, they were about to discover that her husband's was not without its complications either, for on 10 August they interviewed Hugh's friend, Lieutenant Jack Llewellyn Gwynn-Jones.

Jack Gwynn-Jones's name had been hovering around the inquiry from the outset, in all likelihood because some unnamed informant had mentioned him as a frequent visitor to Lieutenant Chevis's bungalow. When looking for a possible motive, the police had apparently asked the servants whether Lieutenant Gwynn-Jones had ever visited the bungalow in the absence of Lieutenant Chevis and received staunch denials. Possibly because their original theory – an affair between Frances and this frequent visitor – had been scotched, Surrey Police did not bother to interrogate the young officer until 10 August, but when they did get round to questioning him, they soon discovered that they had been barking up the wrong tree, for singularly among the various witnesses, Jack Gwynn-Jones evidently did not like Frances Chevis at all.

Gwynn-Jones told the police that he had known Hugh Chevis for more than seven years by the time of his death, having first met him when they were both stationed at Woolwich in March 1924.[41] The pair had become firm friends, constantly in each other's company until Gwynn-Jones was posted to India in February 1927. Their paths had next crossed when Chevis was himself sent to India, where he arrived in March 1930, and the young men were then together again until August that year, when Gwynn-Jones was ordered back to England. After this they did not meet until just after Hugh returned home in late 1930, when 'he told me that he intended to marry Mrs Chevis and I advised him not to.'

Gwynn-Jones did not offer the police any explanation for this abrupt (and probably none-too-welcome) advice, only adding that he had not attended the wedding. By the time the marriage took place, Gwynn-Jones was stationed at Deepcut Barracks and in February 1931 Hugh Chevis was posted there too, allowing the two men to pick up their friendship again. It is evident, however, that Lieutenant Gwynn-Jones's friendship was extended only reluctantly to his comrade's wife: 'I visited him frequently when Mrs Chevis was away, but I think I only dined there once when Mrs Chevis was there.'

Gwynn-Jones told the police that he had first met Frances at the 1926 Grand National (remembering it as the year the race was won by Jack Horner) which she had attended with her husband, Major Jackson. The Lieutenant did not explain how he came to meet the couple, but in the context of the occasion, it would almost inevitably have come about as a result of being introduced to them by some mutual friend or acquaintance, and it is entirely possible that introductions were effected by Lieutenant Chevis, whose own acquaintance with the Jacksons dated from the same year – however, it is equally possible that the honours were performed by some other person known separately to both parties – within this web of army officers and ex-army officers, people who invited one for cocktails and to play golf, or cricket, or tennis, or to come down to the country for a few days' hunting, it was scarcely possible to attend any race meeting or fashionable gathering without coming across someone one knew and thereby gaining yet more introductions to people that they knew and so on.

Whatever circumstances brought about this meeting, either Lieutenant Gwynn-Jones's first impressions were unfavourable, or else he subsequently came to dislike his friend's new love, for he clearly avoided Frances's company when he could, mentioning in an off-the-record chat with Inspector Pharo that he had been invited to join the couple for cocktails on the night Lieutenant Chevis died, but had declined, making the excuse that he was going on leave.

Like several other witnesses, Lieutenant Gwynn-Jones made various comments over and above his witness statement which he probably assumed were 'confidential' as they had been made 'off the record', but while these remarks could not be used in evidence because they did not form part of a signed statement, unbeknown to Gwynn-Jones they were noted down in the interviewing policeman's subsequent report and kept on file. Thus it was recorded not only that Jack Gwynn-Jones had declined a last invitation to cocktails with his close friend, but also a whole variety of other information about that friend which the Lieutenant had evidently not been willing to sign his name against.[42]

Lieutenant Chevis had been 'fond of women', Gwynn-Jones told the inspector. There had been some trouble at Tidworth (which was then, as now, an army base) with the wife of a man there, although he could not remember their names (whether this was a genuine case of amnesia or a tactical one is impossible to say). There had also been a widow who had subsequently married a colonel and had now gone to live in Belgium. Then there was a woman who had lived at Fleet – letters had come from her after Lieutenant Chevis's death, but he (Gwynn-Jones) had destroyed them. In addition, Hugh Chevis had been friendly with Mrs Heap and had lent her money, which had not been returned, but he thought Lieutenant Chevis had ended his acquaintance with Mrs Heap 'because he could not get what he wanted'. To this astonishing litany Lieutenant Gwynn-Jones added that he had seen Mrs Chevis with various men, including one sighting at a cocktail party he had attended in London and another at the Metropole Hotel in Brighton, with 'a tall man'.

Given this list of intrigues, it is a little difficult to take at face value the concluding line of Jack Gwynn-Jones's statement: 'I do not know of anyone likely to do Lieutenant Chevis an injury', since the impression created by his private comments to Pharo suggests a positive phalanx of irate husbands, jealous lovers and would-be seducers of his wife who had a motive, if not much opportunity, to tamper with the handsome young Lieutenant's dinner.

Inspector Pharo had noted in his report that the woman Lieutenant Gwynn-Jones described as living at Fleet was believed to be Iris Coates. Gwynn-Jones had been careful not to provide any names that the police did not already know, but Superintendent Stovell and his team had already been alerted to the existence of Mrs Coates and she was in fact interviewed on the same day as Hugh Chevis's best friend.

Iris Coates was the young wife of an officer in the Devonshire Regiment.[43] The daughter of an army Colonel, Iris had married Captain Ronald Coates in January 1929 when she was only eighteen (the groom was thirty-one). Coates had been posted out to Quetta (then in British India, now in Pakistan) and Iris had followed him out there later, setting sail on 21 January 1930. Hugh Chevis was travelling out on the same boat (by coincidence also bound for Quetta) and Iris had fallen in love with him. When Hugh returned to England in November

1930, she had continued to write to him, but had not arrived home herself until 24 July 1931, four weeks after his death. (Perhaps not surprisingly, Iris's marriage to Captain Coates did not last. The couple were divorced in 1934 and she then married her second husband, Alaric Jacob, with whom she lived in the USA for some years, before returning to Britain. Jacob was a journalist and Iris too became an author, writing a series of historical novels and political works, which were published under her maiden name, Iris Morley.)

Clearly Iris Coates had an alibi and could not therefore be suspected of murdering her lover in a fit of pique, or even of attempting to remove his wife but getting the wrong person – but what of those letters which had been arriving from India? Had Frances Chevis been aware of them? Might they have provoked fury at Hugh's apparent inconstancy? The further Surrey Police delved into the private lives of the Chevises, the more complex they seemed to appear.

CHAPTER THIRTEEN

NO SHORTAGE OF THEORIES

Mrs Coates was not the only person who had been putting pen to paper. Any mysterious death which made the headlines inevitably attracted correspondence and the Chevis case was no exception. Sometimes the letters were from cranks, but many people wrote with the genuine intention of being helpful. On 21 July, Mr W.C. Gay, a baker and grocer from Malmesbury, sent a note to the coroner, asking whether he was aware that the French put some sort of preservative into poultry (though since the partridges had been imported from Manchuria, the relevance of this information was not immediately obvious).[1]

Clarence Roberts, a watch and clockmaker, jeweller and optician (according to his letterhead) of 150 Alcester Road, Moseley in Birmingham, hoped the coroner would not consider him 'presumptuous in writing' and went on to recall that he had read years before that poisoning could occur if a person ate a hare which had ingested Deadly Nightshade, and that some birds might similarly become poisonous if fed on various types of berries. He concluded by saying that, 'As the above may help elucidate the mystery, I am sure you will agree that I am only doing my duty in writing to you.'

John Willes, the proprietor of a guesthouse in Lowestoft, explained that before taking up his current career he had been a farmer, and therefore knew that at cattle markets there was inevitably a 'vermin killer' who sold packets of wheat impregnated with strychnine to put down for birds (to stop them getting at newly planted crops) which might easily be picked up by a partridge. If a 'careless man' then came upon the partridge, he might easily pick it up and sell it at the next market.

Other suggestions were less coherent. One Frederick Fowler wanted to know whether, like him, Mrs Chevis had trouble sleeping at night and heard voices – if so, he could tell her who they were. Someone else suggested the police should investigate J. Hart of Hart's Advertising Agency, since he often travelled to Dublin and resembled the description of the man who sent the telegram, while a Mrs Wilson of Rotherham wrote to Scotland Yard claiming that she had also received a mysterious telegram, which she thought had probably come from Mr Wilson, who she was looking out for on account of personal cruelty, so she hoped they would be able to help her. There was a letter which appeared to be from a child, addressed to 'The Local Police Station, Aldershot near London' and signed 'THE BULLDOG DETECTIVE'. Another correspondent who resorted to capital letters, but was probably not a child, kept the message succinct: 'ONLY 3 PEOPLE COULD DO CHEVIS, COOK, BATMAN, WIFE.'

The Marquess of Hartington telephoned Scotland Yard on 29 July to suggest that the telegram might have come from a land owner called Hartington who lived near Eastbourne (on what basis other than that William Cavendish had somehow confused his own title, Hartington, with Hartigan cannot be imagined), and a few days earlier Cullen Mather, author of one of the first letters to be received, had presented himself at Scotland Yard to enquire whether his letter suggesting that the bird might have been accidentally poisoned with bait laid by Manchurian fur trappers had been passed on to the police, since he had received no reply.[2] One communication which arrived on 2 August stood out above all others – something which Superintendent Stovell described as 'the most astonishing yet received.'[3] It was a postcard from Hartigan addressed to the editor of the *Daily Sketch*.

Even before the *Evening News* published their exclusive on the Hooray telegram, one or two of the other major Fleet Street papers had evidently realised there was 'something in the wind', and resurrected the Chevis story in their pages, trying to dig up a new angle while they waitedx to see what was breaking. The *Daily Express* claimed that Superintendent Boshier, who had investigated the Vacquier strychnine case before his retirement, had been called in to assist Surrey Police, then followed this up the next day by claiming that the police were consulting with Dr Roche Lynch (the Senior Home Office Analyst, who was a bigger name than Ryffel when it came to notorious poisoning cases).[4]

The entirely erroneous suggestion that Roche Lynch had somehow become involved with the case was picked up and repeated throughout August by one newspaper after another, some of whom pestered the analyst for a comment, while others published various comments attributed to him, without bothering to confirm their source, all of which ultimately led the exasperated analyst to pen a letter to the coroner, requesting that he make some sort of announcement when the inquest resumed, pointing out that Roche Lynch had no connection with the inquiry and had not made any of the suggestions imputed to him.[5]

The *Daily Sketch* had a somewhat different take on matters, and under the headline 'Officer's Death Mystery Deepens – Vengeance Theory Suggested' the paper asked, 'Was Lt Hugh Chevis poisoned by an Indian who had travelled to England to wreak revenge?' According to the *Sketch*, while it might sound far-fetched, the police were not ruling out the idea.[6] The campaign for Indian independence was growing and although the British in India continued as if everything was 'business as usual', it was against a background of various forms of political agitation and increasingly frequent acts of violence. That same week the *Daily Sketch* had been among the papers to carry the story of a British officer who had been stabbed to death in a train travelling through the Punjab, the latest in a number of incidents involving attacks on various officials, including other army personnel and a judge.[7]

The Indian vengeance theory had apparently been given credence by 'a very intimate friend' of Lieutenant Chevis, who was quoted as agreeing that 'Oriental Vengeance' was a possibility, saying, 'India is a funny place and an assassin might well come from there.' The *Sketch* strengthened the potential connection by reminding its readers that Lieutenant Chevis's father had been a senior judge in India.

When dealing in 'Oriental Vengeance', it never did any harm to ramp up the 'Mysterious East' angle by intensifying the suggestion of otherworldly forces at work, so the *Sketch* ran a sub-headline: 'Former Husband of Victim's Wife Tells of Strange Premonition', beneath which it was claimed that Major Jackson had told their reporter that while he was staying at Heyford Hills he had experienced a strange sense of foreboding when he picked up the morning paper. Feeling sure that he was about to be confronted with bad news, he had opened the paper and immediately read of Hugh Chevis's death.[8]

The *Daily Mail* also quoted Major Jackson, and though they made no mention of his mysterious premonition, they claimed that the 'Indian Revenge' theory was actively suggested by Jackson to their 'own correspondent in Eastbourne' (by which it is safe to assume they meant the local hack who had managed to doorstep Jackson at the Mostyn Hotel and subsequently sell the story on to all the London papers). 'Knowing the Indians as I do,' the Major is supposed to have said, 'I have little doubt that some of them would go to any lengths to avenge a grievance.' It was 'a very subtle affair', the Major said, and 'it makes me think of native vengeance. Anyone who has served in India will appreciate this theory.'

The reporter also asked whether it was true that Major Jackson had seen his ex-wife since the death of her new husband. 'It is true that I have seen Mrs Chevis since her husband died,' Jackson is quoted as saying. 'I was taking my bulldog for a walk when I met her with her little boy. I had no idea she was in Eastbourne. Naturally we referred to the tragedy, but I made little reference to it. I did not want to make her more sad, because she is one of the best women in the world.'[9]

The *Bournemouth Daily Echo* was among the papers to run enthusiastically with the 'Indian Vengeance' theory. After a somewhat perfunctory report of the inquest on 21 July, the *Echo* had fallen silent on the Chevis case, but with the revelation about the telegram they immediately recalled their local connection, headlining Hugh Chevis as the son of a Boscombe family and sending a reporter posthaste to the home of Sir William Chevis, who refused to confirm or deny the existence of the telegram and declined to offer any theory regarding his son's death.

In spite of Sir William's alleged reticence, the *Echo* was remarkably well informed, noting that there had been an investigation into the sales of poison registered in the Dublin area and claiming that one entry 'may prove of value'. This was almost certainly the purchase made by the coincidentally named

Mr Jackson, which shortly proved to be of no significance whatsoever – but the *Echo* surmised that 'the police believe the man who purchased strychnine on the outskirts of Dublin may be the same man who sent the telegram'. The paper further claimed that great significance was being attached to the fact that the telegram was sent the day before the death was announced and 'it is thought that this indicates the sender had special knowledge'.[10] This particular inaccuracy has persisted in accounts of the case up to the present day – in fact, Lieutenant Chevis's death had been widely publicised in both the English and Irish Press at least forty-eight hours before the telegram was sent – the special knowledge lay not in knowing of the Lieutenant's death, but rather in being aware of his connection to Sir William and Lady Chevis.

The *Daily Sketch* was similarly full of nonsense, informing its readers that a dog had died after lapping water from dishes in which the Chevises' meal had been served, that the Dublin Police had discovered purchases of strychnine logged in the same name as that of the sender of the telegram, and that Hugh Chevis had letters with a Dublin postmark in his possession at the time of his death. Having confidently asserted in Friday's edition that 'it is not considered feasible that the poison found its way accidentally into the bird,' and on Monday that 'it now seems definitely established that Lt Chevis died as a result of foul play', the *Sketch* now had an unidentified 'close friend' of Mrs Chevis saying, 'We have not the slightest suspicion of anyone. It is inconceivable that anyone could have intended any evil toward Lt Chevis. He was the most lovable man, a thorough good sport, without an enemy in the world.'[11]

The *Daily Express* went off on another tangent of misinformation, focussing on the coroner's annoyance that the information about the telegram had got out and adding a complaint from Superintendent Stovell that he had only been told about the telegram on the day that the news of it was broken by the Press and had been 'working in the dark for a month'.[12] (A comment most unlikely to have emanated from the officer leading the inquiry, given that it was completely untrue and contradicted by the *Daily Mirror*, whose coverage made it plain that the English and Irish Police had been collaborating over the telegram for some time.)[13]

On the following day the *Daily Mail* sent their special correspondent, F.W. Memory,[14] down to Eastbourne, where he managed to obtain an interview with Major Jackson.[15] The presence of Mr Memory in the seaside town was an indication of the importance the big London papers were now attaching to the inquiry. In the 1930s, F.W. Memory was already a household name, whose career encompassed missions to cover everything from riots in Palestine to the latest Loch Ness Monster sightings, with big murder stories grist to his mill. The length of the interview suggests that not only did Memory manage to catch the Major as he returned to the Mostyn Hotel, having just taken his pet bulldog out for a drive, but that he also succeeded in getting him talking, perhaps even spending a few minutes with him inside the building. The 'interview' is written as if the journalist and the ex-RAVC officer enjoyed a long cosy chat together, though this is unlikely to have been the case.

Memory described Trev Jackson as a strongly built man of medium height, with greying hair, a close clipped moustache, clear blue eyes and 'the fresh complexion of a man whose life has been spent among horses and dogs'. (The *Daily Express* merely said he was sunburned – though they added that he had 'steely grey' eyes, and 'the bearing of an officer'.) It is interesting that the Major – who had initially been reluctant to discuss anything with the police, now seemed willing to open up and answer questions from journalists, freely informing them that he had spent the weekend of Lieutenant Chevis's death with 'a friend who mounts me when I ride with the Grafton and Pytchley Foxhounds' and recounting again his strange sense of foreboding when he reached for the newspaper which contained the tragic news – adding that he himself was very healthy and not in the least highly strung, which he perhaps assumed to be the prerequisites for a person who experienced premonitions.

It is possible that Major Jackson thought such openness with the papers would defuse public suspicion. He told them that he had written a letter of condolence to Mrs Chevis from his friend's home in Northamptonshire and that 'I still have the greatest reverence and affection for Mrs Chevis. She is the mother of my three children.' He had only met Hugh Chevis once after he and Frances were married, he told the reporter, and that had been as he was going out of a Bournemouth hotel as they were going in. He and the newlyweds had spent about five minutes chatting and 'they seemed very happy'.

While agreeing that the 'Indian Revenge' theory was still on the table, Jackson said there were other possibilities. These included trappers using strychnine to capture the birds, in which case the death would have been an accident, which he sincerely hoped would prove to be the case for the sake of all concerned – although he feared that it was not. How about the Irish connection, Memory wanted to know? 'The Irish are a passionate people,' Jackson said. (In common with most Englishmen of the period, Jackson appears to have had a stereotypical view of Johnny Foreigner, so that Indians, Irishmen and no doubt just about any other race you care to mention were all to some extent suspect.) He knew Ireland, he said, but had not been there since before the war. As for Hugh Chevis: 'Chevis was a fascinating man. Women loved him, men liked him and he was popular. He was so strong that he could pick me up in one hand and you in another.'

Similar sets of remarks were widely reported throughout the British and Irish Press, leading to the suspicion that Memory's interview was not an exclusive but merely a prolonged conversation outside Major Jackson's hotel, parts of which were overheard by other nearby pressmen.

The Dublin *Evening Herald* was among the papers who repeated the information that the telegram had been sent the day before Lieutenant Chevis's death was actually announced in the newspapers, which represented a particular lack of research on their part, since their own paper had carried the story in a paragraph on the front page of the 22nd of June edition, two days prior to the telegram's despatch.[16] The paper also advised its readers that the name used both to send the telegram and purchase the strychnine was false – though since no one knew who had sent the telegram and there were any number of people called Hartigan who might have done so, this claim was only marginally less spurious than the one relating to the date on which it had been sent.

News that the police had called on Major Jackson and asked him to make a statement reached the public the following day. The reporters down in Eastbourne (still no doubt lying in wait for the daily dog walking, which was an essential part of the Major's routine) had no difficulty persuading him to confirm that Inspector Sawkins's visit had taken place – in fact Jackson was becoming quite expansive. He told the reporters more about his visit to Northamptonshire – how he had played tennis and cricket and how a policeman had called at his friend's house in connection with a minor motor accident he had been involved in at Hersham, en route.

He was untroubled by the police's interest in him, he assured the gentlemen of the Press. 'Whatever imputation or direct accusation may have been made against me, I am not the slightest bit concerned and I have the self-confidence of an innocent man.' The policeman had been courteous, he told reporters, interviewing him for about an hour. 'As long as I am not a source of trouble to anyone, I don't mind how people look at me or what people think. The mystery must be cleared up sometime and when that occurs my position will be perfectly plain.' He confirmed that he continued to think Hugh Chevis's death must have been due to foul play – 'I cannot see how it can be otherwise.'[17]

He also talked more about his ex-wife, saying that he had recently bumped into her in Eastbourne and after seeing her he had written, offering her two badges for the Sandown race meeting, so that she could go with a girl friend – he thought it might cheer her up and ease her mind of all the worry. Previous to that he had last seen her on 5 November. 'She rang me up and said she would like to see me for Auld Lang Syne, so naturally I went to see her.' They met at the Grand Hotel and chatted for about half an hour, before a man came to collect her, as they were going to meet her mother and watch the fireworks. 'I thought she was in love with Chevis and so she was,' he said. 'I am broad-minded enough not to want to live with a woman when she is in love with another man.'[18]

This was a reckless admission on Major Jackson's part, implying as it did that far from Frances suing him for divorce on grounds of his adultery, she had actually been in love with another man and he had willingly let her go. Had these remarks come to the attention of the King's Proctor,[19] although the divorce was more than two years behind them, both Trev and Frances could have found themselves back in court, charged with contempt.

Someone must have alerted him to the danger, because two days later the *Daily Sketch* informed its readers that they had received a letter from Henry Flint, a solicitor representing Major Jackson, who wrote: '…the inference might be drawn from the concluding paragraph of your report that Mrs Chevis left him [Major Jackson] because she was in love with Lt Chevis. This was not so, as Mrs Chevis was the petitioner in the divorce proceedings. Major Jackson regrets that your reporter drew an erroneous impression which our client did not wish to convey.'[20]

Meanwhile, Sir William Chevis had also been opening up to reporters. Having originally refused to confirm or deny the existence of the telegram when reporters called on him in Argyll Road, he relented a couple of days later and informed the *Daily Mail's* man that, 'I may have a theory, but unless you have something tangible to support what you think, you may as well keep silent.' A 'stern, grey haired figure', Sir William declined to give any credence to the 'Indian Revenge' theory, saying that his son had only been out in India for nine months and there was no reason to believe he had made any enemies while serving there. He himself had served as a judge in the Punjab for thirty years, he told the reporter, but 'to the best of my knowledge I left not one enemy behind me in India. I returned home some nine years ago and it is hardly likely that any supposed enemy would wait all that time to be revenged on me.'[21]

It is noticeable that after Sir William began speaking with the Press again, a clamour arose to involve Scotland Yard in the investigation. A long article which appeared in the *Daily Mail* on 31 July could almost have been written by the retired judge, containing as it did so many phrases not just reminiscent, but apparently lifted directly from his letters to the coroner and Deputy Chief Constable. 'Let Scotland Yard Get To Work on the Partridge Mystery' the *Mail's* headline demanded. 'At Scotland Yard there are the finest detectives in the world … yet to the amazement of the public no attempt has been made to employ these worldfamous officers to solve the mystery of Lt Chevis's death, although the investigation calls for the employment of highly trained brains.' The *Mail* went on to explain that 'Red Tape stands in the way' because Scotland Yard can only 'intervene' if invited. 'For six weeks Surrey Police have been stolidly pursuing their enquiries and have so far achieved exactly nothing.' According to the *Mail*, had the inquiry been conducted by officers specially trained in this type of investigation, they would have 'speedily indicated a definite line of enquiry'. Instead, all kinds of theories had been bandied about and 'the fact is that the Press has done a great deal more than the enquiries of the police to elicit information. Its power in this direction is receiving tardy recognition from Surrey Police.'[22]

It has been noted previously that unlike some constabularies, Surrey do not appear to have been in the habit of systematically leaking information to the local press – a situation which had presumably led to some bitterness and is probably what inspired a vicious attack included in one section of this particular *Daily Mail* article, which may have been supplied by the local stringer. In this story

Stovell turned on reporters 'in a towering rage'. 'Get out of here,' the report has him shouting. 'I have told you that we can conduct our own enquiries, and we don't want the help of Scotland Yard, or the Press.' When the reporter returned later and attempted to speak to Stovell again, the Superintendent was unavailable as he was 'still busy prosecuting people for having left in a certain vehicle, to wit a motorcar...' If, as is suggested here, Stovell did lose his rag with reporters it is hardly to be wondered at, since they were pestering him continually for quotes and information, and far from being helpful had leaked the story of the telegram contrary to his expressed wishes. Unfortunately, an outburst of this nature would hardly have endeared him to the reporters who invariably justified their intrusive behaviour by claiming that they too were only doing their job and that the police underestimated the amount of help provided by the Press in sustaining public interest and thereby encouraging witnesses to come forward. (In reality, the desperate need to get a quote, a new angle, indeed any snippet which had not already appeared in print was a matter of necessity to many freelancers, who were remunerated under a traditional system called linage or lineage, whereby they only received payment based on the number of lines they provided which were actually used by the paper – no story meant no pay.)

Calls to bring in Scotland Yard continued for some time, perhaps fuelled by Sir William Chevis, or perhaps merely by reporters with nothing new to write. The abilities of Scotland Yard detectives had reached legendary proportions, but the adulation in which they were held and faith in them by the British public in general – and Sir William Chevis in particular – may have been somewhat misplaced. To many people the men from the Yard were super sleuths, with Holmesian powers of detection – the men who could crack a case where the local boys had failed. The truth was somewhat different. The habit of 'calling in the Yard' originated in the nineteenth century, when the vast majority of constabularies had no detective officers at all – a situation which persisted in some smaller or rural forces well into the 1920s. Men from Scotland Yard had become involved in cases outside the Metropolitan area since the reign of Victoria, but the habit of calling on the Yard became more frequent following a Home Office directive in 1904, which formalised the practice. In the wake of this directive, Surrey had been one of the first police forces to call on the services of their colleagues from the Met, following the murder of Mary Ann Hogg in 1906,[23] but folk history has it that the Surrey men were sufficiently underwhelmed that they vowed never to solicit similar 'interference' again. (Although the Chevis case did not occur for another quarter century, memories were long in the police – James Stovell's career spanned both the Hogg and the Chevis enquiries.) At all events, the Hogg murder remained unsolved and this was true of many enquiries handled by the Yard, because, contrary to popular imagination, they could no more conjure up clues which did not exist than could the local men on the ground. While there was some value in calling in the Yard where numerous clues existed, a second set of brains might bring valuable experience or a fresh perspective, or the investigation showed signs of turning into a nationwide manhunt; in a murder where there was little to go on, Scotland Yard was unlikely to provide any real assistance.

The mythology regarding Scotland Yard continued well into the twentieth century, aided and abetted by the media. Britain's first TV police series was *Fabian of the Yard*, which dramatised real cases and included appearances from Robert Fabian, the Scotland Yard detective on whose career the series was based.[24] In 1970, an anonymous serving Metropolitan police officer commented, 'The Yard believes that it is the "cream" of the police service. It is a myth which has been created by themselves and by the Press as a source of good copy.'[25]

Equally there may occasionally have been resistance to the idea of calling in the Yard because of local pride. Quite a number of police forces were strongly opposed to inviting outside help – earlier in the year, Northumberland had resisted the suggestion that they should call in Scotland Yard to investigate the death of Evelyn Foster. In many areas detectives did not receive formal training, but learned the job from their senior officers and this remained the case in Surrey until 1932[26] – it was a method of training which mirrored numerous other walks of life, where men learned their trades by gaining long years of experience of which they were justifiably proud – and these 'university of life' men may have wanted to show the local populace that the investigation was not beyond them. In Surrey, the local constabulary had particularly strong reasons for wishing to bolster their reputation because there had been some potential embarrassments in the recent past. In 1926, Deputy Chief Constable Kenward had made rather a fool of himself over the disappearance of Agatha Christie. Suspecting her husband Archie of murdering her, Kenward had armies of police and volunteers combing pond, heath and woodland for the county's famous novelist, who was all the time holed up in a Harrogate hotel.[27] In 1928, the body of Hilary Rougier had been exhumed and Sir Bernard Spilsbury had declared the death to be 'unnatural', but in spite of a long investigation no charges were ever brought.[28] Then, in January 1931, Surrey Police had undertaken a massive search for the body of a woman called Winifred Parrant, who was said to have been missing for over a year, only to learn a week into an operation which had seen officers digging up areas of common land near Virginia Water, that the young woman was alive and well and living in London.[29] Small wonder then if they wanted to make a success of the Chevis investigation without having to admit defeat and call in outside help.

As well as harassing Inspector Stovell, encouraging Trev Jackson to make damaging remarks about his divorce, and wheedling a quote out of Sir William Chevis, reporters had managed to interview various others involved. They reached Major Campbell before the police did and found him reasonably forthcoming. Campbell told them pretty much what he later told the police: he had originally met Major Jackson in Eastbourne, where the two men found they had a shared interest in hunting and racing and had subsequently exchanged hospitality – Jackson taking Campbell to the races and Campbell having twice invited Jackson to stay in Northamptonshire, once for hunting and once for tennis. Major Campbell said he was aware that his friend was divorced and that his former wife had been married to someone called Chevis, but he knew nothing beyond that, 'We did not discuss our private affairs.'[30]

Gunner Nicholas Bolger was invited to recount the evening of the fateful dinner for the benefit of reporters, though nothing emerged from this exercise that had not already been described at the inquest; and Mrs Yeomans could similarly reveal nothing new save that she had received a letter from Mrs Chevis, as a result of which she was going to join the household at Basil Mansions, and would then be travelling down to the seaside with Mrs Chevis and the children.[31]

Lady Chevis was quoted as saying that she hated all the publicity, but then went on to fuel it further by engaging in a lengthy interview, during which she insisted that her son's death could not have been accidental, and as for the telegram: 'Someone must have sent it. Who was it? The writing was disfigured and the police do not seem able to trace the sender.'[32]

After the gaffe over his divorce, Trev Jackson's short-lived enthusiasm for the Press had waned and he now declined to make any further comments, telling reporters that he had been advised by his solicitor that he had been speaking too freely and should say nothing further. 'I know nothing of the tragedy beyond what I have read in the papers and am only interested because I know the persons concerned.'[33]

The jewel in the crown so far as interviewees went was obviously Frances Chevis, but she had been somewhat elusive. On 28 July, several newspapers included the information that she had returned to London, but their attempts to speak with her were unsuccessful. Papers as diverse as the *Bournemouth Echo* and the *Irish Times* informed their readers that 'a woman who has been Mrs Chevis's constant companion since her husband died, told a Press Association reporter today that "Mrs Chevis is resting in bed. This terrible trouble has been a great shock to her and she is very worried. She intends to stay in London for a few days and then we shall go away somewhere in the country, so that she may have complete rest and quietness. She is most anxious to help the authorities, but she is as mystified by it all as anyone."'[34]

Not every paper met with such limited success, however, for on the same day that virtually everyone else was running this line, the *Daily Sketch* published a long exclusive interview with Frances, given in the comfort of her London drawing room.

CHAPTER FOURTEEN

'BEAUTIFUL WIDOW TELLS HER OWN STORY'

Daily Sketch headline, 1931

Frances presented as 'A slim, tragic figure, dressed in black' according to the reporter (whose byline was 'G.G.').[1] Whether 'G.G.', who claimed to have spent forty minutes conversing with Mrs Chevis in her drawing room, wanted to play up the tragic heroine image, or whether he was genuinely besotted by his subject is impossible to say, but his gushing prose variously described her as 'modest', 'charming', 'lovely' and 'one of the most beautiful women in England', who had 'expressive eyes' and spoke in a 'soft tremulous, half pathetic' tone.

Frances said it was all 'perfectly ghastly' – an expression which had also been used frequently in interviews given by Major Jackson. 'If there was foul play, against whom was it intended? Against my husband, or me, or both of us, answer me that?'

For the benefit of the reporter she recalled the now familiar story of the fatal meal, the ordering and delivery of the birds: 'I have never liked partridge – least of all foreign partridge, which has that peculiar taste one associates with ptarmigan or teal – and so was this. It tasted musty, distinctly musty.' She had served the birds, she said, because, 'I have always done the carving. I did it at home with my mother, I did it with Major Jackson, who was a particularly poor carver, and I did it with Lt Chevis.'

'But there was no carving here?' G.G. queried.

'No, that is true. We just had one bird each. Lt Chevis had the bigger bird, because he was a big man, strong, with a healthy appetite.'

She went on to describe the onset of the illness. 'I will never forget those awful convulsions – it was like a horrid dream – no one who has not been poisoned can know what it was like. Shock after shock goes through one; the body falls away useless, but the brain continues remorselessly. It seemed to last for ages. I lost all track of time. And to think of it for him...'

When the reporter asked if she could think of anyone who might have had a motive, Frances claimed to be dumbfounded by the whole thing and said she had no idea of anyone. 'Might not someone have been jealous?' G.G. persisted. Was it possible that anyone had 'fallen violently in love with you?'

According to the *Sketch* writer's account, 'Mrs Chevis bowed her head modestly. "It is possible of course. These things do happen. In fact it is hardly likely for a woman to live alone in London without it happening. But I can say not since my marriage or for some considerable time before. And violently is hardly the word,' here she smiled in quiet reproach.'

Many things are possible, of course, and one of them is that large chunks of this interview were a work of fiction. Whole sections of G.G.'s account make Frances appear like an eyelash-fluttering idiot in a twopenny novelette – certainly she later claimed that much of what was printed had been made up, and after her experiences with them on 27 July, she did not permit reporters into the house again. In a letter from Frances's solicitors dated 29 July 1931, they stated 'that her life is being made a perfect burden by press representatives who force their way into her flat, then publish lengthy interviews which are based almost entirely on their own imaginations.'[2]

In answer to further probing from G.G., Frances said that she had never heard the name Hartigan before and had never been to Dublin. Nor did she see how anyone could have got at the contents of the meat safe without being observed. There were three bungalows 'huddled close together' and the officers' club nearby, with servants working in and around the bungalows. In addition, she found it inconceivable that their Alsatian dog would not have given the alarm if there had been any stranger about.

Like the *Daily Sketch*, the *Daily Express* claimed to have obtained 'exclusive' access to Frances in her drawing room, which their reporter described as decorated in pale green, with mahogany furniture. (It is unclear whether there really were two separate interviews or only one – the interviews certainly do not read as if they were obtained at the same time, but this may have been a deliberate ploy on the part of the reporters, and both may have been subject to the adjustments of journalistic licence.) Frances told the *Express* that up until Lieutenant Chevis's death she had been spending most of her time down at Blackdown Camp, where 'my husband and I would hold cheery parties', only coming up to London at weekends to spend time with her children. Lieutenant Chevis had been 'terribly fond of game – although I didn't really care for it' – and as a consequence they had eaten partridge, pheasant and grouse regularly.[3]

For the benefit of the *Express*'s man, she had described again the last night she spent with her husband, and when recalling their dreadful agonies had suddenly burst out, 'My God – one ought not to give strychnine to a rat!' She said she simply could not understand how such a thing had taken place, but then added, 'Why, it might happen in any house.'

Frances would later suggest that she had been a reluctant interviewee, and that reporters had 'forced their way into the house'[4] but it is hard to believe that reporters from two national daily newspapers managed to get as far as the drawing room without the agreement of the householder, and the length of the interviews coupled with their cosy tone implies that at the very least she had agreed to speak with them. It is possible that, like Major Jackson a few days earlier, she had reluctantly concluded that it would be better to open up a little. She was certainly concerned about the way she was appearing to the public, because her solicitors had written to Mr Francis, the coroner, on 24 July, expressing concern on behalf of their client that 'an impression seems to have been created by various press notices to the effect that her husband's relations are anxious for a close enquiry to be made and they alone.' This was so entirely contrary to the facts, the solicitors wrote, that their client had requested them to write, placing on record that 'she hopes no stone will be left unturned which may further elucidate the causes of her husband's death.' It was appreciated that the coroner was doing everything in his power to resolve the mystery, the letter went on, but would he be so good as to refer to the contents of their letter when the inquest resumed, in order to dispel the impression created in the press so far, which had occasioned Mrs Chevis considerable distress.[5]

The coroner wrote back a couple of days later, expressing sympathy with Mrs Chevis regarding the fact that 'things [are said in the press] regardless of the feelings of those involved,' but offering no definite commitment to making some kind of statement on Mrs Chevis's behalf.[6] It is probable that the coroner did not perceive it an appropriate part of his role to make press statements on behalf of someone who ranked well up the list of suspects in a murder inquiry, and, moreover, that he was getting rather tired of all the demands being made by the deceased's family. He pointed out in a subsequent letter that thanks to the leaking of the telegram, the press were making the lives of not only Mrs Chevis, but also himself and Inspector Stovell 'a burden', while in yet another exchange of correspondence with Mrs Chevis's solicitor, he rather firmly asserted that yes, he did require her to attend the resumed inquest in August.[7] It is evident from the context that the coroner had been informed, either by telephone, or in a document which no longer survives, that Frances would prefer not to be at the inquest – an entirely unrealistic expectation, since she was one of the principal witnesses. By the beginning of August, the coroner must have been well aware that Surrey police officers had attended Frances's flat on at least one occasion and not managed to gain admittance, whereas representatives of the *Sketch* and the *Express* had been granted interviews in the drawing room, and that while not well enough to attend the inquest she had experienced no difficulty in travelling between her Kensington flat and various fashionable south coast resorts.[8]

By the final days of July, all major participants had flirted with the Press and been bitten by the results. Major Jackson had already made it clear that he would make no further comments, and by 30 July the woman who had two days earlier been smiling modestly upon journalists from the comfort of her 'cosy sofa', was now quoted as responding to a question from a waiting journalist with the words: 'There is nothing more to be said. I am not making any statement. It has got nothing to do with anybody.'[9]

Not easily deterred, the Press pursued Frances down to Hove, where she cancelled the suite of rooms she had booked at her usual hotel, in the forlorn hope of avoiding reporters. Another guest at the hotel was quoted as saying that, 'Everyone here loves her, but it must be the notoriety of the case that has made her shy of mixing with us.'[10]

Alas attempts to maintain anonymity were hopeless. Frances was soon tracked down at a house in the town, and pursued by reporters wherever she went, so that they could report to a breathless nation that she had spent a day on the sands with her three children and their nurse. In an attempt to win their sympathy and persuade them to leave her alone, Frances – who was described as 'obviously distressed' told them, 'I can still say nothing about this affair, nor throw any further light on any aspect of the case. I am still feeling very ill and surely you must understand that my husband's death weighs heavily on my mind. I have come down here to rest and I don't want to see anyone or meet anyone.'[11]

Apart from occasional guarded comments or abrupt denials, there would be no further comments from family members. Only William Kenward, the outgoing Deputy Chief Constable of Surrey, who was retiring on 1 August, seemed willing to be quoted, and he chose to adopt an enigmatic approach, tantalising the Press by informing them that he expected the inquiry into Lieutenant Chevis's death to be wrapped up 'by the middle of next week' adding, 'Then you may find that you have been very wide of the mark.'[12]

Asked about involving Scotland Yard, Kenward laughed and said, 'You can take it from me that you do not have anything less to do when a Yard man comes down here.' The new Deputy Chief Constable, William Bird, would be overseeing the case from now on, he told them, adding the rider that Bird 'knows all about it.' The local reporter working for the *Daily Mail*, who had been spearheading the agitation to call in Scotland Yard, now tracked down Superintendent Bird at home, where he found him scraping whitewash off a window with the help of his two young sons. Evidently annoyed at being pestered on his day off, Bird was clearly in no mind to be co-operative and is quoted as saying that he knew nothing about the case, except what he read in the newspapers, adding, 'You can see I am much too busy to talk about such things.' These comments were reported for the edification of the nation immediately after the remarks attributed to Kenward, presumably with the intention of suggesting that the right hand did not know what the left was doing and that senior Surrey police officers put a bit of DIY higher in their order of priorities than investigating a strange death on their patch. This vicious misrepresentation concluded by noting that Superintendent Stovell also 'professed ignorance' on various aspects of the case when questioned. While the activities of this particular representative of the Press did nothing to harm the investigation, they certainly did nothing to help it either.

This hostile coverage was perhaps all the more surprising because on 30 July the police had given a big boost to the story by allowing the Press to gather in the yard of the police station in Farnham, so that they could obtain and reproduce copies of the form associated with the by now infamous telegram, in the hope that if a facsimile was published someone would recognise the handwriting and come forward. With the telegram form fully in the public domain, everyone in the country could turn detective, pore over a copy of the document which had been completed and signed by J. Hartigan, and try to take a hand in solving the mystery.

CHAPTER FIFTEEN

'IT IS A MYSTERY THEY WILL NEVER SOLVE'

J. Hartigan, 1931

This frenzied coverage during the final days of July had already led to the coroner and the police receiving communications from members of the public who wanted to help, and the release of the telegram form only added to the furore. Principal among the would-be helpers was Mr Milmoe of Dublin, who had identified a man he claimed to have directed to the Post Office with the description of the man who had signed himself Hartigan. It is perfectly plain with the benefit of hindsight that the man Milmoe was describing was actually Major Jackson, whose photograph had appeared in the papers (complete with his bulldog) the day before Milmoe made this claim, and upon whose press interviews this witness had clearly based his conversation with the (presumably wholly imaginary) man.[1]

Various different photographs of Trev Jackson appeared in the press, at least one of which he had evidently agreed to pose for, but others were clearly snapped in the street while he was being waylaid by reporters and one of these included not only Major Jackson himself, but also a woman smoking a cigarette. It is far from clear whether this lady was actually in the Major's company, or merely a bystander, attracted by the group of reporters and as eager as they were to hear what he had to say. This particular picture was widely reproduced and appeared on the front page of the *Daily Mirror* among others, where it was spotted by Arthur Miller, an unemployed sign-writer who lived in Seven Star Road, West Kensington.

Miller visited North Fulham police station next day, where he told the Duty Officer that he recognised the woman in the photograph as his estranged wife, Hettie Letitia Miller, who had left him six months previously to work as a cook at somewhere called Hatden Hill. She had peculiar handwriting, Miller said, so that if he was allowed to see the telegram form (pictures of which would not be released until the following day) he might be able to assist with the inquiry.[2]

As chance would have it, Superintendent Stovell was following up other clues in London on the day that Miller presented himself, so he turned up to interview the man within a couple of hours. Miller said he was sure that he recognised the woman in the photograph as his wife of four years (the estranged Hettie had enjoyed a lively marital history – according to Arthur Miller, she had previously been married to men called Macpherson and Mitchell) and he had last heard that she was working not at Hatden Hill, as the first policeman had noted, but at Haywards Hill in Northampton – an address that was sounding more and more like that of Jackson's friend Major Campbell. 'Her writing is angular,' Miller said. 'I would know it if I saw it.'[3]

Miller was requested to present himself again with a photograph of his estranged wife, which he did. In the opinion of Inspector Allum, who took charge of the matter in Stowell's absence, the woman in the picture bore no resemblance whatsoever to the one who had appeared in the newspaper standing near Major Jackson. More importantly, in the intervening forty-eight hours the London Police had managed to trace Mrs Miller and found her working as a cook at 19 St Mary Abbott's Terrace, Kensington, where she had been employed for five weeks. Prior to that she had been working at a house called The Bluffs, in Haywards Heath. She told the police that she had left Miller because of his lazy habits, and assumed that he had gone to them in the hope of finding out her present address so that he could obtain money from her.[4]

Among literally dozens of communications provoked by the newspaper coverage was one which Stovell described on 3 August as 'the most astonishing development yet'. It was a postcard, addressed to the editor of the *Daily Sketch* and signed J. Hartigan. The message was a simple one:

DEAR SIR,
WHY DID YOU PUBLISH THE PICTURE OF THE "HOORAY" TELEGRAM?
"J Hartigan"

As clues went, the postcard stank from the outset. The original telegram had been sent to taunt the Chevis family more than a month before, and it was reasonable to assume that the sender not only had some personal knowledge or experience of the family, but also that he had some particular grudge against them. It was therefore difficult to see why the mysterious 'J Hartigan' would suddenly decide to take issue with newspaper editors in general or the *Daily Sketch* in particular, merely for reproducing the telegram. Furthermore, while the original telegram had emanated from Dublin, the 'Hartigan' card had been posted in St John's Wood at 3.30 the previous afternoon. Perhaps mindful of the wrath incurred by the *Evening News* over publication of the original telegram, the editor of the *Sketch* did not immediately publish the card, but instead handed it over to the police and its existence was not initially broadcast.

Although the author of the card had evidently attempted to imitate the writing on the telegram form, he or she had not quite pulled it off and a careful comparison of the Hartigan signatures shows that they were not written by the same hand. The 'E's, 'S's, 'Y's and number 1 show obvious differences, while it is hard to imagine why the sender of the postcard would have placed inverted commas around his signature.

This was not the only postcard to come from 'Hartigan', however, for on 4 August someone posted a card in Belfast – this time addressed exactly as the original telegram had been, to Chevis, 14 Argyle Road, Boscombe, Hants. Unlike the missive to the editor of the *Daily Sketch*, the author had eschewed block capitals in favour of a careful joined-up hand:

It is a mystery
they will never
solve
J Hartigan
Hooray

In some accounts of this case, great store is set by these postcards, with the impression given that they might very well have come from the 'real' Hartigan, the sender of the telegram: but the second card, just like the first, had obviously been written by a different hand – a hand which had made considerable efforts to imitate the signature reproduced in the newspaper – but a different hand nonetheless.

The police wasted very little time on them, though they did follow up another anonymous communication from Belfast, which was sent to the coroner on 12 August. This came in the form of a letter, in which the writer claimed that he had genuine information about Lieutenant Chevis's death, but was willing to provide it only on condition that they 'keep my name out of it'. If the police and coroner agreed to provide protection and anonymity, they were to place an advertisement in the *Daily Herald*, addressing the sender as 'Mr Belfast'.[5]

An advertisement was duly placed: 'Mr Belfast; guarantee given, wait to hear from you,' but it elicited no response.

As the date set for the resumption of the inquest drew near, the papers vied with one another for the latest Chevis scoop. All of them seemed determined to keep their readers on the edge of their collective seats, intimating each day that 'sensational developments' were expected and even that an arrest was imminent. Deputy Chief Constable Kenward added fuel to the fire, informing reporters on 31 July, 'While I cannot at the moment indicate the exact nature of the change of circumstances in the case, I can assure you that information has come into our possession which has made it necessary for us to look for the solution in an entirely different direction from that in which our investigation started.'[6]

Superintendent Stovell's movements were scrutinised on a daily basis – one minute he was off to London and the next hotfooting after clues in a variety of other points east and west of Surrey. The *Bournemouth Daily Echo* had him travelling to Essex and Okehampton in the space of a couple of days, as well as following up clues in London and having a conference with the coroner in Surrey.

The Dublin *Evening Herald* spent a great deal of time scotching rumours which they said were circulating round the city, but then replacing them with equally wild stories of their own. There was no truth in the story printed in a Dublin morning paper that the man wanted in connection with the telegram had been traced to County Wicklow, they informed their readers on 6 August, because the man believed to have sent it was under surveillance in London and 'detectives are in possession of details regarding his career.' Scotland Yard detectives were expected to arrive in Dublin soon, they continued, to interview three witnesses, who, it was hoped, would throw considerable light on the affair.

The next day they contradicted themselves again by stating that the sender of the telegram had not been identified, and made no further mention of imminent arrests or the arrival of men from Scotland Yard. While the citizens of Ireland were being encouraged to expect the arrival of English detectives on every boat, back in Surrey Superintendent Stovell was apparently on permanent alert in expectation of 'important documents from Dublin.'[7] The *Sketch* was one of several papers to state that handwriting experts were being put to work on the telegram form, and on 31 July they claimed that information had come to light which suggested that the poison had not been administered to Lieutenant Chevis via the partridge: 'At the moment nothing is certain except that Lt Chevis died the victim of foul play.' (Surviving police files do not support any of these contentions.)

In the same edition they quoted Superintendent Stovell as not investing too much hope in the idea that the solution to the mystery of Lieutenant Chevis's death would be provided by the telegram. 'Even if the writer is traced, he may not be able to throw any light on the death of Lt Chevis.'[8] Only four days later, however, other papers quoted Stovell saying, 'Once the sender of the telegram is found, the solution will be in sight.'[9]

There were garbled stories about the police finding a passenger named Hartigan travelling on a ferry across the Irish Sea on a relevant date – none of which is substantiated by anything in the police records of the investigation – and also that the analyst engaged on the case had variously come up with evidence which proved that the strychnine had been in both partridges, only one partridge, and not in the partridges at all. The *Daily Mirror* assured its readers on 28 July that the man who had bought strychnine in Dublin was thought to be the same man who had sent the telegram, and on 4 August that experiments were to be undertaken cooking partridges which had been impregnated with strychnine. The *Daily Mail* pointed out that the man who sent the telegram appeared to change his mind about what he was going to write and stated with confidence that the first three letters of the message had been altered to HOO, but had originally been HUG: the first three letters of the dead man's name.[10] The *Bournemouth Daily Echo* was among those to repeat an unsubstantiated rumour on 4 August that handwriting experts who had examined the telegram form, having studied the signature, had decided that the sender was not English. (Major Jackson, when asked to comment on the reproduction of the telegram form, said the handwriting did not resemble that of anyone he knew: 'It looks like a groom's handwriting to me.'[11])

In spite of their best efforts to keep the story alive, however, the papers were running out of new things to say. In addition, there was a fresh case to occupy the headlines because, on 4 August, the story of the Kempson murder broke. Mrs Kempson, a 'wealthy widow', had been discovered in her own home in Oxford, where she had been lying dead for at least two days and Sir Bernard Spilsbury had been called in. Headlines such as 'House of Murder and Mystery'[12] began to appear and as the Kempson case increasingly dominated the headlines, interest in the story already dubbed 'The Poison Partridge Mystery' consequently diminished, with most papers falling back on the suggestion that all would become clear at the resumption of the inquest on 11 August.

CHAPTER SIXTEEN

'ONE OF THE MOST MYSTERIOUS POISONING CASES OF RECENT YEARS'

Daily Mail, August 1931

The third and final chapter of the inquest certainly opened amid considerably more public interest than had hitherto been the case. There was a minor scuffle at the door when the large crowd of would-be spectators, some of whom had been waiting for up to an hour to gain admission, discovered that by the time all interested parties and press observers had been accommodated, the space remaining for the general public was limited to a mere ten seats.[1] Everyone was prepared for a 'big production' – there were thirteen witnesses – many more than at any previous sitting, and the public no doubt anticipated sensational revelations and drama galore.

To the solicitors acting for Messrs Colebrooks and Mrs Chevis had been added the presence of Mr Flint, who had a watching brief for Major Jackson. The Major had also turned up to observe proceedings – a perfectly normal state of affairs when one's name had been bandied about in connection with a murder inquiry. The scope of a coroner's inquiry was extremely wide and it was not beyond the bounds of possibility that questions might be put regarding Major Jackson, and prejudicial statements made which needed to be challenged. At this period it was not unknown for the coroner and his jury to 'turn detective' and name a person they suspected of being the guilty party in their verdict – sometimes on the slenderest of evidence. This was of course an extremely dangerous practice, since the coroner's court rarely had all the facts at its disposal and the person so named had little opportunity of mounting an effective defence, but this practice was not outlawed until the late 1970s. (Lord Lucan was the last person to be so named by a coroner's jury in 1975.)

Before calling any witnesses, the coroner spoke about the telegram and said that whether it had any significance to the case or not, sending it 'was a very cruel act.'[2] After complaining about the way the telegram had been published in direct contravention to the wishes of himself and the police, he then announced that two further postcards had been received. He read out the messages from the cards and commented that he had no idea whether or not there was a lunatic abroad, who was responsible for sending these things, because he had no evidence on the point. He went on to mention the numerous letters he had received suggesting ways in which the birds could have picked up strychnine, but said there was no way of deciding this because 'the great handicap in this case is that the birds were destroyed.' Had they been preserved, he suggested, 'we might easily have arrived at a conclusion'.

Not surprisingly, the press focussed a great deal of attention on the postcards, with several papers choosing to headline the question: 'Is there a lunatic abroad?' while others wrote of 'a second message from Hartigan' – as if the origin of the postcards had been definitely established. The inquiry had elicited numerous letters from members of the public, incorporating all manner of suggestions and accusations, so the coroner's decision to single out the two postcards, simply because they had been signed by someone calling themselves Hartigan, was not particularly sensible – and has led to undue weight being attached to these particular communications for almost a century.

Turning to the various statements which had appeared about the police handling of the case, the coroner assured the assemblage that no stone had been left unturned, every effort made to solve the mystery, and that this work would continue. The conduct of the investigation, he said firmly, was one for the Chief Constable of the county and not one for the jury.

Needless to say this did not convince the doubters. The *Daily Mail* published another lengthy attack on Surrey Police the next day, claiming that, 'The open verdict ... should convince Surrey Police that they ought not to have expected to grapple with one of the most mysterious poisoning cases of recent years. Nothing daunted by their failure, they assured the deputy coroner[3] that enquiries would continue ... This penny halfpenny stamp method of conducting important criminal enquiries in the odd intervals between routine duties had had the inevitable unsuccessful result.'

It remains a widely held perception that CID men are able to abandon all other ongoing work and devote themselves exclusively to a single major inquiry for weeks on end. In fact, officers are often required to set an investigation to one side for a few hours or even days in order to give evidence in another case in which they have been involved. The requirements of prosecuting cases through the court – even if it is a case of a relatively minor nature – self-evidently cannot be ignored; and this of course applied to Scotland Yard detectives as well as to regional officers. It is likely that experienced crime reporters on papers such as the *Mail* were well aware of this, but chose to misrepresent the situation in order to further blacken Surrey Police.

The police had failed to 'unearth one iota of evidence' claimed the *Mail*. The *Daily Express* was among those to join in the hail of criticism, opining that after seven weeks the investigation had made no progress. They called on the Home Office to intervene, claiming that there was a precedent for them to go over the head of a Chief Constable and send in the men from Scotland Yard (which again sounds suspiciously reminiscent of Sir William Chevis's letter to the Deputy Chief Constable).

Once he had dealt with the peripheral issues of unwanted publicity and criticism of the police, the coroner referred the jury's attention back to a suggestion made at the first inquest that a neighbour's dog might have died from strychnine poisoning, explaining that since no strychnine had been found in the dog, he did not propose to call any evidence regarding it. He then moved to the main point at issue – establishing how Lieutenant Chevis had met his death – and instructed the jury to forget anything they had read in the press, saying that the evidence 'will not, I think, disclose how strychnine came to be in the partridge...' though 'by process of elimination it will be shown by the evidence of the Assistant Pathologist to the Home Office that we come back to the partridge as the means by which strychnine was conveyed, whether accidentally or feloniously, to the deceased officer and his wife.'

It might be thought that there was a significant degree of assumption and pre-emption in this, since the cause of the dog's death was far from clear, the coroner himself had already referred to the difficulties of inferring anything about the partridges because they had both been destroyed, while there was no conclusive evidence in the analyst's findings that Mrs Chevis had been suffering from strychnine poisoning at all, but the coroner's jury had no reason to know any of this and no doubt accepted his remarks at face value.

The first witness to be called was Captain William Chevis, the brother of the deceased, who gave evidence about receiving the telegram. (Yet another oddity of the case is that Sir William Chevis, in spite of being the recipient of the infamous telegram, and in spite of agitating from the sidelines, did not attend any of the sessions at the coroner's court – though he did expect Surrey Police to call on him in Bournemouth and keep him apprised of what was going on.)

After Captain Chevis, his sister-in-law, Frances, came to the witness's seat and gave her evidence in a low voice. She was dressed in mourning, as was still the custom among those who could afford to observe it: 'a neatly fitting costume and a cloche hat' according to the *Evening Herald*. She evidently found the occasion a strain and nearly broke down, according to the *Daily Express* – although this may have been in large part due to the inevitable scrum at the conclusion of proceedings, when reporters surrounded her, all demanding a comment.

Essentially Frances had little to add to her earlier statement. Asked if there had been any letters, telegrams or other correspondence which might shed some light on the matter, she shook her head. Nor had there been any letters or telegrams found in her husband's pockets after his death. Further questions elicited the information that her husband had neither been insured, nor left a will so far as she had been aware. She knew of no one named Hartigan and having known her husband for five years, she felt that she would have been aware of any friend or associate of his who went by that name.

Had Major Jackson any friends or relatives named Hartigan? the coroner asked. Frances said she did not know – a slightly odd answer considering that she had

known the Major for the best part of a decade, and been his wife for five years –
more than double the length of her entire acquaintance with Lieutenant Chevis.

The coroner wanted to know about her partridge: how had it tasted?

'It tasted musty. There was no bitter or sharp taste.'

The coroner commented that as both partridges were cooked together and
basted with the same fat, 'it amazes me that your partridge should not have tasted
of strychnine', but Frances remained adamant that her partridge merely had a
'very musty, unsavoury taste.'

'Are you quite sure that your husband told Bolger to burn the partridge?'

'Yes, quite sure.'

Asked if she had given the police all possible information, Frances said that
she had, expressing the wish that she could have told them more. 'I have told the
police absolutely everything I can,' she replied again, in answer to a subsequent
question on the subject of her husband's associates.

In the run up to proceedings, it had been implied in some newspapers that
there would be exciting revelations from the Home Office analyst, so there was
probably a frisson of excitement among the press and public when Dr John Ryffel
began his evidence. He read out the list of exhibits he had received, followed
by his report and then took questions. When asked about the total quantity of
strychnine he had discovered, he told the court that he had mixed the material
recovered from Lieutenant Chevis with that from Mrs Chevis, and calculated the
total quantity of strychnine in the dripping and the gravy, and the total amount of
strychnine found was approximately 2 grains (a fatal dose was 0.5 grain) – but this,
he said, was 'an extremely rough calculation' and would depend on what other
materials were employed in preparing the partridge – though why this should
be the case unless he was suggesting that any of these materials also contained
strychnine, Ryffel did not explain.

Asked how he thought strychnine might find its way into a partridge, Ryffel
said that he did not believe it would be possible for a bird to absorb that amount
in life and that it might have been injected into the bird. (Unless there was some
definite evidence of such activity – which there could not be, since the bird had been
destroyed – this was an extremely speculative and mischievous suggestion to make,
implying as it did that there had been some deliberate tampering with the partridge.)

One of the jurors wanted to know why it was that Lieutenant Chevis had been
taken ill a whole hour before his wife, and asked Ryffel if that was consistent with
strychnine poisoning. Ryffel's correct course of action at this point would have been
to explain that as he was not a medical doctor, he was not qualified to answer on
points of this nature, but modesty was never Ryffel's strong suit and confronted with
a question to which he clearly did not know the answer, the analyst's approach was
to waffle, which he did now, offering the convoluted proposition that if strychnine
was taken with a lot of fat, the poison was absorbed far more slowly than if taken by
itself. Quite what this had to do with the juror's question is hard to fathom, since

no one had suggested that Mrs Chevis's meal had been swimming in fat, whereas her husband's had not. Theorising further under the guise of specialist knowledge, Ryffel added that the delay in the appearance of Mrs Chevis's symptoms pointed to her having received less poison than her husband and to the fact that she 'did not pass her food on as rapidly as Lieutenant Chevis' – another entirely speculative statement, but one which led Ryffel to sum up with the conclusion that he was therefore 'not surprised at the lapse of time.'

Superintendent Stovell intervened to point out that strychnine was usually fatal within two hours, whereas Lieutenant Chevis had survived for fourteen, but Ryffel responded that Lieutenant Chevis's breathing had failed at midnight, after which he had been kept alive by artificial respiration.

With regard to the strychnine itself, Inspector Pharo deposed that enquiries had been made at all chemists in the surrounding area of Blackdown Camp, but there had been no record of anyone attempting to purchase strychnine. (He did not add that similar enquiries had been made in Dublin, Eastbourne, or the area of London immediately surrounding Mrs Chevis's flat.)

Mr Maskey, the Sanitary Inspector for Frimley and Camberwell Urban District Council, who in line with normal routine had been called in to investigate suspected food poisoning or contaminated foodstuffs, gave evidence that he had taken charge of the remaining partridges from the stock at Messrs Colebrooks and found nothing wrong with them. There had been no other complaints regarding that batch of poultry or that supplier. The birds he obtained from Colebrooks had been analysed at the Ministry of Health Laboratory with no result.

Philip Bowser, Hugh Chevis's brother officer and a guest on the evening of his death, was called as a witness, but could add nothing material to the case. There had been nothing unusual about his host or hostess that evening, he told the coroner. Both had appeared in perfect health. Lieutenant Chevis had been a popular officer and he and Mrs Chevis had appeared very happy. The Lieutenant had no enemies that he could think of.

Nicholas Bolger was required to give evidence yet again, but his account of the affair was just as before. He was absolutely definite that Lieutenant Chevis had instructed him to have the partridge burned. In answer to questions put by Mr Rose and the jury, he explained that it was a perfectly accepted practice within the household to burn rubbish and things left over from the table – the kitchen was equipped with an Ideal Boiler specifically designed for the purpose. He also stuck to his story that Mrs Chevis had told him that Lieutenant Chevis was suffering from strychnine poisoning while they were together in the kitchen, just before Mrs Chevis was taken ill. 'She said the doctor had said that Lieutenant Chevis was suffering from strychnine poisoning. I am quite certain about that.'

Mrs Yeomans was called and was similarly unable to add any new information, except to agree with Mr Ricketts, who represented Colebrooks, that if she happened to be out, the delivery men were authorised to simply leave things in the meat safe – although what possible relevance this had cannot be imagined, since Mrs Yeomans had not been out on the day in question, and both she and William Noyes agreed on this point.

She was followed by the three witnesses who had handled the partridge before it arrived at her kitchen door. Firstly Charles Tyler, the shop manager at Colebrooks, who gave evidence as to the numbers of partridges in stock and the receipt of the order.

After Tyler the court heard from Fredrick Downs, a poulterer who had been on the staff at Colebrooks for twelve years. Colebrooks was a large business, he told the court, and he was engaged in the preparation of poultry twelve hours a day, from 8 a.m. in the morning to 8 p.m. at night. He described how he had prepared and dressed the birds while Noyes waited, drawing them, trussing them, dusting them with flour and finally wrapping them in paper – including a piece of beef fat in the parcel – an aid to cooking not mentioned by Mrs Yeomans, who had referred only to the use of dripping derived from the previous day's lamb. Mr Ricketts – who seemed to specialise in introducing irrelevance – asked where Downs had obtained the beef fat and Downs said that he had received it from Noyes. As Noyes was the van driver, rather than someone who worked on the premises, Noyes had presumably obtained it from Tyler when he collected the rest of the order from the stock room, but Mr Ricketts seemed satisfied to let the matter of the beef fat rest.

A juryman asked whether Downs had done anything to 'buck the birds up', but Downs denied this. Mr Rose asked if he had noticed any shot left in the birds, but Downs said he did not think they had been shot and thought it more likely that they had been snared. He had not seen any shot, at any rate.

William Noyes was called and explained yet again that he had received the birds from Tyler the shop manager, had watched them being prepared by Downs, and had then delivered them to the bungalow.

Dr Attenborough gave evidence of his arrival at the bungalow, where he found Lieutenant Chevis having convulsions. He had removed the patient to Frimley Cottage Hospital in his car, where his stomach had been washed out under anaesthetic.[4] After this the convulsions became even more violent and an injection of magnesium sulphate had been administered. This had diminished the convulsions somewhat, but at 12.15 respiration had ceased. The team of doctors continued with artificial respiration for some hours, but eventually they were forced to concede defeat.

Sitting through this evidence must have been immensely distressing for those present in court who had known and loved Hugh Chevis – the awful ordeal of his death further underlined when Dr Attenborough spoke of having performed a subsequent post-mortem on the 'well developed, muscular body, which was marked with abrasions and bruising... as a result of the artificial respiration'. The cause of death had been asphyxia due to acute poisoning from a convulsant agent, probably strychnine, Attenborough told the court. All Lieutenant Chevis's organs had appeared normal apart from the meningeal vessels, lungs and bronchi, which had been congested as a result of asphyxia.

One witness in whom the press took little or no interest was Ivy Thorne, the uniformed nurse who had arrived at the inquest by car with Frances Chevis. Ivy Blanche Thorne's testimony was largely ignored by the newspapers and in the coroner's file her answers survive only in note form, without the questions which provoked them. It is therefore impossible to do more than piece together and infer her evidence from what survives. In response to the coroner's questions, she explained to the court that she lived with Mrs Chevis at her London flat. On the evening of 20 June she had received a telephone call from Mrs Chevis at about 9.15, as a result of which she had contacted Mrs Chevis's own doctor, Dr Gibson, and they had travelled down to Frimley Cottage Hospital together, from whence they had collected Mrs Chevis and taken her back to London. When questioned about the timing of this journey, Miss Thorne said there had been some delay in leaving the flat, because she had to wait for the arrival of the night nurse (presumably because she could not leave the three children alone). She estimated that she eventually left the flat at ten minutes past eleven, but it is unclear at what time she called for Dr Gibson, or at what time they eventually arrived at the hospital. She does not appear to have been asked at what stage a private ambulance was engaged to transport Mrs Chevis, and nor do we learn precisely what was said during the telephone call between the bungalow and the flat.

Ignoring these potentially important points, the coroner instead followed the correspondence obsession which bedevilled the case, asking Nurse Thorne about the clothes belonging to Mrs Chevis which she had collected from the hospital that morning, and whether there had been any telegrams or letters in the pockets. Miss Thorne said the hospital had given her a receipt for Mrs Chevis's things, which she had taken straight back to London with her. There had been no letters or telegrams in the pockets.

On the face of it, Nurse Thorne's part in the affair was peripheral, yet the point which everyone seems to have missed is that her account of the evening simply did not match up with that of Frances Chevis. Both women gave evidence of a single telephone call. According to Frances Chevis the call had been made at some time around 8 o'clock, before her husband had been taken ill, and the purpose of the call had been to enquire after the health of her son Peter. Yet according to Ivy Thorne, the call had been made at around 9.15 and as a result of this call she had alerted Mrs Chevis's doctor and set in motion the events which would lead to Frances being spirited away from the hospital before the police had the opportunity to take a statement from her. Frances would hardly have asked her nurse to arrange for Dr Gibson to attend her at 8 o'clock, unless she somehow knew that she was about to be taken ill, while according to her own evidence, by 9.15 she was prostrated with the awful symptoms of strychnine poisoning and presumably unable to make a telephone call at all.

CHAPTER SEVENTEEN

'WE WILL NOT DROP OUR INVESTIGATIONS'

Superintendent James Stovell, 1931

The inquest ended on a note of uncertainty. Mr Francis said, in his summing up, that there was 'not a shred of evidence' to show how the strychnine came to be on the birds and informed the jury that they would have to return an open verdict, which they did.[1]

As the major participants in the drama attempted to leave the building they were mobbed by enthusiastic newsmen. Superintendent Stovell assured reporters that, 'We will not drop our investigations. They will continue as searchingly as before the verdict of the coroner's jury.'[2]

Frances Chevis managed to escape to her waiting car, brushing aside enquiries with the words, 'No. Not now. I am very ill.'[3] Her ex-husband was marginally more forthcoming, saying that it was all 'as much a mystery as ever.'[4] Faced with a reporter from the *Daily Sketch* he apparently became positively loquacious, asking, 'Who would have wished to break up a home which was of the happiest? I always knew that Lieutenant Chevis and his wife were most happy. Is it not strange that the police have never questioned me on any detail other than my movements at that time? Yet I know more of the family than anyone. They have never asked me to explain any theory I might have had. As for myself, I have never had anything to hide.'[5] Though the *Sketch* described this brief statement as 'an exclusive interview with Major Jackson', it reads suspiciously as if their reporter has stitched together a series of one line answers to questions put outside the inquest, possibly inventing a couple of things along the way, before adding an anti-police slant which suited the thrust of the articles about the case which had been appearing in various papers the day before. Certainly the police statements provided by Major Jackson indicated that he *had* been asked about matters other than his immediate whereabouts on the penultimate weekend in June – and if he did have some theory as to the death of Lieutenant Chevis, there is no indication that he had made any attempt to share it with the police either on the previous occasions when they had interviewed him, or subsequently.

In a quote which does sound more authentic, Major Jackson said, 'It is the first inquest I have attended and I certainly don't want to attend another. Mrs Chevis looked to me very ill. I glanced in her direction once or twice and she seemed to be on the verge of tears. I did not speak to her.' (It should be pointed out that this may have been as much from lack of opportunity as anything else. Reports of the proceedings make it clear that Mrs Chevis and the other witnesses were initially escorted into a side room and then to a designated seating area in the court, whereas Major Jackson and his solicitor had seats in a separate part of the room. In the general scrum to avoid the Press at the end of the proceedings, no one would have had much opportunity for a chat.)

In spite of a last ditch attempt to stir up the embers of the story – on 11 August, the *Evening Herald* in Dublin reported the inquest under the headline 'Inquest Sensation: Hooray Telegram Followed By Postcard' – without the 'sensational developments' with which the Press had been tantalising their readers during the preceding fortnight, interest in the 'Poisoned Partridge' case was waning, particularly as the killing of Mrs Kempson in Oxford was providing new excitement, with an ongoing manhunt and the suspect – Henry Daniel Seymour – finally tracked down in Brighton and arrested for her murder on 17 August. (He would go on to face trial and be hanged later in the year.)

Though the hearings were over and the verdict in, it still fell to Mr Francis to deal with an aftermath of correspondence. Dr Ryffel was swift off the mark to submit his bill for settlement, enclosing it in a letter written the day after the inquest, in which he commented: 'The Chevis case was certainly of great interest and I do not see what other verdict could have been brought in. May I express the pious hope that the police are able to elucidate the mystery of the Hartigan telegram and the postcard.'[6] (It is somehow typical of Ryffel that he wrote postcard singular, rather than postcards plural – accuracy never being his strong suit.)

Ryffel himself had managed to create more work for the coroner with his 'gravy' gaffe, about which the coroner received a letter from a Mr L.J.A. Schulty of Winchester Road in Twickenham, who queried how the strychnine could have got into the gravy, and if so why Mrs Yeomans, who stated in evidence that she had tasted the gravy before serving it, had not tasted the poison in it.[7] There is no evidence that the coroner replied to the majority of letters he received from members of the public, but he made an exception with Mr Schulty – perhaps because the point could have been an important one. (Had it been possible to accept Ryffel's 'strychnine in the gravy' evidence at face value, it would have been an indication that the gravy had been adulterated with strychnine after if left the kitchen, and that the gravy, rather than the partridge, had been the medium by which Lieutenant Chevis had been poisoned.)

Mr Francis wrote back promptly, telling Mr Schulty that his was the first 'outside' letter that he had replied to since the inquiry began. 'I would like to remove your misapprehension ... there were two gravies – the small portion under the dripping after it had set and the separate gravy made and served with the meal. It was the gravy under the dripping which had set and was poured off after basting which contained strychnine and tasted bitter. This was not tasted by the cook and never reached the dinner table.' He went on to explain the ingredients with which Mrs Yeomans had made the gravy served in the gravy boat, which 'had tasted perfectly alright.'[8] It is quite possible that on receipt of the letter Mr Schulty scratched his head over the notion of 'two gravies' and wondered why, if the analyst and now the coroner wanted to describe the meat juices, or 'jelly' as the darker section of dripping was more generally known, they spoke of gravy, rather than using the terminology in common parlance.

Mr Francis continued to receive letters for a few days after the inquest. F. Pecks of Norwich wanted to know whether it had occurred to anyone that the poison may have been in the herb the bird was stuffed with?[9] (In fact, the birds had not been stuffed with anything.) While S. Rickett of Southsea wrote to say that five members of the family of Lord John Russell 'nearly succumbed to eating foreign partridge in 1842' and the particulars of the case could be found on page 62 of *The Recollections of Lady Georgianna Peel* compiled by her daughter, Ethel Peel.[10]

There is nothing to record whether or not the coroner tracked down a copy of the volume in question, but the present author has done so. The anecdote in question occupies only a few paragraphs, detailing how a friend of the Peel family (a judge called Halliburton) had made them a gift of a partridge imported from Nova Scotia, which the Peels decided to share for supper. The bird was divided into five necessarily very small portions and no sooner had each tasted their share than they knew at once that they had been poisoned. Their family physician, Dr Julius, attended and by a fortunate coincidence he happened to be aware of potential problems with Nova Scotian partridges, and explained to the family that at certain times of the year these partridge ate berries which, while having no effect on the birds, rendered their flesh unfit for human consumption. Dr Julius told the family that they had been saved from death by the fact that each of them had only eaten a minute quantity of the bird.[11] Although the family were prostrated by the poison and could not even move from the dining room, there is no mention in this account of the dramatic convulsions which inevitably accompany strychnine poisoning and it is far more likely that they had come into contact with a different toxic substance.

More than one kind of partridge was found in Nova Scotia at the time and while the Birch Partridge were hunted and consumed, the Spruce Partridge was avoided as the Black Laurel berries which formed part of its diet were poisonous to humans.[12] It rather sounds as if the bird which had found its way to the table of the Russell family fell into the latter category (apparently as a result of an honest mistake, for the family remained friends with the extremely apologetic Judge Halliburton). A number of other letters were received by both the coroner and the police, mentioning the issue of birds and poisonous berries, but the crucial point was that the Black Laurel berries contained not strychnine, but cyanide, which brings on quite different symptoms.

There were plenty of other letters in a similar vein. Mr J. La Touche of County Wicklow had also stumbled across possible elucidation in his own personal library, writing as late as December 1931 to say that he had been reading back numbers of *The China Journal of Science & Arts*, where he had come across references to partridges being poisoned by Chinese fowlers and then exported. He did not want to send the relevant journal to the police, as 'it would spoil my series' but he had taken the trouble to type out the article and enclose it with his letter.[13]

Not everyone obtained their theories from the printed word: the usual crop of letters from spiritualists offered a variety of suggestions from the Other Side (Spiritualism had enjoyed a level of unsurpassed interest during the 1920s and early '30s, probably as a result of the enormous loss of life suffered during the Great War and subsequent influenza pandemic). Someone suggested that the police obtain samples of handwriting from everyone called Hartigan, in order to compare them with the writing on the telegram – starting with Major General J. Hartigan CMG DSO. A London correspondent claimed that the handwriting on the 'It's a mystery' postcard was characteristic of the penmanship taught in the Civil Service, 'as any tutor for Civil Service Class II will tell you,' and 'Curious of Birmingham' wrote on 12 August, wondering if there had been a cruet on the table – the obvious implication being that had strychnine been secreted within it, Lieutenant Chevis could have added the fatal dose to his partridge himself, when he seasoned his dinner.

The case seems to have provoked particular interest among the citizens of Birmingham, for another of their number wrote a long, rambling letter claiming to have known Major Jackson in Eastbourne many years ago. If Major Jackson was viewed with considerable suspicion, even more people were keen to point their finger at Bolger, whose nationality not only created a coincidental link with the origin of the telegram, but also awakened the widespread anti-Irish prejudice which lurked in many English minds. Some put forward as a proposition that it must have been Bolger, simply by virtue of his being Irish and a Roman Catholic. A man who worked as a postman in the Republic wrote to point out that if Bolger was from the South of Ireland, he must have known people called Hartigan, as it was such a common name there.

Bolger was also accused by people who should have known better. Sir William Chevis (who as an ex-judge might have been relied upon to keep an open mind and weigh actual evidence against mere prejudice) wrote to the police casting suspicion on Bolger, and even Frances Chevis toyed with a theory about the batman, writing to Superintendent Stovell while she was in Hove, speculating that surely the birds must have been tampered with en route from the kitchen to the dining room, which only left Bolger. Was it possible that he had done this under orders from someone else, she wondered? Someone who had terrified him into keeping silent? She ended by saying that it was 'all ghastly' and admitting that her theory about Bolger was 'far-fetched'.

The unfortunate batman was questioned again, and made to go through his entire eleven-year army service, culminating in the two years he had spent at Blackdown Camp, to which he had originally come as batman to Lieutenant Ross, who had been the occupant of 'D Hut' prior to Lieutenant Chevis – but nothing emerged from this which linked him to the telegram, or offered any reason why he should take it into his head to poison the officer he served.[14]

One of the various letters sent directly to Sir William Chevis reported some suspicious remarks which the sender had allegedly overheard in a London pub. It was passed on to Surrey Police who dutifully investigated, but quickly established that there was nothing in it.[15] Another anonymous correspondent, sheltering under the alias 'No.6', wrote to the editor of *The News Chronicle* claiming that the telegram had been sent by James Hughes of Aldershot – 'I am sending this information at considerable risk to myself'. This message arrived on a postcard which was initially thought to have come from The Union Jack Club in London and the police hoped that the number 6 might be an enigmatic clue to the identity of the sender. However, their enquiries produced no James Hughes who had any possible connection to the Chevis family and while the Union Jack Club confirmed that they had a Room No. 6, it had been unoccupied for at least a week by the time the postcard was sent – and in any case they denied that the card in question was one of theirs.

An anonymous accusation against Mr J. Dill Smith, a barrister, proved similarly unpromising. Mr Dill Smith was traced to his home at Sidcup in Kent, where he said that he knew nothing about the dead man, except that they had both been to Charterhouse School at the same time, but he had not known Lieutenant Chevis well as they had belonged to different houses.[16]

Other suggestions majored on the idea of a Sinn Fein revenge killing. Hugh Chevis had never been to Ireland, so it was difficult to see why Sinn Fein should have had the slightest interest in him, but naturally the rumour mongers had been at work and while pursuing enquiries at Blackdown Camp, Inspector Pharo was asked by Major Walsh whether it was true that Sir William Chevis was the judge who had tried the Connaught Rangers? (It was not.)[17]

An ex-serviceman wrote to point out that army signallers were taught to write the text of a telegram in capitals letters, then sign their own name in joined up handwriting, as 'J Hartigan' had done, and any number of people wrote to reinforce the point made early on by Superintendent Brennan of the Dublin Police that Hartigan was a common name in Ireland.

Many of those who communicated in writing about the case hid behind aliases, or simply left their letters unsigned, but after the 'mystery they will never solve' postcard, no one else wrote to anyone concerned with the case representing themselves as J. Hartigan.

Towards the end of August 1931, however, another note bearing the message 'Hooray Hooray Hooray' did come into the possession of the Irish police, initially as a result of its having been misdirected by the postal authorities.[18] The note had been posted in Dublin and the intended recipient was Miss Viola O'Reilly, who lived in London. The Garda men returned to the Hibernian Hotel, where they found (perhaps not surprisingly – given that O'Reillys are even more prevalent in Ireland than Hartigans) that two persons of that name had been staying there during the critical period in June, but when traced, neither guest had any connection with the Chevis family or any knowledge of either the telegram, the postcard, or this latest note.

Undeterred, the police turned their investigations toward the intended recipient's family, but by October they were able to inform Superintendent Stovell that the note had originated with Viola O'Reilly's mother, who had sent it as a joke on learning that a particularly unpleasant relative had died in France and left them both some money. All the family were now 'very annoyed' with the sender, 'for causing all this bother.'

Although the investigation teams on both sides of the Irish Sea had received dozens of communications and suggestions regarding the telegram and the 'Hooray' postcards, none of them had identified the handwriting on the original form, as had been initially hoped when the facsimile was released to the Press. While the postcards were clearly from hoaxers, the telegram itself remained a potential clue and the police in Dublin and Surrey made every attempt to link it to the crime. As well as checking the registers of the Hibernian Hotel and dozens of poison registers, they checked the passenger lists of boats crossing from England to Ireland between the date of Lieutenant Chevis's death and the date of his funeral, but Detective Sergeant Doddy ('in pursuance of diligent enquiries') soon found that the ferry passenger lists were not even supervised by company employees, but worked on the basis of voluntary compliance, with only those passengers who hoped to get their arrivals or departures listed in the local papers, for example football teams, or professional men such as doctors and solicitors, generally bothering to complete the details.[19]

Just how much could be deduced from the telegram? It has been suggested that the sender had some special knowledge of the death of Lieutenant Chevis, which he could not have known in the ordinary course of events. Some retellings of the case have gone even further, suggesting that only the murderer could have known about Hugh Chevis's death at the time he sent the telegram, as there had been no public announcement in Dublin at that point, but this is incorrect. Although Eire had been an independent republic for almost a decade by 1931, it was still the habit of its national newspapers to pick up stories from across the water – just as they had been doing for centuries. A sample front page from Dublin's national papers at this time quite often contained relatively little Irish news at all – English murder trials and the tennis at Wimbledon featured prominently and in this spirit, a brief report of Hugh Chevis's sudden death had appeared on the front page of Dublin's *Evening Herald* on Monday, 22 June, under the heading: 'Food Poisoning

– Death of a Royal Artillery Officer at Blackdown'. It was a brief item, stating that Lieutenant H.G. Chevis had died at Frimley Hospital on Sunday, and that the suspected cause of death was food poisoning.[20]

Clearly then there was no mystery at all as to how 'J Hartigan', or indeed just about anyone else in the British Isles, could have got to know about the young officer's death. However, where 'Hartigan' did show special insight was in making the link between Sir William Chevis and the dead man. The Dublin papers did not even provide the deceased officer's full name, still less mention any of his family connections, and nor did the London dailies. The exception appears to have been the Bournemouth newspapers, who, on the same day that the story was breaking in brief elsewhere, published a much lengthier item, which not only stated that the deceased was the son of Sir William and Lady Chevis, but also gave their address as Mountain Ash, Argyll Road.[21] It seems likely, however, that 'Hartigan' did not derive his information from the Bournemouth papers, not only because he was unlikely to have seen them in Dublin, but also because he did not address his telegram to Mountain Ash, Argyll Road (which was the correct spelling) but to 14 Argyle Road. So while nothing can be stated with absolute certainty about the identity of 'Hartigan', it does appear that he was someone who knew enough of the Chevis family that as a minimum he could identify one of Sir William and Lady Chevis's sons from their initials alone.

There may be a small clue in the telegram's being erroneously addressed to 14 Argyle (rather than Argyll) Road. Someone who knew Bournemouth well or habitually used the address in correspondence would surely have got this right, so it is likely that 'Hartigan' had to look up the address, then failed to recall it correctly. Being in possession of the address was not in itself particularly suggestive, since it was listed in Bournemouth directories and against Sir William's entry in *Who's Who*, both of which sources were easily accessible to anyone determined to trace the ex-judge's whereabouts, whether they happened to be on the mainland or in the Republic.

Turning to the handwriting on the form, Major Jackson had dismissed it as looking 'like a groom's'. In making this observation the Major was not implying that grooms have a particular handwriting style, but rather that the writing did not appear to be representative of a well educated person – it did not resemble the handwriting of anyone he knew – for which read anyone of his own social class. The capital letters do appear somewhat clumsy – though it could be argued that this was all part of a cunning attempt to disguise the sender's identity – and perhaps the error in spelling Argyll was all part of this same subterfuge, as was the clumsy start to the message, where the sender had apparently been forced to alter the initial letters.

The spelling of Hooray provides another source of speculation along class lines. Hooray has long been an acceptable written alternative to hurrah and appears to be gradually overtaking it in popularity, but prior to 1900 and well into the twentieth century, hurrah was much more widely used when writing the word.[22] Today we associate the term 'Hooray Henry' with the British upper classes, but in the 1920s and '30s, the upper and middle classes said 'Hurrah' and even writing in the 1970s Jilly Cooper quotes a children's nanny saying, 'Vulgar children say "Hip Hip Hooray"...We say "Hip Hip Hurrah".'[23]

Can anything else be gleaned from the wording? All manner of theories have been promulgated regarding the telegram. Several newspapers pointed out that the first word of the telegram had been altered, and at least one suggested that 'Hartigan' had originally written 'HUG' – intending to start the message with the dead man's name – and thereby demonstrating that he knew what it was. This may be correct. 'Hartigan' might have initially planned to word his message along the lines of 'Hugh Dead Hooray' – which would not have increased the word count (and thereby the cost) – but might have generated curiosity in the mind of the assistant behind the counter, who would have accepted a triple cheer as a perfectly routine message, being of course unaware that the recipients were mourning a death, rather than celebrating a wedding, a birth, or a win on the Irish Sweepstake. It could equally be that 'Hartigan' simply made a slip of the pen, missing out the second 'O' in Hooray, but almost immediately realising his mistake and altering the letters. Yet if 'Hartigan' did intend to write HUGH this essentially tells us little more than we can already deduce – that he was familiar enough with the Chevis family to recognise who they were from their initials alone and therefore by inference knew what H.G. stood for.

In 2011, a BBC Radio 4 programme about the case[24] suggested that J Hartigan was an anagram of RAJ HATING. This fell in rather neatly with the notion that Hugh Chevis's death was one of a series of assassinations which took place during the period, and were part of the campaign for Indian Independence, but there are some obvious difficulties with this notion, not least that the sender of the telegram did not appear to be Indian, that Lieutenant Chevis had spent only a very short time in India, and that all the other murders and atrocities had been carried out on the Indian sub-continent. Terrorists by their very nature hope that their actions will invoke terror. In order to maximise this possibility they tend to make clear their responsibility for any deaths, explosions or other criminal acts they have undertaken, rather than masking their activities under obscure anagrams which take half a century to decode.

Even the child who wrote to the police about the murder calling him or herself 'The Bulldog Detective' very sensibly debunked the 'Indian Revenge' theory, pointing out that an Indian seeking revenge would surely have attacked Sir William Chevis, the long-serving judge and implementer of Imperial rule, rather than his son. (The Bulldog Detective's theory was that a fellow officer had poisoned Lieutenant Chevis in a fit of jealousy.)[25]

At the same time, the Indian connection cannot be dismissed as unimportant. The telegram was sent specifically to the victim's parents, rather than to his own address, his brother, his widow, or the newspapers in general – which was an odd course to adopt if 'Hartigan' had a grievance against Lieutenant Chevis, but the most obvious route to follow if he had a grudge against one of the Lieutenant's parents.

On 26 July, Sir William Chevis told reporters that, 'To the best of my knowledge, I left not one enemy behind me in India',[26] but this statement is at best hopelessly optimistic. There are probably few judges, however fair minded, whose decisions have met with the universal approval of all those who have appeared before them and, as a long-serving judge in British India, Sir William was a member of a profession reviled by whole sections of Indian society. Members of the judiciary were among those singled out for attack – and although these incidents had increased in number during the late 1920s and early '30s, they had been occurring well before Sir William's retirement in 1922. In 1908, for example, two women named Kennedy were killed following an attack on their carriage in Muzaffarpur, which had been carried out in the mistaken belief that it contained a local judge.[27]

After a period of relative stability which had lasted for almost fifty years, there had been considerable tension in the Punjab (where Sir William Chevis spent most of his career) in 1907, when Lajput Ral and Ajit Singh, two Lahore lawyers who would undoubtedly have been known to Sir William (who served as a judge in Lahore from spring 1908 onwards), began to speak out at public meetings.[28] Sporadic instances of civil unrest and rioting continued for some years and in 1915 it was necessary to institute a Special Commission for the trial of political offenders. In 1919, William Chevis was commended for 'rendering valuable services in India in connection with the War' and this was almost certainly linked to his role in these Special Commissions.

Indian resistance to British rule had been growing steadily for decades and was the subject of almost daily demonstrations in the streets, yet it was seemingly still possible for a judge to retire from India in blissful ignorance of the way his role (and by definition therefore himself personally) was perceived. The notorious General Dyer, who orchestrated the Jallianwala Bagh (or Amritsar) massacre, remained convinced not only that he had acted correctly during this brutal military intervention, but also that all right-thinking Englishmen agreed with him. Dyer continued to insist that his action in shooting unarmed civilians had restored order and saved lives, to the end of his own.[29] The episode in Amritsar took place on 13 April 1919 and reverberated around the Empire, but the British in India continued to believe that they were fair, particularly in the way they dispensed justice, and that the vast majority of Indians were loyal in the face of this 'benign' authority and wanted them to stay. The truth seems to have been rather different, with a variety of sources expressing concern about the way justice was dispensed in the Punjab (as well as other parts of India).

By the time William Chevis arrived in India in December 1885 there was a well established judicial system, split into seven tiers which dealt with cases according to their relative seriousness or perceived monetary value.[30] Like the entire Civil Service system in British India, the lower ranks were administered by a vast army of clerks and lesser officials recruited from the native population and Chevis would have leapfrogged the bottom tier of the court system altogether when he took up his initial appointment as Assistant Commissioner 3rd Class in Lahore. By 1893, he had risen through the ranks of Commissioners to be appointed a District Judge (in Simla), which enabled him to hear criminal and civil cases with no limit on value, and to hear appeals from the five lower levels of the courts. Only the Chief Court in Lahore had a greater authority and by 1904 he would be elevated there – initially as a temporary Additional Chief Judge and later by way of a permanent appointment. The Chief Court in Lahore, where William Chevis would dispense justice for the best part of twenty years, was a magnificent building, complete with 95ft-high marble towers, courtyards and fountains, in itself a statement of confidence about the governance of the region in general and what transpired within its walls in particular – but such confidence was sadly misplaced.

Writing in 1914, Sir Bampfylde Fuller claimed that 'the brusqueness of manner and harshness of command [employed by many officials] upset Indians of all castes'.[31] Day Krishna Kapur, who wrote a history of the Judiciary in the Punjab in 1928, commented of the Victorian period that: 'the system of administering justice in the Punjab... was full of shortcomings and fraught with many failings',[32] and that while Indian officials at the bottom end of the system were often corrupt, inefficient, or lacking in appropriate training, Commissioners and District Judges were 'high-handed'. The Lt Governor said of the Punjab judiciary in 1890 that they had 'a want of sympathy with the common people which the court ought to have'.[33] According to another student of the Raj, Lawrence James, the British officials – who had never enjoyed sufficient numbers or military might to survive if the whole population had risen against them – enjoyed a life of luxury, amid periodic fears of unrest and rumours that their servants were about to murder them in their beds. James is among the authors to make the point that much of the pomp and display – riding on elephants for tiger shoots, lavish picnics, and a rigid social order with pomp and ceremony galore, may have grown out of the need to appear splendid and invincible. While the British remained 'convinced that without them India would sub-divide into tribal chaos and civil war...Isolation among a population which could never be wholly trusted bred arrogance and a feeling that any concession would be interpreted as appeasement and weakness. Prestige mattered and at every level had to be appeased.'[34]

Far from Sir William having made no enemies, this picture gives plenty of scope to imagine the existence of a positive regiment of disgruntled defendants, petitioners and others, not all of whom were necessarily of Indian extraction, since the courts heard cases brought by and against persons of all nationalities. No complete list of cases heard by William Chevis survives and nor were cases of a minor nature automatically reported in the newspapers, so it is possible that

J. Hartigan was one such disgruntled litigant. In a long judicial career, it is entirely feasible that William Chevis made a determination against a Mr Hartigan in a lower court, on a matter (which appeared to him at least) as too trivial to be memorable or noteworthy. However, a Digest of the major appeal cases heard at the High Court in Lahore between 1908 and 1914 (which happens to cover the initial six years when William Chevis was first appointed there) survives in the India Office Collection at the British Library and it is immediately noticeable from these documents that very few non-Asian names appear in the lists. Statistically the sheer weight of the native Indian population made the appearance of a member of the European minority in court a rarity, and this alone might have been sufficient to make any case involving a European into a memorable one. (Such cases were also noteworthy because the rules for trying a European differed from those set down for trying an Indian, inasmuch that a jury made up of at least 50 per cent European or American men had to be empanelled to hear it.)[35]

While a courtroom injustice is the most obvious possibility, the truth is that grievances may stem from a variety of sources. Sir William's high-handed attitude toward Surrey Police and his anti-Irish prejudice against Bolger may offer us clues to the potential for making 'enemies' both during the exercise of his judicial powers and also outside the courtroom. We have no way of knowing what kind of man William Chevis was to work with. In workplaces and professional hierarchies all over the world, rivalries, petty jealousies and even hatreds abound, leading some individuals to take unpleasant (sometimes anonymous and frequently pointless) revenge on their colleagues. The author is aware of a company team-building event which resulted in two separate participants suffering injuries (a broken nose and a considerably bruised posterior) which, while represented as accidental, were incurred as a result of another employee's desire to 'even a score'; the internet is awash with news stories of people who have tormented colleagues with hate mail, while some go even further – believing that colleagues had ruined his career at Concordia University in Montreal, Dr Valery Fabrikant shot four of them dead in 1992. The sending of one telegram, gloating over a family's unhappiness, pales into insignificance by comparison.

Nor is Sir William's career the only potential source of problems. His surviving grandson remembers him as a kindly old gentleman, whereas his wife Amy was 'a martinet'.[36] In rigidly snobbish, protocol ridden British India, it was all too easy to give or take offence and perhaps it was the high-handed Amy who had put someone's nose out of joint – figuratively speaking – at some long forgotten soirée. But here too we encounter a difficulty, for the Europeans in India were not all that populous, and surely some kind of major social incident would have been memorable – yet the name Hartigan rang no bells with the Chevises. Again we may be up against a genuine lapse of memory – and the fact that what is to one person a never-to-be-forgotten slight or social humiliation, may pass all but unnoticed to everyone else and be swiftly forgotten by the perpetrator.

There undoubtedly were men by the name of Hartigan serving in India at various times. No comprehensive records of those employed in the British Indian civil service exist, but prior to Irish Independence, substantial numbers of Irishmen took up careers in the Indian Civil Service and other parts of the Empire. (It was said that Irish graduates dominated the Indian Medical Service.) Trinity College in Dublin had an Indian Civil Service School, where students could train for the Civil Service Examinations which were the passport to a career on the sub-continent, and hundreds of recruits travelled that academic route throughout the Victorian era and beyond.[37]

In the Proof of Age Records relating to the Indian Civil Service there is a Jeremiah Hartigan, who was born in Middlesex in 1880 (making him an ideal age to fit with the sender of the telegram) but only about 5 per cent of these records survive, suggesting by the law of averages that had a full roll call been available, there would have been plenty of other J. Hartigan's to choose from.[38] Ships Passenger Lists (also incomplete) record various J. Hartigan's leaving for India, perhaps to travel, but more likely in connection with careers and business interests. A John McKnight Hartigan appears in the Bombay Staffs Corps list of 1879 and a Sergeant Henry Hartigan was awarded the VC following his gallantry during the Mutiny in 1857 – though he was certainly not sending telegrams from a Dublin Post Office in 1931, as he died in 1886 and was buried in Calcutta. *The Times of India* variously makes reference to a Lt Col M.M. Hartigan, Brevet Colonel E.R. Hartigan, Major E.A.S. Hartigan, Major E.R. Hartigan and Major Collis Hartigan (who is recorded as attending a fancy dress ball in Poona in October 1901). It could well be argued that whilst none of these latter men had initials which matched the one on the telegram, they may have had disgruntled brothers or sons, who felt moved to send a spiteful telegram to Sir William and his lady in revenge for something suffered by a beloved relative.

In 1909, a Corporal Hartigan – initials unspecified – gave evidence in an arson case which came before the Indian courts, but William Chevis was not the presiding judge and there is no obvious connection. Another Hartigan was employed at the High Court premises in Calcutta – he crops up in stories recorded in *The Times of India* in 1869 and again in 1883, so it is likely that his career overlapped for at least a short time with that of William Chevis, but again no initial is provided and again there is no obvious connection, as Calcutta was in an entirely different jurisdiction to that where Chevis spent his career.

Searching for the right Hartigan is a veritable needle in a haystack operation – and in all probability a fruitless one. All of the Hartigans cited above and many more *could* have been involved at some time in a dispute or unpleasantness involving William or Amy Chevis, or merely resented the status enjoyed by the couple – but it is equally likely that Hartigan – just like Hibernian, was a name invented on the spur of the moment to cover the sender's true identity. If the sender had really intended to remind the Chevises of some past injustice, it is likely that he would have made himself somewhat plainer, so it is reasonable to conjecture that the man who sent the telegram had no intention of giving himself away. If he knew the couple well enough to recognise their son from his initials alone and to know that they had retired to England, then it is reasonable to suppose that had he provided his real name, they would probably have recognised him immediately too.

Where was the possible satisfaction in an anonymous telegram? The coroner rightly described it as a cruel act, for at the very least the sender would surely have guessed that such a message would heighten the couple's distress. It is worth reflecting that the effect on the Chevises was likely to be unpleasant, whether or not they knew who was responsible – some would argue that an anonymous message has a more sinister overtone. Nor does anyone have to look very far for 'Hartigan's' motive in keeping his own identity a secret, for it can be surmised that the sender may have been genuinely afraid of revealing himself. Sir William had once exercised considerable power and influence and any ex-underling now reliant on a Civil Service pension might have been reluctant to risk the possibility of forfeiting it for alleged misconduct. (Such fears were probably unfounded, but the wheels of government have been known to grind in mysterious ways, and the rights of employees and pensioners were considerably less well defined or defended than they are today.) It is also possible that the sender feared the existence of some legal penalty for sending a nuisance communication – so the long-borne grudge was revenged anonymously, with Sir William and Lady Amy none the wiser as to the name of their tormentor, and meanwhile 'Hartigan' was content to jeer from afar – deriving a perverted satisfaction from the knowledge that he had enjoyed 'the last laugh' at the misfortune of an old adversary.

Although the police moved heaven and earth in their attempts to trace 'Hartigan' it must have become increasingly clear to them that they were wasting their time. In common with the 'Bulldog Detective' and the present author, the investigating officers concluded that the genesis of the Hartigan telegram lay either in some unrelated incident in Sir William Chevis's past, or was from a hoaxer who had nothing to do with the family at all. As early as 31 July, Superintendent Stovell was quoted as 'not placing too much hope on this mystery within a mystery ... even if the writer is traced he may not be able to throw any light on the death of Lt Hugh Chevis.'[39]

Although various sections of the Press repeated Stovell's remarks, they continued to emphasise the telegram as a key point in the case. The 'Hooray' telegram helped to keep the mystery going and made it seem akin to one of the fictional murders beloved of their readers, whereas the police retained a more prosaic view of life, in which murderers do not usually decamp to another country and send a telegram, taunting the victim's relations. In one of his case summaries dating from 9 August, Chief Constable Nicholson agreed that 'tracing the sender [of the telegram] will lead nowhere... [and] is probably irrelevant to the case.'[40] 'Hartigan' had no obvious connection with the death of Lieutenant Chevis and although policemen on both sides of the Irish Sea diligently pursued 'the Man in Grey' for some weeks, their interest in him was never greater than when they briefly thought it possible to identify him with Major Jackson – for essentially Surrey Police's suspicions had always centred on suspects closer to home.

CHAPTER EIGHTEEN

'A TALKIE TALKIE MAN'

Harry J. Jennings, 1931

From the very outset of the case Major George Thompson Trevelyan Jackson understandably figured large in the thinking of Surrey Police, for if anyone had a motive to murder Hugh Chevis, this must surely be the man? To an outsider at least, Jackson had been the man who had everything – a beautiful young wife, a luxurious home, three children, and unlimited funds with which to indulge his penchant for the Good Life, with strings of polo ponies and regular trips to the South of France – until his role was usurped by Hugh Chevis, who had replaced him in Frances's affections and to all intents and purposes had broken up his marriage. By the summer of 1931 Hugh Chevis looked set to enjoy all that had been Major Jackson's, while the latter was left with his army pension and a modest private income, living in a series of hotels, bereft of his wife and children. (It was a period when many children never saw their natural father again following a divorce – either because the circumstances had been acrimonious, or because it was deemed 'good form' to step aside completely, in favour of the new love in a former partner's life.) Under the circumstances it would hardly be surprising if Major Jackson bore Lieutenant Chevis some resentment, and from this it scarcely took a giant leap to imagine him exacting a painful (and permanent) revenge.

Faced with the rejection of divorce and estrangement from his children, Jackson reordered his life just as the majority of men in his situation would have done – effectively continuing as far as possible as if nothing had happened. It was the era of the stiff upper lip – grown men did not 'bleat' about missing the kids. He and his friend Major Campbell would not be likely to speak of their 'private affairs' – an English gentleman conversed about the cricket, the racing results and the weather – he did not unburden himself on the subject of his private life. Nor was it remotely remarkable for a middle-class man with appropriate means to live in a hotel. Many single men opted to live at a hotel or their London club, rather than keep up an establishment alone. The practice had much to recommend it, for a hotel provided all the comforts of home – regular meals, laundry, shoe cleaning and daily newspapers – without the bother of managing servants, dealing with tradesmen's bills, or arranging repairs for the roof. Most good hotels accepted caged birds, or well-behaved dogs, many provided garaging for motorcars, and the other guests and residents made for company at meal times and in the evenings. Long-term residents were a regular source of income to seaside hotels in the 1930s, though their numbers would diminish steadily as hotel prices rose in comparison with the cost of other kinds of accommodation. Even so, the practice was still sufficiently commonplace that the BBC TV comedy *Fawlty Towers*, first broadcast in 1975, included long-term hotel resident Major Gowen (beautifully played by Ballard Berkeley) – a recognisable type who had seen service abroad, was much interested in the cricket results, liked a flutter on the horses and was forever enquiring about the arrival of the daily newspapers.

Suspicions against Frances's ex-husband were no doubt heightened at the outset of the investigation because Trev Jackson initially did nothing to allay them, refusing to tell the police where he had been during the weekend of Hugh Chevis's death, or to discuss anything with them regarding his ex-wife or his divorce. He appeared to be a reasonable physical match for the sender of the telegram and there had even been a man called Jackson staying at the Hibernian Hotel. (Though the police would soon come to realise that the numbers of men called Jackson made for even greater complications than did the numbers of men called Hartigan.)

To Surrey Police, Major Jackson may also have come across as the sort of retired officer who might not have been averse to taking the law into his own hands – for it was rumoured that out in the Tropics a chap who took another fellow's wife might be found with a bullet in the head and no one any the wiser. There is no doubt that Jackson *was* one of a type – the sort of man without whom no country house party in the 1930s would have been complete (invariably played by the actor Nigel Bruce in films of the period) who would ultimately be caricatured as a Major Gowen: clipped accent, plus fours, knowledgeable about dogs and horses, who rode to hounds, played cricket and tennis, used a monocle to read, and could be guaranteed to bump into acquaintances in the paddock at any race meeting. Whether or not they were genuinely handy with a revolver in a tight spot, however, such men definitely had an honour code – whatever Major Jackson thought about his ex-wife in private, he would not besmirch her reputation in public – because such conduct was not the act of an officer and a gentleman. The Major Jacksons of the world had a good poker face and it may initially have appeared to the police that he was being very careful to guard the secrets of his hand.

Even now it is difficult to divine Trev Jackson's true feelings about his second divorce. To the newspaper reporters who surrounded him on the doorstep of his Eastbourne hotel, he had implied acquiescence to the divorce – suggesting that he had not wished to stand in the way of Frances's happiness with Hugh Chevis. He spoke glowingly – almost affectionately – of Hugh and Frances's happiness together. Yet behind the scenes a more complicated picture was emerging. Dorothy Heap told Inspector Pharo that she had been surprised when she heard about the divorce, as she had believed the Jacksons to be happy together[1] – and though Major Jackson refused to discuss the details of his divorce with the police, records reveal that he initially attempted to contest it. (Another friend of Hugh and Frances Chevis had provided a statement telling the police that he understood Major Jackson had not contested the divorce because he could not afford to.[2]) Moreover, while the divorce had been granted on grounds of Trev Jackson's adultery, two out of three of the named respondents had protested their innocence and the police soon assembled an abundance of evidence that whatever extra-marital activities the Major might or might not have been engaged in during the spring of 1928, the catalyst in his divorce had undoubtedly been the arrival of Lieutenant Hubert Chevis and his romantic overtures to Frances.

Jackson himself told the police about letters he had received on his return from a trip to France, alleging misconduct between his wife and the dashing young Lieutenant who had been introduced into their household in 1926. Friends of Lieutenant Chevis such as Jack Gwynn-Jones and Peter de Havilland told the police that they had initially been introduced to Frances and Trev Jackson by Hugh Chevis around this time, implying that Lieutenant Chevis and Frances Jackson, once acquainted, seem to have spent a lot of time frequenting the same race meetings and parties,[3] but confirmation that Frances and Hugh had been lovers well before she initiated divorce proceedings against her husband came from Frances herself, who confirmed in an interview with the police that she had been 'living with' (a polite euphemism for sleeping with) Hugh Chevis for four years.[4] It is unclear from the context whether Frances intended this to be understood as four years prior to his death, which would date their affair to at least mid-1927, or whether she meant four years prior to their marrying in December 1930, but either way, it was possible to conjecture that Major Jackson found himself at first cuckolded and then perhaps cornered into a divorce by someone with unlimited funds on her side.

In addition to Trev's undoubtedly having a motive, Frances had informed the police that her ex-husband was 'an artful, vindictive man' who had hated Hugh Chevis, and that no one ever knew where they stood with Trev Jackson, or what he might do.[5] In a separate letter to Superintendent Stovell, written the day after the final inquest hearing, she asked, 'Are you satisfied about Major Jackson? I know him well and watched him yesterday [at the inquest] and his face was a study. He always told me (when I was still living with him) that if I went on seeing Hugh Chevis, he would ruin his career. As I knew he had no influence in the Army, I took no notice.'[6]

In this same letter, Frances claimed that she could not get Jackson's expression at the inquest out of her mind. 'His uneasiness struck me very forcibly... He is a really queer man. Are you sure his alibi is all right – or is his friend "a really good friend"?'

The police may not have read too much into such statements since they emanated from a woman who was herself the prime suspect in the case. It is unlikely that Major Jackson was the first husband to mouth threats against the man who was having an affair with his wife, and while it seems almost de riguer for every wronged husband to shout, 'I'll kill him,' relatively few ever go on to do so. Jackson's expression may have been no more than a manifestation of unease at having to attend the inquest in the knowledge that he too was apparently a suspect. Moreover, it is not unknown for couples who have been happily married for many years to take a very different view of one another in the wake of an acrimonious divorce, sometimes astonishing friends who thought they had known the parties well, with allegations that a former partner was in reality artful, vindictive, a liar, bully, blusterer, philander and all round peculiar after all. (A suggestion was made in a booklet produced about the case that Frances may have been suggesting to the police that Major Jackson was a homosexual, but describing a man as 'queer' in 1931 had no such connotations among the general public, who would speak of any oddity as 'queer', merely meaning that it was strange or unusual. During the 1920s and '30s, *The Tatler* ran a regular series under the heading *Queer Stories*, which had absolutely nothing to do with homosexuals and there is not the slightest shred of evidence that Trev Jackson was attracted to his own sex.)[7]

In spite of expressing her suspicions about Jackson, Frances admitted during the course of the same letter that she had 'no right to... doubt his alibi, or cast suspicion on him'. Either shortly before, or soon afterwards (it is impossible to be sure because Frances was in the habit of sending undated letters) she had written to the police suggesting that the murder had been committed by Bolger, which hardly implies that she was convinced of Jackson's guilt, and in a subsequent interview with the Chief Constable of Surrey, Frances admitted that 'someone must have done it' and the only person she could think of was Major Jackson.[8]

Irrespective of Frances's own suspicions, the police did their level best to establish a link between Trev Jackson and the death of Hugh Chevis. They followed up the Jacksons who had stayed in the Hibernian Hotel and purchased strychnine respectively, but were unable to establish a familial connection. Forced to accept that Jackson's unimpeachable alibi placed him firmly in Northamptonshire, they explored the possibility of his using an agent to perform the deed and send the telegram, returning to Major Campbell's establishment to enquire whether Jackson had written any letters while he was a guest in the house.

Major Campbell evidently thought this a ridiculous line of enquiry – it was an era when the postal service was a standard medium of communication, used with far greater frequency than the telephone. Letters posted in the morning would arrive the same day. Friends kept in touch by letter, issued invitations and wrote thank you letters. Business transactions were conducted by letter, condolences sent. It was therefore an unusual day when a gentleman *did not* need to write some letters and stationery was generally provided in a guest's bedroom for the purpose. Major Campbell confirmed that his friend had written some letters, which would have been placed on the hall table, where they were collected by the butler and handed over to the postman when he next called. Asked whether he knew any of the intended recipients, Major Campbell replied stiffly that, 'When friends are staying with me, I do not examine their correspondence.'[9]

The butler at Heyford Hills was similarly unforthcoming, telling the police, 'I simply pick up the letters and hand them to the postman. I do not notice to whom they are addressed.'[10]

Still with a potential accomplice in mind, the police instigated enquiries about the friend who had accompanied the Major on the first part of his journey to Northamptonshire, but this turned out to be Mrs Lawrence, the same woman with whom it had been intimated that Trev Jackson was carrying on an affair, and nothing was uncovered to indicate that Mrs Lawrence had anything to do with the case, or for that matter that there was anything improper about her relationship with Major Jackson.[11]

They also took an interest in one Benjamin Fieldhouse, who was believed to be a nephew of Major Jackson's[12] and had a criminal record. Fieldhouse used the alias J.J. Jackson and appears to have been a small time conman, who was convicted of obtaining credit by fraud, but he was soon ruled out from playing any part in the matter, since he had been in prison for almost a year by the time of Hugh Chevis's death.

Jackson's training as a vet also proved a source of suspicion, since this obviously meant that he knew about poisons and how to use them. Ryffel's wholly unsupported assertion that the poison could have been introduced into the birds by means of a hypodermic needle appeared to point in Jackson's direction, but he assured Superintendent Claydon of Eastbourne Police, who interviewed him on this and other matters in the wake of Ryffel's inquest appearance, that he had not practiced as a vet since 1923 and as a consequence had no strychnine or syringes in his possession.[13] The police also theorised that Jackson might have shown Frances how to use a syringe, or that she might have picked up this knowledge from him, but although Trev agreed with Claydon that his ex-wife might have seen him using a syringe when she visited him in his surgery, he said that he had certainly never shown her how to use one, or provided her with one.

Anxious to explore every possible avenue where Major Jackson was concerned, the police even queried the fate of the first Mrs Jackson, but they soon established that Mabel had died of natural causes.

Members of the public also entertained suspicions where Major Jackson was concerned. Ernest Briant, the proprietor of a Bournemouth garage, sent the police a copy of a letter the Major had written to him in 1928 regarding an unpaid bill, because Briant considered that the handwriting on the letter resembled the handwriting on the telegram form, though neither the police nor the present author agree with him.[14] The contents of the letter implied that Trev Jackson was short of money in June 1928, though this is scarcely to be wondered at since he was in the midst of divorce proceedings and cannot necessarily be taken as any reflection of his usual financial position.

Mrs Amelia Jackson of Chorley Wood wrote to Surrey Police at the end of August, claiming that her husband, Major Eric Jackson, was a cousin of Trev's and suggested that the police call on her as soon as possible, since she had a great deal to say which could be of interest to them. (Sunday afternoons, she said, were the best time to call.) Superintendent Stovell seized on this lead with alacrity, arranging to visit Mrs Jackson within forty-eight hours (on a Sunday) and his enthusiasm is hardly to be wondered at, given that among other things Mrs Jackson stated in her letter that her husband – from whom she had been estranged for three years – was constantly travelling to Ireland, from whence he shipped back horses, hounds, dogs, and motorcars under false names, and that one of his aliases was J. Hartigan. As if this were not enough, Mrs Jackson also thought she might have met Lieutenant Chevis, who she thought was one of two officers who had called at the house to see her husband about some horses he was selling.[15]

By the time Superintendent Stovell arrived Amelia Jackson had become much firmer in her conviction that Lieutenant Chevis had visited the house to look over some horses, and placed the visit three years previously. She also considered that the writing on the telegram form looked like her husband's, though she could not say for certain that it was his – but she was no longer quite so sure about the relationship between her husband and George T.T. Jackson, now saying only that she thought her husband had a cousin in Eastbourne and another in Bournemouth and that one of his cousins had served in the RAVC. More disappointing still from Stovell's point of view, she retracted her original assertion that her husband used the name Hartigan, now saying instead that he used 'many names'.[16]

There is nothing in the police files to indicate that this was taken any further, perhaps because enquiries revealed that the two coincidentally named majors were not cousins (the present author has found nothing to suggest that they were related), but more likely because they had already wasted time over another estranged spouse (Arthur Miller – see chapter fifteen) who had hoped that by suggesting their missing partner was in some way involved in the case, they might persuade the police to reveal their whereabouts. Certainly Mrs Jackson's statement 'He left me several times, but I found him again, then he gave me the slip' was suggestive. Nor does Major Eric Jackson sound quite the fly-by-night that his wife's allegations regarding his nefarious activities first suggest, for during her statement to Stovell she admitted that he not only paid all the household bills, but also sent her a regular allowance.

Earlier in August the Metropolitan Police had been approached by a man with the unpromising name (for a witness at least) of Tosh, and like Amelia Jackson he excited the interest of the investigators with potentially suspicious information about Major Jackson.[17]

Herbert Tosh made a statement explaining that he had married his wife Gertrude in 1903 in London. Later they had gone out to India, where he had been the proprietor of a machinery business in Cawnpore. While staying at the Charleville Hotel in Mussoorie in 1906 they had encountered Major Jackson, who was then stationed in Lahore, and Mrs Tosh had fallen violently in love with the man: in no time at all informing Herbert Tosh that she wanted to be rid of him, so that she could be with Major Jackson. Not long after these unpalatable revelations Tosh had suffered from violent stomach pains one evening and became so ill that he was confined to a nursing home for a week – he thought he had been poisoned – indeed that his wife and Major Jackson had attempted to poison him.

On their return to London in 1907, the couple had separated and Mrs Tosh had died of salpingitis[18] at the end of the year. Herbert Tosh told the police that he was not sure whether his wife had 'lived with' Major Jackson either before or after their separation, but he was convinced that the man whose picture he had seen in the newspapers was the same man with whom his wife had been infatuated and who had been party to an attempt on his life.

Mr Tosh was described in the initial police report as a man 'of a very excitable nature' who appeared to be 'deeply embittered against Major Jackson' as he believed that Jackson had been responsible for the break up of his marriage.

Stovell was interested enough in Mr Tosh's story to ask Superintendent Minter of the Metropolitan Police to have a further chat with him, and Minter arranged to do so, writing to inform Stovell that he did not agree with the impression of the officers who had first encountered Herbert Tosh and described him as 'excitable' and 'suffering from delusions'; but although Minter found Tosh rational and fully convinced that the Major Jackson he had seen in the newspapers was the same man who had wrecked his home life, the superintendent also drew out the admission that it had never occurred to Mr Tosh until now that either his wife or Major Jackson had attempted to poison him, and that his admission to the nursing home could well have been connected with his kidney stones and other internal troubles. (Mr Tosh had an operation to remove his appendix and deal with his kidney problems on his return to England in 1907.[19])

Minter did not query in his report, although he might well have done, whether Mr Tosh would really have been able to recognise the officer from a newspaper photograph, almost twenty years after the original events, or how it was that Mr Tosh did not appear to be aware of Major Jackson's Christian name, which he probably would have been, had there been genuine intimacy between the Major and his wife.

The police concluded that there was nothing in the allegations and there is no evidence that Trev Jackson was the heart-breaker in this case, for while it is true that Jackson served in India at various times,[20] he did not attain the rank of Major until 1915, so to anyone who had known him in 1907 he would have been Captain Jackson – another detail which had apparently escaped Mr Tosh. In addition, the police were coming to appreciate that there were an awful lot of men called Jackson who had served in the British Army, including a not insignificant number who had served in the RAVC.

One witness who could provide a Jackson–Hartigan connection gave a statement to the police in Felixstowe, saying that he had known a retired army vet called Jackson in 1916. This Jackson had been a great friend of a Patrick Hartigan, himself an ex-army officer, and the two men had at one time lived together. Mr Hartigan had eventually met with a most unfortunate fate, being killed in an accidental fall from a hotel window while on a visit to Liverpool for the Grand National. Mr Fraser (the witness volunteering the information) recollected that this particular Jackson had eventually married a Miss Van der Pool.[21]

Though it was transparently obvious that Trev Jackson had not retired from the army by 1916 and had never been married to a Miss Van der Pool, the police obligingly forwarded a photograph to the local police, so that Mr Fraser could confirm that it was not the same man. If nothing else this story served to confirm the considerable numbers of Jacksons and Hartigans who had at one time or another taken the King's shilling.

In a final despairing attempt to get something useful on Jackson, the Chief Constable of Surrey Police arranged for a private investigator called Harry J. Jennings to stay at the Mostyn Hotel and attempt to worm his way into the Major's confidence. Three of Jennings's reports survive in the form of letters to the Chief Constable, written on Mostyn Hotel notepaper. Quite aside from the underhand tactics now being employed in the hope of persuading Trev Jackson to incriminate himself, there is something deeply unpleasant about the tone of Jennings's letters, which archly refer to Major Jackson as 'my friend' – presumably lest they should fall into the hands of any third party and reveal the identity of the person being spied upon. To make matters worse, the letters all read as if Jennings was determined to put the worst possible construction on even the most innocent actions and remarks of his quarry.[22]

In the first letter, written on 26 August, Jennings informed the Chief Constable that he had managed to manoeuvre himself into sitting next to Major Jackson at dinner the previous evening, so that they ended up having coffee and cigars together afterwards and chatting for almost an hour. Jennings also managed to engineer a casual chat before breakfast next morning and sat beside the Major again at lunch, though he went on to explain that as there were 150 visitors staying in the hotel, he had to spend a certain amount of time mingling with the other guests in order to provide himself with cover. He complained of being 'handicapped by the fact that the Mostyn does not possess a licence' as this obviously prevented him from persuading the Major to become more expansive over a drink. His initial impression was that, 'He is a braggart... but nevertheless an astute man of the world' and as a result the most Jennings would promise was that 'I will do my best to make him talk if possible.'

By the following day Jennings was able to write that he had gained the friendship of his target to the extent that Jackson had taken him out for a drive in his motorcar – a grey two-seater, with a 'dickey seat'. They had visited Langney, where the Major had shown Jennings over his dog boarding kennels and on their return, when they passed The Crumbles,[23] Jennings had turned the conversation to murder, but Jackson had made no reference to the Chevis case.

Jennings felt that his efforts had only gained his 'friend's' confidence up to a point – which was hardly surprising, given their relatively short acquaintance, but the investigator assured the Chief Constable that he would be 'playing him a very light line, or he may take fright'. Attempts to lure Trev Jackson into a separate licensed hostelry for a drink had fallen flat, since the Major said he was presently 'chained to the water wagon', and to Jennings's further disgust the man was evidently on friendly terms with a local solicitor, Mr Mayo, whom he suspected of advising Jackson to be cautious about what he said to anyone. In spite of the upbeat tone of his communication, Jennings had little to report aside from the fact that Jackson had confided that he was a qualified vet, who had held a commission in the army, that he dressed for dinner, though his day suits suggested that he might be strapped for cash, and that he had confided the information that he had travelled a good deal and once been quite wealthy – none of which was exactly a secret.

In his final surviving report, written on 28 August, Jennings claimed that he and his 'friend' were now sharing confidences and exchanging views on politics and women. The confidences did not appear to amount to very much – or even relate to information that would normally be accounted confidential. According to Jennings, Jackson 'boasted' of his former wealth, influential friends and past good times, which included trips to Ireland to purchase black horses for the Life Guards, though given the tone of Jennings's correspondence, the reader is forced to question how boastful these statements of fact actually were and how much effort Jennings had put into engineering the conversation onto these topics in the first place. He quoted Jackson as saying that 'having seen all there is to see, his only remaining pleasure in life is to bring pleasure to others.' 'This is typical of our friend,' Jennings wrote, adding that as Jackson was 'a naturally talkie talkie man' he might eventually touch upon the questions which most interested the investigator, if he was patient.

The Chief Constable had evidently run out of patience, however, for he called off the surveillance which was no doubt proving expensive, since the police were presumably not only paying Jennings for his time but also picking up his hotel bills.

In one of her letters to the police, Frances had queried whether the friend providing her ex-husband's alibi was 'a really good friend', but Jackson's alibi was backed up not only by his friend's household, but also by at least two other police forces, because the Major had been involved in a collision en route to Heyford

Hills, which had resulted in a visit from the Northamptonshire constabulary over the same weekend. A further reference to a brush with the police over alleged 'careless or dangerous driving' – this time in Eastbourne – appears in one of the Major's interviews with the Eastbourne Police,[24] and it might be construed from this that Trev Jackson was an exceptionally careless motorist.

In truth, the general standard of driving in the 1930s made the highways and byways of Britain extremely dangerous and the numbers of accidents, death and injures in proportion to the numbers of cars on the roads was far worse than it is today. Although there had been an ever increasing number of lorries, cars, motorcycles and bicycles on the roads since the turn of the century, the concept of a 'Highway Code' was still in its infancy (the first ever edition was not published until 1931) and many provincial newspapers included helpful hints for motorists, such as the advice that 'it is courteous and safe to negotiate a left-hand corner by keeping into the gutter, because oncoming cars tend to meet in the middle of the road on bends, giving every possibility of a collision'.[25] Even more frequently encountered were the regular weekly columns of local 'Road Casualties'. Many motorists appear to have accepted the possibility of 'a spill', or even a fatality, as a natural hazard of life with driving – and in particular driving at speed – a legitimate leisure activity which ought not to be regulated by the authorities, any more than was taking to a horse and galloping across the countryside. Alex Woodward Hill, who had pulled out of a side road and thereby caused a three vehicle pile-up in which (apparently by some miracle) no one was seriously injured, complained to the Press that, 'I suppose the person coming out of the side road always gets the blame.' A young woman stopped by a police constable for running a red light and driving on the wrong side of the road, merely laughed in the officer's face – not apparently because she had been drinking, but because she was astonished that he should perceive any problem with her activities; while a motorist who had driven onto the pavement and knocked down a nine-year-old child, explained himself by saying that after he restarted his car (which had stopped suddenly in the middle of the road) he had not realised that the wheels were pointing towards the pavement.[26]

The driver responsible for injuring the nine year old had only driven a car on a dozen previous occasions and clearly had little idea of how to control the vehicle, and in this lay a big part of the problem, for driving tests would not be introduced until 1 April 1935, which meant that anyone over the age of seventeen could get behind the wheel of a motorcar without the benefit of a single driving lesson. They could also drive as fast as they liked because, by 1931, the earlier speed limit of 20mph had been abolished (not least because it had proved impossible to enforce it) and the introduction of a 30mph limit for built up areas was still several years away. The first set of traffic lights did not appear in Britain until 1927, the first pedestrian crossings in 1934, and the vast majority of road junctions did not benefit from Give-Way signs or white lines, while traffic islands were virtually unknown. With some two-and-a-half million motor vehicles on the roads, the situation had become increasingly dangerous and chaotic.[27]

The number of fatalities on Britain's roads was rising steadily and in 1934 there were 7,343 – the highest number yet recorded.[28] Trev Jackson was one of these statistics: he died at around 10.30 on the morning of Tuesday, 27 November 1934, having lingered in hospital for almost three days with injuries which included a fractured skull. Major Jackson had been on his way from Bournemouth to Aldershot (where he had planned to watch a first round FA Cup match) when he crashed his car while attempting to overtake another vehicle. The car had run onto a grass verge, dropped into a ditch and overturned, pinning the two occupants inside, from whence they had to be extracted by rescuers. His passenger, Miss Phyllis Littler, of Parkstone, was uninjured.[29]

At the time of his death, Trev Jackson had been living for some months at the Meyrick Mansions Hotel in Bournemouth. On learning that his former guest had died, the hotel proprietor paid tribute to the Major, saying that he was, 'a good sportsman, crack polo player and was to have contested the final of a golf trophy tomorrow.'

The character of George T. T. Jackson is something of an enigma. His ex-wife described him as a bully, a liar and a blusterer, painting a picture of a generally cruel and vindictive man, but it is difficult to know how much of this was coloured by a marriage which broke down and the tragic events which followed soon afterwards. Trev has been portrayed as a womaniser, but the circumstances of his divorce from Frances are far from clear cut, and during the murder investigation in 1931 the police failed to unearth any evidence which supported the suggestion that Major Jackson was carrying on with anyone else's wife, or even had a particular lady friend.

This being said, the Major appears to have had no shortage of female friends. The glimpses of his life which survive not infrequently place a young woman alongside him in the two-seater, and even if the Major's expressed desire to 'bring pleasure to others' extended no further than giving lifts and escorting young women to sporting events, it is reasonable to conjecture that he was an attractive man and good company – otherwise these invitations would surely have been declined. Men evidently enjoyed his company too. It is unlikely that Major Campbell would have invited Jackson to his home in Heywood Hills if he had thought him in any way untrustworthy (Major Campbell had an unmarried daughter living at home), that he would have been welcome at Maidwell Hall, the home of Sir Reginald Loder, or that Jackson's brother officers would have voted him captain of the RAVC Golf Society six years on the trot. Major Jackson was the subject of a half-page obituary in the *Journal of the Royal Army Veterinary Corps*, which recorded that 'he was held in high esteem by his brother officers' and 'will be greatly missed.'[30] He was described as a 'great sportsman' at a time when this was one of the greatest compliments a man could be paid, implying not just a high degree of skill, but also an attitude of courage and fair play. (In 1933, the author Sir John Foster Fraser wrote: 'Most of us would prefer to have inscribed on our tombstones "He was a good sportsman" to anything else.'[31])

Was Trev Jackson's letter offering his ex-wife two badges for Sandown Races a bizarre gesture of cruelty, or a clumsy attempt at sympathy from a man who thought nothing was more calculated to raise the spirits than a day of fresh air and good sport?

Irrespective of his true nature, there can be little doubt that Major Jackson was not responsible for the death of the man who supplanted him in Frances's affections. He could not have been anywhere near 'D Hut' on the weekend in question and there is no evidence that he managed to engineer the affair via a third party. The notion of the Major (complete with his usual plus fours) creeping around the side of the house to the meat safe and injecting the partridges with strychnine is from first to last absolutely ridiculous – but then the notion of anyone doing this is equally so. The bungalow stood on a military camp, where any unusual activity was far more likely to be noticed than in an ordinary suburban street. There were other occupied buildings nearby and at least two dogs (the Evereds' spaniel and the Chevises' Alsation) liable to give the alarm. The assassin would have needed to choose his/her moment carefully – not least to ensure that there was any meat in the safe at all – and although there was a window of a few hours between the delivery of the birds and their extraction from the safe for cooking by Mrs Yeomans, 20 June was a warm day, with the ever-present risk that someone would decide to spend some time out in the garden.

The possibilities of an outsider tampering with the meat before it reached the oven were remote in the extreme and this was summed up by the anonymous correspondent already quoted, who claimed that 'only three people could do Chevis, cook, batman, wife.'

CHAPTER NINETEEN

ONLY THREE PEOPLE

The Irish connection suggested by the 'Hooray' telegram guaranteed that Nicholas Bolger was the subject of considerable police scrutiny, but they found nothing in his background to connect him with Dublin, or anyone called Hartigan. There can be no denying that Bolger was also a victim of anti-Irish prejudice. Civil strife and 'divided loyalties' were recent issues and men like Bolger, who had joined the British Army prior to Irish independence, occupied an anomalous position, with the distinct danger that they would be regarded with suspicion on both sides of the Irish Sea.

Quite aside from having no motive to murder Lieutenant Chevis, Bolger appears to have had less opportunity to tamper with the food than anyone else in the household. Bolger said in evidence that he had not seen the partridges delivered and had been unaware of what was on the menu until he asked Mrs Yeomans when he arrived for work at around 6 o'clock in the evening. This appears to be borne out by William Noyes, who had delivered the partridges, and by Mrs Yeomans, who received the order, unwrapped the birds, put them on a plate and then put the plate into the meat safe, neither of whom thought that Bolger had been around during this transaction. While we cannot be sure of the exact time of the delivery, it seems likely that it occurred after Bolger had served the Chevises their lunch and gone home for his own.[1]

It is possible to stretch a point and allow the possibility that Bolger tampered with the contents of the meat safe when he returned to 'D Hut' at 6 p.m. that evening (it would be reasonable for him to assume that some sort of meat or fish for the evening meal would have been in there and the dogs might not have barked at the arrival of someone well known to them), but to make this conjecture it is also necessary to provide Bolger with some strychnine and a motive – neither of which he appears to have had. It was also very risky for Bolger to open the meat safe, since he had no excuse to do so, if anyone had spotted him there. Once Mrs Yeomans brought the birds into the kitchen for cooking, the batman would have had no further opportunity to get at them until he carried the cooked partridges from the kitchen to the dining room, and here it should be recalled that the building in question was a modest bungalow rather than a baronial mansion, in which the journey from kitchen to dining room would normally occupy no more than a matter of seconds. While it is just remotely possible that Bolger – for reasons we cannot possibly guess – managed to add strychnine to his officer's dinner, it is hardly likely. The police questioned Bolger again and again, but this seems to have been largely prompted by external suspicions. One particular aspect which may have told in his favour with the police was that his evidence remained consistent throughout and has a calm, sensible quality to it. By 2012 Nicholas Bolger had been dead for many years, but his daughter, Patricia, told the author that her father had been a very gentle, quiet man, and that 'calm and sensible' were precisely the words she would have used to sum him up.[2]

Mrs Yeomans had the greatest opportunity to lace her employers' dinner with strychnine, but she was not a promising suspect either, for, like Bolger, she had the reverse of a motive since the Lieutenant's death left her without a position (a very difficult situation for a self-supporting widow). The police checked up on the fate of her first husband and established that he had died of an abscess on the brain – not a condition easily confused with poison – and Mrs Yeomans too had every appearance of being an ordinary domestic servant with no mysterious past.

Assuming that strychnine had been introduced into one of the partridges by a member of the household, once the cook and the batman had been ruled out, only Hugh and Frances Chevis were left. The possibility of a suicide pact gone wrong was considered and dismissed by the police, together with any idea that the strychnine had been taken as some kind of sexual stimulant, since quite aside from anything else neither of these theories fitted the evidence provided by Bolger that Lieutenant Chevis had summoned him back to the dining room and complained about the taste of his meat. There was also a faint chance that husband had intended the poison for wife, but this hardly appeared the most logical of ideas, because Frances had been clear from the outset that she always served the meat, so placing strychnine in one of two birds which then passed out of your control, with the 50/50 chance that the wrong one would end up on your plate, was a suicidally stupid way to go about killing anyone, even if you had a motive for doing so.

In spite of this the police did not immediately rule out the possibility that Hugh Chevis had made an unsuccessful attempt on his wife's life, for there was the ever-present issue of Frances's wealth. Stories of impecunious charmers marrying wealthy heiresses were legion – in fiction if not in fact. Serious consideration was given to the idea that the whole business had been plotted to bring about Frances's demise, but had gone awry, leaving the 'wrong' person dead. In furtherance of this theory, the police questioned what would have happened to Frances's fortune in the event that she, rather than her husband, had died.

They discovered that under the terms of Frances's will, Hugh Chevis would have received a lump sum plus £500 a year, but along with this came responsibility for the three children, who would only come into their shares of the estate at the age of twenty-five, so effectively Frances was a better financial proposition alive that dead. (There had been a similar provision for Trev Jackson under previous wills, but since the second marriage and the drawing up of a new will, as the police report succinctly put it: 'he is out of it altogether'.)

In spite of ingenious suggestions about water jugs and cruets, the fact of the poison being in or on the partridge seems incontrovertible. It was the partridge alone which tasted bitter, and we do not have to rely on Frances's word for this because it was what her husband told Bolger and also what he told Dr Bindloss later that evening. We can also be reasonably sure that the strychnine had been introduced into the partridge before it was cooked, because Ryffel – however incompetent in regard to isolating other samples in his tests – could confidently assert that he had found traces of the poison in the dripping – somewhere it could not possibly have been if poison had been introduced after the cooking process. (Common sense suggests that if introducing the poison to the meal at the table, the partridges would not have been the chosen medium, since any kind of powder or foreign substance would have shown up easily on the exterior of a roasted bird, while attempting to conceal anything inside it would have been impossibly fiddly when compared to, say, stirring something into the gravy boat.)

As well as there being traces of strychnine in the dripping, Mrs Yeomans almost certainly sent a certain amount down the sink when she washed up the roasting tin and it seems highly likely that this is what killed the Evereds' family pet, who had the misfortune to be in the wrong place at the wrong time. That the dog from the adjacent bungalow just happened to exhibit symptoms associated with strychnine poisoning and expire the self same evening seems a coincidence too far, and it is therefore reasonable to infer that the chemist, William Million, was mistaken in his results. It is true that Inspector Pharo's sample of drain water did not contain any of the poison either, but there is no suggestion that the sink was not used between the dinner-time washing up and the policeman's visit next day, so by the time Pharo collected his sample from the sink drain, it is likely that the far too much waste water had flushed through to leave any residual strychnine.

With Bolger, Mrs Yeomans and Hugh himself out of the picture, we are left with only one person in the house – and here we finally have someone whose behaviour was not only suspicious but who also appeared to have a motive. There is the fact that on the morning of her husband's death Frances was whisked away to London, where she managed to avoid making any statement to the police for almost a fortnight. Bolger contended that Mrs Chevis had informed him that her husband was suffering from strychnine poisoning prior to her receiving this diagnosis from the attending doctor – how had she known? Then there were her own symptoms: why had the strychnine not reacted upon her immediately, as it had with Lieutenant Chevis? Was it possible that Frances had been faking? Thanks to Ryffel's gaffe with the samples of vomit, there was no out and out proof that she had ever been suffering from strychnine poisoning.

Frances represented herself as a heartbroken widow who had adored her husband, but it did not take the police long to see a possible fly (or perhaps even a number of flies) in the ointment, and like so many of the issues which surrounded the case, clues had arrived via the postal system.

Iris Coates had been writing to Hugh Chevis since his departure from Quetta in November 1930, and though Jack Gwynn-Jones had destroyed the letters which arrived from Iris after his friend's death, some of her earlier letters had survived and were still in the bungalow at the time of Hugh's death, which meant that Frances could easily have discovered and read them at any time. The letters were subsequently burned, but we can conjecture their contents from the observation made by Superintendent Stovell in his notes on the case that, 'Iris Coates appears to have been madly in love with the deceased.'[3]

To Surrey Police it was easy to see any number of reasons why Frances Chevis might have wanted her husband out of the way. Here was a woman who had gone through a divorce in order to be with the man of her dreams, only to find that in the run up to their wedding he had been engaged in a love affair with another woman. Nor was it difficult to construct other scenarios in which her second marriage had turned sour within a matter of months. Accustomed to a glamorous life in London, how would Frances adapt to the lot of an army wife, inhabiting a series of small bungalows in dull military encampments? Had she perhaps begun to question Hugh Chevis's motives for marrying her in the first place? She candidly admitted to the police that he had been 'in rather an awkward position [financially]' when they met, so she had 'helped him out', and once they were married she had paid all his bills.[4]

Whatever anyone else may have thought, at the beginning of August Frances Chevis was still the number one suspect so far as Major Nicholson, the Chief Constable of Surrey, was concerned. In his notes on the case, penned on 9 August, he wrote: 'I consider Mrs C is still under the most grave suspicion.' He wrote that he thought her quite clever enough to appear passionately fond of her husband and yet to have disposed of him and, moreover, could not see anyone else who had a motive. (By now Major Nicholson had concluded that the telegram was an irrelevance and thought it most unlikely that the poison had found its way into the birds accidentally.) It was the Chief Constable who pointed out that as the ex-wife of a vet, it was possible that Frances knew how to use a hypodermic syringe and that she might even have obtained one from her former spouse. He reckoned that she had had access to the birds both before and after they were cooked and might have hoped that the death would simply be ascribed to food poisoning. It was also a matter of common knowledge, he noted, that 'more wives poison their husbands than the other way around.' (It was for many years the traditionally held view that women were much more likely to use poison than men – statistics prove otherwise.)

By this stage it had also become apparent to the police that Frances seemed to have as lively a love life as did her husband, and the Chief Constable noted that 'she is a passionate woman and highly sexed.' Major Nicholson evidently considered this not only an unusual and potentially dangerous combination, but also a situation well outside his normal comprehension, and he advised Superintendent Stovell to 'look into this sex business' with 'Spilsbury or Roche Lynch, or some other leading women's doctor'.[5]

Geoffrey Nicholson is remembered as a pioneering moderniser of police practice, but although only thirty-six years old in 1931, his attitude to women seems to have been deeply conventional and anything but modern. Throughout the Victorian era it had been accepted (in public at least) that decent women found sex distasteful – overly promiscuous women could face not only social stigma, but might even be incarcerated in a lunatic asylum and treated for nymphomania – and these attitudes lingered on for years in many sections of British society. Like Mr Francis the coroner, and so many others at the time, Nicholson appears to have been bamboozled into believing that the regular team of Home Office expert witnesses were the font of all knowledge when it came to anything remotely touching on the medical, and thus listed Spilsbury (a pathologist who never treated living patients) and Roche Lynch (whose medical career had long since diverged into analytical chemistry and toxicology) as equally likely to be of assistance when it came to gynaecological matters as a 'leading women's doctor'.

There is no record that Superintendent Stovell followed up his boss's suggestion to 'look into this sex business' with Spilsbury, Roche Lynch or indeed anyone else. The inquiry team did, however, pursue the question of extra-marital affairs, interviewing suspected paramours such as Iris Coates and John Blair, and following up a portion of a letter from a thirty-one-year-old woman in Cheshire, apparently written to Lieutenant Chevis in April 1931, which had been discovered among his effects after his death. The piece of paper in question had been torn off so that it was only possible to read the address and date on one side of the notepaper, and the end of one sentence and beginning of another on the reverse. While there could be no doubting the nature of the relationship between Hugh and Iris Coates, and a question mark hung over that between Frances and John Blair, the scrap of correspondence from Evelyn MacLennan proved entirely innocent.[6]

Miss MacLennan lived with her father in Cheshire, from whence she kept up an occasional correspondence with Sir William and Lady Chevis, to whom she had originally been introduced by an aunt who lived in Boscombe. As a result of this she had also become friendly with Hugh, although she was at pains to inform the police that she had not 'been acquainted with his personal habits or private affairs'. She had written to Lieutenant Chevis's parents in April 1931 to tell them that her mother had died and in his reply, Sir William told her that he would be passing the letter on to his son, who would also be writing to her in due course (he had not got round to doing so by the time of his death). The torn off address and seemingly ambiguous phrases on the preserved part of the letter made perfect sense in this context.

Although Frances was hardly likely to have murdered Hugh Chevis for money, the police checked further into Hugh's financial affairs and established that he had not been insured and had not left a will – very probably because he had nothing much to leave. Frances had received his clothing, personal effects and saddlery, while Captain William Chevis had paid off his brother's £5 overdraft at the bank. Of the remaining items at the bungalow, the food had been shared between Mrs Yeomans and Nicholas Bolger, the drink taken to Frances's London flat, and Frances's jewellery had been retrieved by Mrs Edge, the wife of Major Edge, and returned to Frances.[7]

Mrs Edge's involvement was a source of considerable irritation to Frances and she lodged a complaint with the police about Mrs Edge 'apparently having free rein of the bungalow'.[8] There is no doubt that the bungalow was scarcely treated as a secure crime scene. As well as Mrs Edge, the servants had free access both before and after the arrival of the police, Captain William Chevis visited the bungalow, but did not remove anything so far as the police were aware, and the bungalow was 'cleared up' by Nurse Thorne and Mrs Chevis's chauffeur at some subsequent point, when they removed a variety of the couple's possessions including a suitcase containing personal papers and correspondence. The police belatedly decided to take an interest in the contents of the suitcase several weeks later, only to discover that they had been burned.[9]

It had undoubtedly occurred to the police that Frances might have engineered her husband's murder with the aid of an accomplice, and there is more than a suggestion in the files that they flirted with the notion of collaboration between herself and Trev Jackson. On the face of it this would appear ridiculous: Frances had after all left the Major for Lieutenant Chevis. Yet Jackson had spoken affectionately of Frances to the press and refused to discuss the circumstances of his divorce with the police, while at the same time managing to imply that his marriage had been broken up by Hugh Chevis, rather than imputing any blame to his young wife. Was it possible that on discovering Hugh's treachery with another woman, Frances had turned to an old love for succour? Support for the possibility came from Frances's trips down to Eastbourne in the wake of her husband's death, and towards the end of July she took the children down to Hove, where she rented a house in Salisbury Road, a location within easy motoring distance of Major Jackson's Eastbourne lodgings less than twenty-five miles away. It was presumably with this possibility of collusion in mind that while Harry J. Jennings was snooping on Trev at his hotel, PC George Hector was simultaneously keeping Frances under covert surveillance.[10]

Like Jennings, PC Hector began his operation on Tuesday, 25 August, noting in his report that he was handicapped by the nature of Salisbury Road, which was a quiet residential street with few opportunities for concealment or loitering. At 10.30 in the morning he saw three children emerge from the house accompanied by a large, heavily built woman, who Hector took to be a cook (almost certainly Mrs Yeomans, who had been invited to take up employment with Frances and travelled down to Hove with the family) and a short, slim woman, dressed as a children's nurse (presumably Ivy Thorne). Hector followed them as they made calls at various shops and when he observed the cook making a call from one of the telephone kiosks in the Post Office, he nipped into the adjacent kiosk in order to listen in, but learned nothing more edifying than that Mrs Chevis wanted the car brought round at 11.30.

Having pursued the little party as far as the beach, where the children settled down to play on the sand, Hector returned to Salisbury Road in time to see the arrival of a large Minerva car (registration YU 2970) driven by a chauffeur in grey livery. The chauffeur was a tall, broad shouldered man of 'military appearance', clean shaven with dark hair and a swarthy complexion, who seemed very attached to the lady he was driving and walked arm-in-arm with her. Hector evidently managed to get a good look inside the car, which he observed to hold some 'very expensive goods' including a squirrel fur coat left on the back seat. He ended his report by requesting that someone check the ownership of not only the Minerva, but also a Morris saloon which was regularly parked outside the house, registration number PN 5247, and suggested that it might be helpful if he was provided with a photograph of Mrs Chevis in order to help him make a positive identification.

It can scarcely be credited that Hector was given no idea what his suspect looked like before he was sent to watch the house and report on her movements, but this was evidently the case for the following day he received his photograph and was consequently able to report that the woman who had appeared on affectionate terms with her chauffeur was not Mrs Chevis – presumably it was Audrey De Villiers Pritchard, the registered keeper of the Minerva motorcar. The Morris saloon, meanwhile, transpired to be Frances's own vehicle, rather than one belonging to an overly frequent or suspicious visitor.

This second report was as disappointing as the first. Mrs Chevis had been observed seeing the children off for the beach in the morning and then sitting alone in the front room from time to time during the day. She went out for a walk between 3 p.m. and 5 p.m. in the afternoon accompanied by 'the larger servant', but only to a local public garden known as St Ann's Well, and the most exciting thing Hector could find to write about this was that her black dress 'is cut rather low at the neck'. The only car Hector noted in the street was an open, four-seater Talbot, registration YL 4383, which was driven away by a man of military appearance at about 6 o'clock in the evening. It is unclear from the report whether the man had actually been visiting Frances's premises and, thanks to the military service to which an entire generation had been subjected, few middle-class men between the ages of thirty to fifty did not have a military appearance. By 6.30 the blinds were pulled down and all was quiet according to Hector, who presumably then went back to his lodgings for some much needed supper.

PC Hector was not the only person taking an interest in Frances's movements. She was still being dogged by the press (Hector himself notes that a reporter had called at the front door two days running and been sent away) and although he informed his superiors that he did not believe the household suspected that it was being watched, one cannot help but think that Frances, her children or servants must have observed the man lurking in Salisbury Road and following them as they went about their day-to-day routines.

On day three Frances left the house with one of the children, drove to the station and took the fast train to London. Mother and child returned the same day and the car was removed by an assistant from Baker's Garage, in Second Avenue, where it was being kept when not needed.

On day four Frances saw the children off as usual, then left the house with 'an elderly lady' (this was probably her mother, who lived in Hove at the time). They visited several shops and a bank, before joining the children, who were playing on Hove Lawns (a popular spot on the seafront). They returned to the house for lunch and the whole party left in the car at 3.15, and though Hector took up the pursuit (it is not recorded what kind of vehicle was made available to him, but it may well have been a bicycle) he lost them and could only report that they returned to the house at 8.30 that evening.

One can imagine the collective yawns at Headquarters on receipt of the constable's next instalment detailing day five, which again set down how the children left the house with the nurse at around 10.40, how Frances and the elderly lady walked to Hove Lawns together at 12.35, how the party returned for lunch a little while later, and then at 3 o'clock Frances and the nurse drove with the children to the beach again. Hector's opinion is not recorded, though one feels that whatever excitement there had initially been for him in this undercover operation, it had long since ebbed away. The later reports are merely a flat recitation of an ordinary seaside vacation, not even enlivened by references to fur coats, low cut necklines, or men with a military bearing. On 30 August he asked whether or not he was to continue the operation, as if required to stay any longer in Hove he would need to book more nights with Mrs Snow at 17 Hova Villas, where he was staying. A pencil note on the bottom of the report ordered the cessation of the surveillance just one week after it had begun.

Surrey Police had focussed heavily on the possibility of collusion with Major Jackson, but seemingly failed to notice another, slightly less obvious candidate for the role of Frances's accomplice. Not everyone had been entirely blind to this possibility however – at the end of July the Force received an anonymous letter addressed to the Chief Constable and dated 26 July. Written in an educated hand on good quality notepaper, the letter is reproduced here in full:

> *Sir,*
>
> *With regard to the poisoning of Lt Chevis I must tell you that a hospital nurse of the name of Thorn broke up Mrs Chevis's first marriage – coming as a maternity nurse to Major Jackson's baby boy – she then settled down as children's nurse to Mrs Jackson and probably resented the second marriage. She has a hatred of men and is a very strange character.*
>
> *Was she at the bungalow at the time of the poisoning?*
>
> *Yours truly.* [11]

There is nothing to suggest that the police paid this particular letter any more regard than they had the musings of 'The Bulldog Detective', Curious of Birmingham, or any other of a myriad of correspondents. It was a surprising omission, for the letter has the ring of authenticity – not necessarily in its accusations, but rather inasmuch that it was clearly written by someone who was familiar with the Jackson household in its Bournemouth incarnation. The present author has been unable to trace any mention of Nurse Thorne's name in the newspapers until well after this letter was received and in addition the correspondent was correct in his/her assertion that Miss Thorne had first been engaged to attend Frances in the run up to her son Peter's birth in 1927 and had been with the family ever since – information which was definitely not in the public domain.

It is possible that the police dismissed the thinly veiled suggestions that Frances might have been enjoying some sort of relationship with the 'man hater' (a frequent euphemism for lesbian at the time) because they were reasonably confident that the Jackson marriage had come apart for completely different reasons, but there is also a vague sense that, much as in an Agatha Christie mystery, servants (unless they happened to be Irish) were not really considered as serious suspects. In this the investigation was somewhat remiss.

Even assuming that Frances was not unusually close to Ivy Thorne, there was evidence that she relied on her greatly. It is clear from the list of people originally told of the existence of the 'Hooray' telegram that Nurse Thorne was taken into her mistress's confidence on the matter. Ivy Thorne seems to have assumed a role similar to that of a companion or secretary to Frances, often acting as a spokesperson for her mistress in a way that a mere family nurse or nanny would not normally have done. It was Nurse Thorne who informed Captain William Chevis that there had been a letter of condolence from Major Jackson in Northamptonshire, [12] Nurse Thorne who informed the police of Frances's availability or otherwise when they wished to speak with her, and in all probability she was the woman at Basil Mansions who told the press that Mrs Chevis was too ill to see them – a woman described in the papers as both 'a friend' of Mrs Chevis and 'Mrs Chevis's constant companion'.[13]

It was the loyal and indefatigable Nurse Thorne to whom Frances entrusted the task of removing private letters and papers from the bungalow and this was the same woman to whom Frances had placed a telephone call on the night of the fatal meal – a telephone call which had resulted in the arrival of the Nurse to rescue Frances from the cottage hospital. All in all, Nurse Thorne flits through this story like a persistent phantom, ever present at moments of crisis, and rather than enquiring about purchases of strychnine made in the name of Chevis, the Metropolitan Police might have done equally well to ask about any purchases made in the name of Thorne, particularly since Frances was not in the habit of running her own errands.

At quite an early stage in the inquiry, Mr Francis's suspicions led him to query exactly how much strychnine had been isolated in the sample of vomit obtained from Frances, and Surrey Police approached Ryffel with the same question a couple of weeks later, but Superintendent Minter did no better with the disingenuous analyst than had the coroner, reporting back that 'Dr Ryffel stated that he did not consider very clear evidence was given by Dr Bindloss at the inquest as to what extent Mrs Chevis was poisoned.'[14]

It was Ryffel at his most infuriating. Had he separately analysed the samples provided from each patient, the police would have had definite evidence as to the presence or otherwise of strychnine in Frances Chevis's vomit, but thanks to the analyst's bizarre decision to combine the two samples, they had no definite evidence one way or the other. Faced with a question which highlighted his own lack of competence, Ryffel typically tried to sidestep the issue by suggesting that blame for any uncertainty lay elsewhere.

Could Frances have introduced the strychnine to the partridge? As mistress of the house she not only had access to the meat safe, but, if observed investigating the contents, could easily have invented an excuse – saying that she thought the door was not closed properly, or perhaps alleging that she had noticed an unpleasant odour. She was perfectly placed to hang around in the garden waiting for an opportune moment because, as the lady of the house, she could go wherever she liked.

Where could she have obtained the poison? Certainly not over the counter of a Knightsbridge chemist unless she wanted to court suspicion, but here we must bear in mind that Frances had plenty of cash at her disposal and while recreational drug use was not widespread in the early 1930s, nor was it unknown, so it is entirely possible that Frances had a contact, or could have obtained the substance she required from a friend of a friend.[15] Could such a transaction have been undertaken without risking discovery, once the death of Hugh Chevis became known? Given that traders in illicit drugs are not generally queuing up to reveal the names of their customers to the authorities, we must assume that it could.

Frances herself had suggested to the police that one might expect discretion to the point of perjury from members of one's own circle, asking Superintendent Stovell in a letter querying Major Jackson's alibi, whether his friend was 'a really good friend' – the clear implication being that *really* good friends would lie for you. Again one is forced to question just how good a friend was Nurse Thorne and what precisely passed between the two women during the phone call made on the night of Hugh Chevis's death.

1 Lieutenant Hugh Chevis. (By kind permission of Major Bill Chevis)

2 Mrs Frances Chevis.

3 The photograph of Major Jackson which was circulated by Surrey Police. The child he was holding by the hand has been scratched out. (Surrey Police Files)

4 Sir William Chevis. (By kind permission of Major Bill Chevis)

5 Lady Amy Chevis. (By kind permission of Major Bill Chevis)

6 Major William Chevis, brother of the deceased, during the Second World War. (By kind permission of Major Bill Chevis)

7 Hugh Chevis's grave in Aldershot Military Cemetery. The inscription reads: 'In ever loving memory of Hubert George Chevis Royal Artillery, beloved husband of Frances Chevis, died June 21 1931 aged 28 years. Until the day breaks.' (Author's photograph)

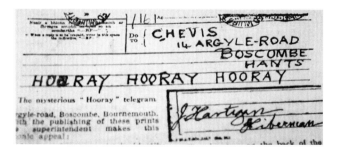

8 A copy of the original telegram form as it appeared in the newspapers. (Surrey Police Files)

POST CARD.
THE ADDRESS TO BE WRITTEN O

THE EDITOR,
    DAILY SKETCH
        200, GRAY'S INN RD
            W.C. 1.

9 & 10 The London postcard. (Surrey Police Files)

LONDON.
1ST. AUG. 1931

DEAR SIR,
        WHY DID YOU
PUBLISH THE PICTURE
OF THE "HOORAY"
TELEGRAM ?

    " J. Hartigan "

POST CARD
THE ADDRESS TO BE WRITTEN ON THIS SIDE
BELFAST
AUG 4
12¼ PM
1931
ONE PENNY

Chevis
14 Argyle Road
Boscombé
Hants
England

11 & 12 The Belfast postcard. (Surrey Police Files)

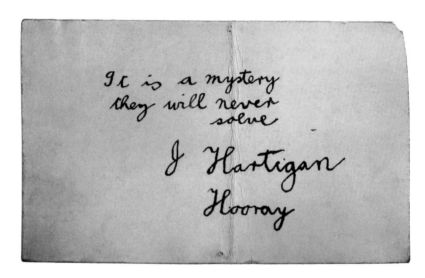

It is a mystery
they will never
solve

J Hartigan

Hooray

13 Frances awaits her car at the conclusion of the inquest. The woman on the left of the picture may be Ivy Thorne. (Getty Images)

14 Frances leaves the scene, still pursued by reporters. (Getty Images)

15 Frances's children, from left to right, Pauline, Peter, David and Elizabeth. (By kind permission of Charles Jackson)

CHAPTER TWENTY

'NO JUSTIFICATION TO SUSPECT HER AT ALL'

Major Geoffrey Nicholson, 1931

On his appointment as Chief Constable in 1930, one of the improvements introduced by Geoffrey Nicholson was a system whereby he personally read the reports of all indictable crimes which were under investigation by his force.[1] Where he felt it appropriate he involved himself in case conferences and made suggestions, and he appears to have taken a particular interest in the Chevis case, which is hardly surprising given its seriousness. Nicholson did not allow his summer holiday to interfere with this aspect of his work, and continued to correspond with the Deputy Chief Constable during a sojourn on the Isle of Wight. From the letters they exchanged, it is clear that although Nicholson favoured Frances Chevis as chief suspect, his newly appointed deputy, William Bird, was not so sure. In a letter to his boss written on 13 August, Bird queried why, if Mrs Chevis was a poisoner, 'wouldn't she have got rid of Major Jackson that way, instead of bothering with a divorce?'[2]

There is a degree of naivety in Bird's approach here, since he appears to be suggesting that if someone employed poison on one occasion, this necessarily meant that they would invariably do so on every other occasion when someone vexed them or stood in their way. In fairness to the Deputy Chief Constable, there was a widespread belief around this time that poisoning was almost invariably a serial offence, reinforced not only because some notorious poisoners really had claimed multiple victims, but also thanks to several cases which involved multiple alleged victims and are now suspected to have been miscarriages of justice.[3]

Bird's failure to comprehend the position with regard to the ease or otherwise with which a party might obtain a divorce is far less excusable. As previously stated, England's divorce laws were draconian and in practice it could be extremely difficult to get a divorce. If there was the slightest suggestion that Frances had been enjoying the attentions of another man, then unless Hugh Chevis was willing to co-operate with her as had Trev Jackson in 1928, her chances of getting a divorce from him were extremely slim.

Bird also cautioned his superior against 'going too far' along 'sex lines' as he felt that attempting to make too many enquiries in that area would lead to 'various individuals bringing in their solicitors'. He did agree that the telegram was something of a red herring, and even speculated that the whole business of the telegram might have been no more than 'a press stunt'.

Major Nicholson had no doubt seen copies of the letters which Frances had sent to the inquiry team, one of them wondering whether Bolger had somehow tampered with the partridges en route to the table[4] and the other a much longer letter, which, as well as casting suspicion on her ex-husband by questioning the genuineness of his alibi and claiming that he had loathed Hugh Chevis to an extreme, took time to thank Superintendent Stovell for his efforts to solve the case, apologising for the fact that she had not thanked him at the inquest, but explaining that she had been 'a bit upset.'[5] She was very grateful for all his hard work and trouble, she wrote, and would 'go on wishing hard that your efforts may be rewarded.' 'You won't give up yet, will you? I do ask and ask you not to.'

The entire letter is mercurial in nature, moving swiftly from describing Jackson's 'intense hatred' to admitting that she has 'no right to accuse him', from her gratitude at Stovell's attempts to 'solve the ghastly process of my husband's death' to the almost childlike plea that Stovell wouldn't give up on the process. The letter ends by reiterating her thanks for all the officer's efforts to date and the addition of a jokey postscript that, 'The reporters are still enjoying Hove air! I just won't see them unless they trip me up in the street.'

It must have been very difficult to decide what to make of such a letter, which was hardly the regular run of the mill correspondence received from a victim's widow or a major suspect in a murder inquiry. Among other things, the Chief Constable wanted to know what the leading officer in the case made of the woman at its centre and perhaps remained sceptical when Stovell responded that he had now interviewed Mrs Chevis on several occasions and observed nothing in her manner to indicate that she had any guilty knowledge.[6] Within a matter of weeks, however, Geoffrey Nicholson would have the opportunity to meet Frances and make a judgement for himself, because on 15 September he spent almost two hours with his chief suspect and made copious notes of the visit, either as it occurred or shortly afterwards.[7] It is not explicitly stated that Frances had made a prior appointment to see the Chief Constable, and though the report could be read this way, it is equally possible that she unexpectedly dropped in at Police Headquarters and asked to see him.

Whether expected or not, she was shown in at 3.30 and immediately enquired whether there was any news and how the investigation was going. Major Nicholson replied that he did not expect any developments at the moment and then asked whether he might put some questions to her, saying that she did not have to answer anything if she did not want to, but Frances apparently had no objection to telling him anything he wished to know and began to respond with what to the Chief Constable seemed like disarming openness.

Nicholson asked her about her will and Frances said that over the course of the past few years she had made several, and 'as a matter of fact, made rather a habit of making wills'. Her first ever will had been made when she married Major Jackson – he had not pushed her into it in any way, but he had suggested that it would be a good idea. (Until Frances married and came into her fortune, there would have been very little point in her making a will, as she effectively had nothing to leave and in the event that her death had taken place prior to inheriting the money left to her by her father, it would have devolved onto other legatees.) She explained that she had made other wills since the one suggested by Major Jackson, at least one of which had been made at the suggestion of her solicitor (this may well have been to take into account the need to provide legacies for an increasing number of offspring) and she had made her latest will after marrying Lieutenant Chevis. Major Nicholson asked if this new will had been at his suggestion, but she said it had been made entirely of her own volition. (In fact, it would be normal practice to make a new will, as marriage negated any previous testament.)

Having worked the conversation round to documents of one sort or another, Major Nicholson asked her about the letters and papers which had been removed from the bungalow. Frances confirmed that all her late husband's paper had been removed from the bungalow by her nurse and her chauffeur, who had brought them back to London in a suitcase. She had looked through all the correspondence, she told him, but not read any of it closely before it was all burnt. It had mostly been bills and love letters from her husband's 'other lady friends'. Among other items retrieved from the bungalow by the servants, she had received an unopened money box in which she found a swimming medal and a letter from the wife of an officer in the Devon Regiment (presumably Iris Coates).

She explained that she had made a complaint to the police not just because Mrs Edge had apparently enjoyed freedom to roam around the bungalow at will and remove her jewellery, but also because the police had not taken or read the letters when they had the opportunity to do so, rather than asking about them later when they had been burned and it was therefore too late to follow up any clues which might have been contained therein. This was an eminently reasonable point: Inspector Pharo had visited and 'searched' the bungalow at least twice prior to the arrival of Nurse Thorne and the chauffeur, reporting that he had found no correspondence excepting 'a few invitations for dinner and some bills', whereas according to Frances there had been love letters from Mrs Coates and other female friends in the plural. While Pharo's initial search was typical of a somewhat cursory investigation into what had initially been thought no more than a suspected food poisoning, Frances could hardly be blamed for burning letters when she assumed that the police had already taken the opportunity to remove anything they required.

The Chief Constable left the letters to one side for a moment – perhaps a little taken aback at the ready manner in which Frances admitted that her husband had had other 'lady friends' – asking her instead about Nurse Thorne, who Frances described as 'very reserved'. She told him that Miss Thorne was a certified midwife who had come into her employment about four years ago when her youngest child was born and stayed on as the family's nurse. Nicholson asked why it was that the nurse was 'so reserved' (from which we can probably construe a reluctance to open up to his officers) and Frances said she thought it was 'because Thorne knows about my peccadilloes and has decided to keep her mouth closed.'

No doubt suitably encouraged to feel that no subject was off limits, the Major put it to Frances that although she and Hugh Chevis had appeared publicly in love with one another, each had no immediate knowledge of the others affairs and both 'went their own way'. Frances agreed that this was so, but said that all the same she had been very much in love with Hugh and he with her – they would have been married sooner if he had not been posted out to India just before her divorce came through.

How had married life turned out for them, the Chief Constable wanted to know? Frances admitted that she had found it a trifle irksome at the beginning, particularly living at the Queen's Hotel in Farnborough, after being accustomed to a much more lively life and good times in London, but that had soon worked off and she had been happy to be finished with her past life.

'What is your real outlook on life at the moment?' he asked.

'Anything to be happy,' Frances replied. 'I was happy then...'

Major Nicholson moved on to ask her about possible motives for the crime, and Frances said that at first she had assumed it was an accident, but had later 'been rather forced to the conclusion' that someone must have done it on purpose, and the only person she could think of was Major Jackson. 'He has no guts, but living with him as long as I did, I got to realise that he was an artful, vindictive man. He hated Chevis – he had good reason to hate him. I consider he is a blusterer.'

Nicholson continued the gentle interrogation by reminding her that many people would say it was she herself who was the most likely agent of Lieutenant Chevis's demise, another statement with which Frances readily agreed, though she continued to insist that Trev Jackson was 'a cunning liar' and that no one knew where they stood with him, or what he might do. The Chief Constable asked whether she had suspicions of anyone else, but apart from Jackson she had no suggestions to offer: 'I could never get to the bottom of Bolger, but at the same time, would not want to suggest that he had anything to do with it.' As for Mrs Yeomans, Frances agreed with Major Nicholson that if she had had any involvement whatsoever in the death of Lieutenant Chevis, she would have given herself away at once under cross-examination at the inquest. (Mrs Yeomans had now left her employ, Frances said, for reasons she did not entirely understand. Mrs Yeomans had made some vague statement to the effect that she was planning to get married, but Frances could not decide whether to take it seriously and the present author can find no evidence that she actually did so.)

Not including the ex-cook, Frances told the Chief Constable that she currently employed four female servants in her London home including Nurse Thorne, and there was also a chauffeur who had been working for her for six years. It was he who had driven Nurse Thorne down to Frimley on the night when she and Lieutenant Chevis had been taken ill. She understood that some members of the public had been suggesting that she was carrying on with her chauffeur but that was not the case.

Now that they were on to the role of the servants on the night of the poisoning, Major Nicholson could easily have asked Frances to clarify at precisely what point in the evening she had telephoned her London flat and asked Nurse Thorne to come down to Surrey, but in common with everyone else he appears to have missed the potential significance of this and asked instead about other details to do with the serving of the meal. Frances explained yet again that she always served the meat, after which they helped themselves to vegetables. All the serving dishes were put on the sideboard and they helped themselves from there, she said, because the dining table was so small.

Towards the end of the conversation Frances made perhaps the most surprising intervention yet, asking whether the police would have any objection to her going out to India, because she had a 'flave' for a man who had recently gone out there – although she said she was not travelling with the specific intention of seeing him there. The Chief Constable told her that the police had no objection.

She left at 5.20, thanking Nicholson for all that the police had done so far and reiterating her willingness to give them any help she could. In return, he told her that he 'would always be glad if she would let him know of anything where she thought Surrey Police could be of help, so that somebody could go up and see her.' (While one presumes that this offer of assistance extended only as far as the inquiry into her husband's death, it reads as if the gallant Major was putting his force at her disposal for whatever whim happened to come to mind.)

Nicholson's thoughts and observations on this session form the finale to the report. He noted that Mrs Chevis was absolutely calm throughout the entire interview and at no stage attempted to fence, or evade a question, also recording that she had a curious manner when speaking 'which suggests an American accent.' She was 'undoubtedly a woman of the world, who has tasted the good things in life.' Nicholson was also of the opinion that 'she feels the death of her husband very much... at one point she almost dissolved into tears when asked about her life with him.' He no longer doubted that in being married to Hugh Chevis she had achieved 'a state of bliss' and now that he was dead she longed to find the right man and settle down to a happy married life. In conclusion, the Chief Constable stated that he felt 'no justification to suspect her at all.'

CHAPTER TWENTY-ONE

'ACTUAL PROOF IS STILL MISSING'

William Bird, 1932

It would be all too easy to assume that Major Nicholson was a sucker for a pretty face and had simply become the latest man to have fallen for Frances's feminine charms and wiles, but while it is true that the Major may have been to some extent both charmed and disarmed, by mid-September he had another reason to doubt his earlier suspicions about his favourite suspect – although he did not share these developments with her.

The earliest suggestion that Lieutenant Chevis's partridge might have been impregnated with poison by accident appears to have come from Cullen Mather. The manufacturing agent, who happened to be staying in Hove at the time of Hugh Chevis's death, read about the case in the *Daily Telegraph* and wrote to the editor of the paper, requesting that rather than publish his letter it should be forwarded to the appropriate authorities.[1] Significant numbers of those who wrote to the coroner, police and even to the newspapers sincerely intended to be helpful and Mr Mather clearly fell into that category, believing that he had important specialist knowledge to bring to the table. Mather had business interests in India, Burma, Ceylon, the Malayan States and China, and, having spent most of his life in Asia,[2] felt that he had an insight into various practices there about which he correctly assumed the general public in Britain would have little idea.

Mather explained that Chinese and Manchurian trappers routinely used strychnine to obtain foxes and other animals for the fur trade and that since birds were equally liable to pick up the poison: 'if game is imported from Manchuria there would always be this risk to the consumer.'[3]

The letter was promptly passed on to the police as its author had requested, but it does not appear that they initially took a great deal of notice of it, probably dismissing it as merely one among many letters suggesting everything from accident to supernatural interference – although it was also one of the letters they forwarded to the coroner, since he clearly had to be alerted to any possibility of accidental death.

The vast majority of correspondents no doubt appreciated that neither the police nor the coroner was likely to respond to individual letters from the public (although as we have seen, when the inquest proceedings were eventually concluded, Mr Francis did reply to one or two such letters) but having written his letter, Mr Mather was not content to let the matter rest and on 24 July he called in at Scotland Yard, seeking confirmation that the letter he had written a month before had got through.[4] Although the note forwarded to Surrey Police by Scotland Yard implies that Mather was merely complaining that he had not received a reply, it is more likely that Mather's visit to the Yard was prompted by genuine concern, because he had evidently been following the case and had no doubt read a report of the inquest proceedings held a couple of days earlier, in which the emphasis had been on the possibilities of foul play, with no evidence at all brought regarding the possibility that the birds could have picked up the poison by accident. Murder was a capital offence in 1931 and Cullen Mather may well have approached the police because he entertained a genuine anxiety about the possibility of a miscarriage of justice resulting from inadequate information.

Deputy Chief Constable Kenward received the note from Scotland Yard and passed it to Stovell, commenting that Mather's explanation 'is quite feasible [and] warrants a certain amount of thought'.[5] From this point onwards Surrey Police began to explore the possibility of accidental poisoning more seriously and it may have been with Mather's information in mind that Kenward told reporters on 31 July that enquiries would shortly be completed, at which time they would find that they had been 'very wide of the mark'.[6]

After replacing Kenward on 1 August, Deputy Chief Constable Bird appears to have taken over this particular aspect of the inquiry and in a letter to the Chief Constable on 13 August, mentioned that he was 'still on the track of the partridge being poisoned before it arrived in this country'.[7] Major Nicholson did not initially favour the theory, however, asking why, if this was a regular practice among trappers, had there been no other deaths of the kind.[8] It was a fair point. If Manchurian fur trappers were regularly leaving strychnine about for birds to eat, how was it that only a single partridge in two consignments had managed to pick it up? Why weren't partridge eaters dropping by the dozen every year?

More significantly, the idea of the partridge having died itself as a result of consuming poison, which had then lingered in the bird's system and resulted in the death of Lieutenant Chevis, had been pooh-poohed by the expert analyst in the case. The coroner had consulted John Ryffel on the point and the analyst had written back on 14 July, assuring the coroner that accidental ingestion by the bird was highly unlikely, whereas introducing a hypodermic syringe full of strychnine into the dead bird would 'fit the facts'.[9]

Ryffel's opinions inevitably carried a good deal of weight, so it is important to consider them in detail. Ryffel claimed that if a bird took a fatal dose of strychnine, it would presumably die before the strychnine was absorbed into its system, but this assumption is of itself incorrect. Although strychnine is a fast-acting poison, its fatal effects occur precisely because it is swiftly absorbed into the nervous system, leading to seizures and death. Indeed, strychnine is so quickly absorbed that administering an emetic to make a victim vomit back the poison is not considered a worthwhile form of treatment. Ryffel's contention that the poison would get no farther than the crop before its progress was arrested by the death of the bird was therefore wrong.[10] To make matters worse, Ryffel based his conclusion that the tissues could not have absorbed enough strychnine to kill a human being on the idea that the bird had been gutted and its innards removed, prior to its being exported (thereby ruling out any gradual post-mortem absorption) but this too was incorrect, as Ryffel could easily have established if he had troubled to read the witness statements with which he had been provided, or listened to the evidence brought at the inquest, where Frederick Downs, the poulterer who worked for Colebrooks, specifically stated that he had drawn the birds on 20 June, before singing them out, trussing them, dusting them with flour and then handing them over to Noyes for delivery.[11]

It is clear that either a member of the investigation team or a member of the public alerted the Press to the story of the Manchurian trappers, for several papers picked up the point around the end of July, with the *Daily Express* referring to 'an extraordinary method of trapping partridges' in its 29 July edition, but 'extraordinary' as the method might be, it did not make for nearly such exciting copy as engaging in further agitation that Scotland Yard should be called in, or reporting that a Dublin man thought he had recognised the sender of the mysterious telegram, and these angles were given considerably more coverage, with the papers giving very little credence to the idea of an accident.

However, the police were not so fickle as the newshounds and continued to follow the issue up, so that in notes following the progress of the investigation, alongside a list of questions about the state of the deceased's marriage and his finances, there appear questions about how long it takes strychnine to be absorbed into the flesh of a partridge, whether there were any similar cases on record and what were the possibilities of the poison already being in the bird when it arrived in the country – against which Stovell had noted that it was difficult to 'get anything definite on the matter.'[12]

One obvious way of discovering more was to experiment by cooking partridges which had been impregnated with strychnine – several people had written to the police suggesting this course and on 4 August the *Daily Mirror* claimed that such an experiment was about to be undertaken, but in fact it was not until the end of the month that Ryffel (who had initially been reluctant to undertake this particular task, writing to the coroner that it might be better if someone else did it)[13] took charge of four partridges, prepared for cooking as the originals had been, and embarked on an unusual culinary experiment. (Ryffels's reluctance to become involved in cooking the partridges is a little odd – he was to be paid for his time as usual and although cooking a sample before testing it was probably outside his usual sphere of activity, it would certainly appear to be much closer to his area of expertise than to that of anyone else in the case, as it definitely came under the heading of scientific experiment and analysis.)

Ryffel initially cooked two of the birds in a dish in a gas oven, having first applied three grains of strychnine hydrochloride to the breast of one of the birds.[14] He basted the birds in fat during the cooking and reported that when cooked the birds looked 'very slightly different' – though he did not explain in what way they looked different, or whether he meant by this that the poisoned bird was in some way distinguishable from the one to which strychnine had not been directly applied.

He tasted the treated bird and found it to be very bitter, as was 'the small amount of gravy separated from the fat'. The second bird merely tasted 'musty'. The 'clarified fat' did not taste bitter, but it did give a small yield of strychnine. Apart from the breast of the contaminated bird, the only appreciable source of strychnine was in the 'gravy', with the remainder of the fat and the breast of the other bird yielding only 'negligible' amounts.

Ryffel then injected a solution of 3 grains of strychnine hydrochloride in 7cc of water into the breast of one of the remaining birds before cooking this pair in identical fashion to the first two. His results were pretty much indistinguishable from those derived in the first test, with again 'a slight difference in appearance', a very bitter taste from the treated bird, a trace of strychnine in the breast of the untreated bird, traces of strychnine in 'the dripping' and 'a considerable amount in the gravy'.

The analyst considered that either method of application was consistent with the Chevis case, although he still considered that the amount of strychnine found in that case suggested an original application of more than three grains.

All in all the report was a classic piece of Ryffel-ism. While it did establish that the experiments demonstrated cross-contamination by basting, which produced only negligible amounts of strychnine in the second bird, much else was shrouded in confusion. Contriving to use three different expressions for the clarified fat and meat juices did not particularly help matters – and did the birds look appreciably different to one another or not? Did they look sufficiently 'different' to normal, uncontaminated birds that a woman experienced in cooking partridges might have been expected to notice?

In addition, Ryffel's conclusion stated as hard fact something which was little better than mere conjecture, because since he had been unable to make any tests whatsoever on the original bird which had poisoned Lieutenant Chevis, he had based his idea of how much strychnine must have been originally ingested (which is in itself quite different from how much strychnine was in the flesh of the bird) on an analysis of bowls of vomit reserved from two different people and the amount of strychnine he had found in a bowl of dripping. This was at best no more than a guestimate and could in no way be realistically comparable with the results of his latest experiments. To further cloud the issue, if anyone in receipt of this document had troubled to go back and check Ryffel's original report in July, they would have discovered that the analyst's original opinion was that 'the total quantity of strychnine associated with the partridges cannot be less than 2 grains'[15] whereas he was now confidently stating that his earlier results had indicated 'much more than 3 grains'.

Surrey Police seem to have been less easily satisfied than the coroner and evidently queried certain points with Ryffel, because on 22 September, the latter responded to a question regarding the appearance of the birds, by saying that the birds to which strychnine had been added 'would pass muster',[16] and by early October Superintendent Stovell was reporting that he had spoken to the analyst again and on this occasion Ryffel admitted that he had had to 'climb down' regarding parts of his original report.[17]

Meantime Major Nicholson had questioned why – if ingestion of strychnine by the bird had been the cause of death – had there not been other cases? It was certainly the case that people were not dropping like flies after eating partridges, but in spite of this there is a substantial body of evidence to support the possibility that this was how Lieutenant Chevis met his death.

To begin with there was ample evidence that substances ingested by a game bird in life could have a detrimental or even fatal effect on any humans who subsequently consumed the birds. The Peel family's experience with Nova Scotian partridge (mentioned in Chapter 17) was sufficiently well known in Britain that the danger of eating certain types of North American partridge was mentioned in books of medical advice such as *The Household Physician*, an indispensible volume then found on the bookshelves of many homes.[18] The birds in question became dangerous only after eating certain types of berry which, while harmless to them, were deadly to humans, and though this is not precisely the scenario which was being suggested by Cullen Mather and others, the principle – of toxic substances being passed on in the flesh of the bird – was essentially the same.

Although there were no known cases of humans being poisoned after eating birds contaminated with strychnine, there were fairly regular reports of this occurring among their canine friends. In fact this was such a frequent occurrence that it was mentioned in the 1935 Report and Recommendations issued by the Poison Board, who, when advocating greater restrictions on the sale of strychnine, pointed out that farmers, gamekeepers and so on were in the habit of laying strychnine-impregnated birds to kill vermin, which were found instead by other animals – usually foxhounds or domestic pets – and consumed with fatal consequences. In 1935 it was still legal to purchase strychnine over the counter as a pest killer, but the Board's recommendation was to restrict the sales to medicinal use.[19]

Reports of these animal fatalities frequently appeared in local and occasionally in national newspapers. A positive spate of strychnine-related fatalities among Hampshire livestock in March 1932 included three foxes, two domestic dogs, some draghounds from the Royal Artillery pack, and various wild birds, and it was suggested that the origin of the problem lay in poisoned grain which had been consumed by creatures other than its intended target.[20] In 1938, the laws relating to the sale of strychnine were strengthened in accordance with the Board's recommendation, but they were relaxed again less than two years later, in order to control vermin for more effective wartime food production,[21] so countrymen continued to lay strychnine-laced grain – or more often dead birds which had been contaminated with strychnine – in order to tempt their prey. Cases of poisoned foxhounds and beagles were the ones which tended to make the news, but there were probably just as many domestic pets lost to the practice whose deaths to an unidentified poison went unrecorded.[22]

In spring 1982, after poisoned birds were discovered at Ravenglass in Cumbria, the RSPCA pointed out that though long illegal, the practice of poisoning birds (often pigeons) with strychnine, then leaving them out for 'vermin' was a continuing problem, and frequently led to the death of both wildlife and domestic pets. A huntsman weighed in to mention the risk to foxhounds, who, he said, often experienced a slow and painful death as a result of the practice, and Mr Richard Porter of the RSPB said that it was only a matter of time before a human life was lost as a result of the practice.[23]

Condemning the practice was one thing, but discovering the individuals responsible was quite another and prosecutions were rare. In 1919, a rat catcher named George Lea was brought before the courts after he caused the death of three dogs on the Duke of Westminster's estate by laying poisoned baits, but Lea was the exceptional (and apparently particularly stupid) case – he appears to have been called in to deal with rats and to have assured the Duke's agent, Major Kerr, that the baits would be harmless to domestic animals.[24]

(Not every poisoning of a domestic pet was accidental. In 1908, John Mansfield of Ilford, Essex, was found guilty of poisoning his neighbours' dog with strychnine because its barking had annoyed him, a scheme perhaps inspired by the case against a John Spencer of Leicester which had been reported earlier in the year. Responsible for a series of burglaries, Spencer had been in the habit of carrying meat laced with strychnine, in order to silence any dogs he encountered in the course of his evening's work.[25])

Mr Porter of the RSPB was by no means the first person to have sounded the alarm on the possible risk to humans. Back in 1946, a widespread alert was published after the theft of a chicken from the back seat of a motorcar in Edinburgh. The bird had been 'treated' with strychnine, the intention being to lay it as bait for a fox, and it was feared that if cooked and consumed the bird could prove deadly. Fortunately the thief read the newspapers and the bird was recovered before any harm ensued.[26]

As far back as 1914 concern was expressed after a number of wood pigeons poisoned by strychnine were found in the Scarborough area. Dead birds had been found within a five-mile radius of the town and the report noted how fortunate it was that none of them had been eaten[27] – yet in spite of these anxieties being aired from time to time, there do not appear to have been any definite reports of anyone in Britain dying as a result of eating a contaminated bird, and there were relatively few unexplained strychnine deaths. On the contrary, there appears to be some degree of evidence to suggest that a human being – unlike a dog, for whom a much smaller dose was fatal - could consume a bird poisoned with strychnine and survive the experience.

On 10 March 1911, *The Times* was among the newspapers to report that Arthur Banham of Feltwell, Norfolk had been fined for laying grain poisoned with strychnine in order to catch wild birds. He had 'recently despatched about 80 larks to London ... all destined for human consumption'.[28] As well as the consignment for London, Banham had also attempted to export some additional birds to Paris. The report does not explain whether the entire consignment was recovered, but even assuming that it was, Banham's activities appear to have been on such an industrial scale that it is difficult to believe it was his first offence, or that he was the only individual engaged in producing food for the table in this way. Numerous letters received by both the police and the coroner from a variety of sources suggested either that the partridge had been poisoned accidentally when the bird picked up poisoned grain intended for some other creature, or that it had been poisoned deliberately in the 'Banham' manner. The Banham case alone leaves little doubt that these stories of birds being poisoned deliberately with the intention of introducing them onto dinner tables were not apocryphal.

Cullen Mather's story of fur trappers leaving poisoned birds out in order to kill their quarry without spoiling the pelts with visible signs of shot is supported by no lesser authority than the 1911 St Petersburg Conference of Fur Trappers, where concerns were expressed that sable was in danger of rapid extinction thanks to the widespread practice of trappers using strychnine baits.[29] Mather's persistence and genuine concern evidently impressed the police, for when Mather offered to do what he could to find out more about the possibilities of accident on his return to the Far East, Surrey Police were happy to accept. Mather's correspondence with Deputy Chief Constable Bird therefore continued and in December 1931 he wrote from The Astor House Hotel in Shanghai, reiterating his conviction that the bird had picked up the poison grain by accident, and saying that he was continuing to look into it.[30]

Another correspondent with experience of life in Asia who developed a special interest in the progress of enquiries was Arthur Sowerby, editor of *The China Journal of Science & Arts*. This was the publication which had been drawn to the attention of the investigation by Mr La Touche, and it seems likely that either La Touche, or more likely Cullen Mather, had contacted Sowerby and drawn the case to his attention, for by December 1931 he too was writing to the police in Surrey from his offices in Museum Road, Shanghai, on the subject of accidental ingestion of strychnine by partridges.[31] The item in *The China Journal of Science & Arts* originally provided by Mr La Touche certainly made for interesting reading in the context of the death of Lieutenant Chevis.

The piece had been contributed by a Mr F.H. Williams and appeared in a regular section of the magazine called *Shooting and Fishing Notes*.[32] The main body of the text was concerned with shooting Sand Grouse, but Williams also included an anecdote about an encounter he had with a group of Chinese game hunters, who, after drinking a considerable quantity, confided in Williams how they had recently captured a large number of partridge. According to their story, the hunters went into the mountains and selected or hollowed out a suitable bowl in the rock, where they placed water. The water froze overnight, but would always thaw by midday, attracting the wild partridge to drink there. The hunters replenished the water each day and after allowing time for sufficient numbers of birds to get into the habit of drinking there, they one evening added strychnine to the water, returning next day to collect the dead birds and transport them down to Ching-wang-tao, where they sold them to ships in the harbour.

Williams himself considered the story authentic, firstly because it had been relayed to him in great secrecy, secondly because he had noted the absence of partridges in the district and, thirdly, because he had bought a pair of partridge himself and having eaten them been unexpectedly sick – an illness for which he now felt he had an explanation.

Although there are some difficulties with this – Williams's own illness does not appear to have much in common with strychnine poisoning, and it seems a trifle unlikely that the Chinese hunters would really have shared trade secrets with him, even under the influence of alcohol – the method of trapping the birds en masse is credible and would produce better results than merely sprinkling poisoned grain which might only trap one or two birds at a time. If Arthur Banham had come up with a similar scheme in Norfolk, then why should not his counterparts in China? Williams places his hunters in the area of Ching-wang-tao, today more commonly known as Quinhuangdao – but whatever the spelling, an area indisputably located within what was once known as Manchuria – the origin of Lieutenant Chevis's partridge.

It is worth noting at this point that both Frances Chevis and Frederick Downs, the poulterer who prepared the birds at Colebrooks, told the court that they had observed no signs of shot. In the opinion of Downs, the birds must have been trapped or snared – although the absence of shot could equally have indicated that the poisoned bird had been picked up from the ground where it had expired.

Privately the investigation team began to incline more and more to the theory of accident, so that on 19 January 1932, Deputy Chief Constable Bird responded warmly to Cullen Mather's latest letter, thanking him for all his efforts and concluding, 'Although actual proof is still missing and the chances are it will never be definitely ascertained from whence the strychnine that caused the sad death of Lt Chevis came, your letter is of invaluable help to us in reaching our conclusions in this case and your "strong suspicions" strengthens very much our belief that the poison was in the fatal bird when it entered this country.'[33]

CHAPTER TWENTY-TWO

ACCIDENT OR MURDER?

While the Chevis case was not quite a Nine Day Wonder, media interest faded soon after the inquest, as was invariably the case where no further information was forthcoming. The police investigation continued into the autumn and winter, but was ultimately inconclusive. The idea that the partridge could have been poisoned, either accidentally or deliberately, before it ever arrived in England gradually became the favoured theory of the senior officers in the case, and this appears to have been passed on to at least one or two members of the Press, because the *Daily Express* and some other papers ran a story in January 1932 stating that it was 'now generally accepted' that the poison had been placed in the partridge by Manchurian fur trappers, initially hoping to attract foxes, who had then somehow mixed this bird up with a consignment of uncontaminated partridges destined for the table.[1] This rather garbled explanation of the affair concluded by saying that questions were liable to be asked in the next session of parliament regarding the transportation of foodstuffs from abroad.

This prediction proved correct when J.P.L. Thomas, the Member of Parliament for Hereford, asked Sir Hilton Young, the Minister of Health, if he was aware that Manchurian partridge were being imported into the country, and whether the Minister was satisfied with the conditions pertaining to the birds. The Minister replied that Manchurian partridges were subject to the same conditions as any other imported foodstuffs, adding that in 1930, the year for which most recent figures were available, the total amount of game imported (among which Manchurian partridges would have represented a tiny fraction) had only amounted to 20cwts.[2]

While the police erred towards the theory of an accident, they inevitably accepted that the matter was far from clear cut. In October, Stovell had interviewed Lewis John Lacey, a fur buyer based in London, who assured the Superintendent that in the dozen years he had been buying fur in Manchuria, Mongolia and Japan, he had never encountered, or even heard of strychnine being used to trap birds destined for consumption, or for that matter to trap wild animals for the fur trade either.[3]

A further stumbling block was the complete absence of any other known case of a human being dying as a result of eating a bird which had been poisoned in this way. It was a point not lost on Superintendent Stovell, who included it in more than one of his lists of questions and answers in Surrey Police files. Several correspondents who had written to draw attention to the possibility that the partridge had imbibed the strychnine in Manchuria also admitted this difficulty in their letters, including Mr La Touche, who had first alerted the police to the story in the *China Journal of Science & Arts*, and who mentioned in his original letter that while he had no reason to doubt the authenticity of Mr William's account, he had himself been a customs official in Ching-wang-tao and never encountered the practice.[4]

Oddly there is no indication in the files that the police ever shared their favoured theory with Lieutenant Chevis's family. Hugh's widow left the country while the investigation was still ongoing,[5] but his father continued to 'campaign for justice' in his own particular way, writing to the Chief Constable in typical bombastic style in December 1931:

> Sir,
>
> It is nearly six months since our splendid son was so diabolically poisoned with strychnine. Is anyone troubling themselves to continue enquiries in a really trained detective manner? We will give a reward and I am sure Mrs Chevis will also, if the really guilty person can be procured. The 'Hooray' telegram was sent from Dublin <u>either to take away suspicion from the guilty person in England</u> or it was sent by someone who knew that their diabolical plan had <u>succeeded.</u> The partridge was poisoned by someone between the time it was ordered by telephone on 19 June and the time it was put on my son's table on the evening of 20 June. It was cleverly planned and from that 'Hooray' telegram this <u>is</u> probable proof. The batman is Irish. He is with Major Edge at Deepcut. Please ask him where he (Bolger) was during the time our son was at Okehampton from 6 – 19 June. I want to know.[6]

It will be noted that Sir William remained under the impression that he was entitled to issue orders to members of the Surrey police force and one feels a degree of concern for the numerous defendants who must have appeared before him in the course of a very long judicial career, if the forgoing is in an example of Sir William's powers of reasoning when confronted with a given set of circumstances: it is not at all clear how Bolger's whereabouts during the period in question could have been evidence in the case, and in fact the police had established from the outset that Bolger had been at the camp in Devon with Lieutenant Chevis, as would naturally have been expected, since he was the officer's batman.

In addition, it is difficult not to sympathise with Sir William's colleagues and underlings, if the hectoring attitude which the retired judge continued to display in his correspondence with Surrey Police was in any way typical of the manner in which he generally conducted himself – for while allowances must be made for personal grief, these glimpses of Sir William in full flow rather beg the question why a long-suffering clerk or court servant had not been tempted to poison the judge's partridge long before.

If Sir William received a written response to this particular missive, it has not survived in the police files. In the twenty-first century, it is customary for a UK police force to appoint an officer to liaise with the family of a murder victim and keep them as fully appraised as possible with the progress of the case. While this was not the norm eighty years ago, the relationship between a victim's family and the investigators might be strengthened if a strong bond of sympathy grew up between them; however, it was equally likely to be adversely affected by a lack of co-operation, or perceived unreasonable behaviour on the family's part. The police gradually warmed to Frances Chevis, but Sir William's behaviour alienated them from start to finish with the result that although by December 1931 they had pretty well made up their minds that Hugh Chevis's death had been a tragic accident, they elected not to share this information with his family.

It is apparent from Sir William's letter that he had convinced himself of two things: firstly that his son had met his death as the result of a 'diabolical' plot, cunningly conceived by a clever killer, and secondly that Surrey Police were not up to unravelling the mystery. The decision to fob Sir William off with a non-committal response about police enquiries continuing was entirely understandable, since recent experience suggested that if they were completely candid with him, he would leak their conclusions to the Press, accompanied by a lot of bluster about how the police could not see the plain fact that it was a murder, with the consequent re-ignition of the whole anti-Surrey Police furore.

While no record of the police response has survived, we know that they did not share their conclusions about the strong possibility of an accident, not only because descendants of both Sir William and Frances Chevis remained unaware that this was the official conclusion, but also because of a later letter received by the police from Sir William's surviving son, Captain William Chevis.

In the Chevis family it was certainly not a case of 'like father like son', for while Sir William's rudeness became a hallmark of the case, his elder son emerges as a very different kind of man, glimpsed now and again taking on the organisation of his brother's funeral, quietly settling his debts without troubling Frances over the money, acting as go-between over the telegram, appearing at the inquest to give identification evidence, and occasionally writing in the politest of terms to the coroner, or the police. In July 1932, he addressed a letter to Superintendent Stovell in precisely this vein, apologising for bothering him, but explaining that he had heard a rumour that the sender of the 'Hooray' telegram had been identified and apprehended, and asking whether it would be possible for the Superintendent to let him know the truth or otherwise of this? Stovell responded by return, saying that there had been no truth in the rumour and, true to form, the Captain politely acknowledged his response and thanked him for his trouble.[7] One cannot help wondering whether the police might have been more candid with the family if they had only had to deal with Captain Chevis.

There is no further evidence that Sir William continued to correspond with Surrey Police. He died in 1939 and is buried (with Lady Chevis, who survived until 1943) in Boscombe East Cemetary. Unusually for a man who had enjoyed such a prominent career, his passing does not appear to have been recorded in the local newspapers – it was a far cry from the Glory Days in India, when the Chief Justice of the Punjab threw garden parties in his honour.[8]

Meanwhile his daughter-in-law, Frances, had slipped out of his life. Major William Chevis, grandson of Sir William and nephew of Hugh, believes that he and his brother played with Frances's children, but that these meetings pre-dated his uncle's death and it appears that the families did not keep in touch afterwards. This is not altogether surprising and nothing sinister should be read into it. Frances had only been a member of the Chevis family for a matter of months by the time of her husband's death, and lived in a different part of the country.

In November 1931 she took a trip to India, just as she had told the Chief Constable she intended to. Whether this resulted in a reunion with her current 'flave' we have no way of knowing, but if there was a relationship it did not last, because just over two years later the news broke that Frances was to remarry. Her bridegroom was Gerald Braham, manager of 'Isobel's', a Mayfair dress shop which had become famous as the first entirely British fashion house. Their Regent Street premises were accessed via silver bronze gates and a magnificent staircase led to the first floor salon, where the models paraded dresses for prospective clients on a black marble dais. Only the super-rich could afford to patronise the premises, while Isobel herself had become so famous that she was accorded celebrity status in her own right.[9]

The tabloids seized on the marriage as an opportunity to appraise their readers of Frances's status as an heiress (a point which they had seemingly failed to grasp back in 1931), referring to the news of her engagement as 'an echo of the partridge death mystery' – an epithet both insensitive and inaccurate.[10] According to the Press the couple had known each other for some time and no definite plans had yet been made about the wedding. Frances and her bridegroom may have been understandably disingenuous with the Press, for in fact they were married within the month and set off for a honeymoon in New York on 28 February.[11] The birth of their son, David, in December the same year sparked another flurry of stories, with the *Daily Mirror* perfectly illustrating how inescapable is a murder for the family of the victim, with the line 'The birth of a son to Mrs Frances Howard Braham of Basil Mansions announced yesterday, recalls the famous poison partridge mystery'.[12]

Whatever the birth suggested to the Press, it is unlikely that thoughts of Hugh Chevis's death were constantly uppermost in the minds of Frances and her growing family. They continued to reside mainly in London, though Ships's Passenger Lists record trips abroad from time to time and Frances continued to indulge her fondness for Monte Carlo and the South of France. She was there in September 1939 when war broke out and with typical determination and not little personal risk, drove herself and the three oldest children back to the coast and obtained a cross-Channel passage, regardless of the advancing German armies.[13]

The war separated her from her husband Gerald (who, although over forty at the outbreak of war, served in the Royal Fusiliers and then the Army Ordnance Corps) and the relationship did not survive. Her daughters Elizabeth and Pauline were married in 1949 and 1950 respectively, the ceremonies followed by a reception at Claridges, and both girls were given away by their brother Peter, who had also married in 1949. In 1951, Frances herself trod the matrimonial path for the fourth time.[14] Husband number four was another retired army officer, Brigadier General William Neilson Bicket, who was almost twenty years her senior and, like Frances, had grown-up children. The marriage lasted until it was dissolved in 1969.

At the age of sixty-nine, Frances was married for the final time. Her choice was again a retired army officer, Colonel John Rayson, and they elected to live abroad, choosing the gentler climate of Monte Carlo, where Frances died in 1972, not quite two years after becoming Mrs Rayson. She was outlived by both Colonel Rayson and Brigadier General Bicket – Gerald Braham (who had also remarried) died in 1957. Her death attracted no publicity. It was forty years since the poison partridge mystery and the case had been generally forgotten by all but the family themselves and occasional students of crime, for whom the question still remained – accident or murder?

CHAPTER TWENTY-THREE

HAT-TRICK OF MURDERS

The Wallace Case, the Foster Case, the Chevis Case: three infamous, unsolved deaths which occurred within barely six months of one another, all of which have enjoyed the status of classic murder mysteries, though only one of them is irrefutably a murder at all.[1] In common with many mysterious deaths in the early part of the twentieth century, the case of the poison partridge will never be solved. Certain facts can be deduced, but no one will ever be able to state with absolute certainty how Hugh Chevis met his death in June 1931.

Unlike some of the alleged arsenic murders which occurred in the 1930s and earlier, there can be no doubt that the cause of death was the ingestion of poison – in this case strychnine. The distinctive symptoms were present and strychnine (which, unlike arsenic, does not occur naturally in human beings) was isolated in the deceased's vomit and his organs. In addition, it is reasonable to believe that the strychnine was introduced into the Lieutenant's system via the partridge served to him at dinner. Irrespective of the evidence of his widow on the subject, Hugh Chevis informed both his manservant and at least one of the doctors who attended him that it was the partridge – and only the partridge – which had tasted bitter. Thus while it is possible to promulgate a whole series of speculations about the presence or otherwise of cruets and water jugs on the Lieutenant's dining table, the question of how the poison arrived on Hugh Chevis's plate is essentially confined to the question of how it was introduced into the partridge.

With the possible exception of the bird consumed by his wife, we know that none of the other partridges in the consignment had been contaminated – or at least contaminated to a dangerous level – for those which remained in the warehouse were specifically tested for strychnine, while the attendant local publicity would surely have guaranteed that anyone else in the area who had purchased a partridge and found it unsatisfactory would have registered the point with the suppliers or the police.

If the evidence of the delivery driver, William Noyes, is to be believed – and there is no reason why it should not be – we know that it was impossible to tamper with the partridge en route to the Chevis's bungalow, because the van was never left unlocked. Even assuming that the van was not locked, it is difficult to construct any realistic scenario in which an assassin sneaked up while Noyes was not looking and introduced poison into the game. Aside from anything else, the partridges had been wrapped up in paper, and after interfering with them the perpetrator would have had to re-wrap the package in such a way that Noyes would not notice it had been tampered with. In addition, he or she would have had to somehow know that Lieutenant Chevis's dinner was travelling on that day in that particular van and followed the van until an opportunity to get at the contents arose – and even if we were to assume that the poison was not specifically intended for Lieutenant Chevis, but had been randomly introduced with no particular victim in mind, these conjectures are not remotely likely.

Once delivered, the partridges spent several hours in an outside meat safe when they might just conceivably have been tampered with by some mysterious agent of a 'diabolical plot': but had such a person existed they would have had to evade the interest of both Lieutenant Chevis's Alsation dog, his own household, his neighbours, their servants, and anyone else who happened to be passing by. On the face of it, this too has much to argue against it and nothing much to recommend it.

Equally unlikely is any scenario involving Ellen Yeomans or Nicholas Bolger. Mrs Yeomans had opportunity, but no motive and, as stated previously, stood to lose her position by the death of Lieutenant Chevis and presumably therefore every reason to want to keep him alive.

Indeed the lack of motive is a problem in respect of pretty much any suspect, since Hugh Chevis appears to have been an immensely popular man, with no one having anything but good to say of him, in spite of his reputation as a ladies' man. Yet here we come to the one possible source of motive – for while the notion of a jealous ex-lover stealing into the garden to tamper with the contents of the meat safe has very little to commend it, the presence of incriminating papers in the bungalow in the shape of love letters from Iris Coates and possibly others, surely provided ample motive for the Lieutenant's bride of six months?

There are a number of pointers in favour of Frances having been the guilty party. Motive has already been touched on and she is one of only three people (the others being Ellen Yeomans and Hugh Chevis himself) to whom the meat safe was easily accessible that afternoon. Obtaining a restricted drug ought not to have presented an insurmountable problem to a woman who had access to almost unlimited funds and at least one extremely discreet, loyal servant. Frances always served the meat at the table and could therefore have ensured that her husband received the 'dosed' bird.

Then there are various aspects of her behaviour on the night of his death. Bolger, who enjoys the distinction of being the most logical and consistent of the witnesses, was certain that his mistress told him that Lieutenant Chevis was suffering from strychnine poisoning before she was taken ill herself, although the attending doctor swore on oath at the inquest that he had not shared this diagnosis with her.

Her own symptoms did not manifest themselves until after the doctor had arrived to attend her husband – perhaps when she had witnessed the effects of strychnine and was able to mimic them. Thanks to Ryffel's decision to mix samples from husband and wife together, there is no forensic evidence to prove that Frances had ever ingested strychnine and we have only her word for it that her bird tasted strange – though we do know that she tasted a portion of her husband's bird, because he told Dr Bindloss this.

Then there is the mystery of the telephone call. Frances told the police that she telephoned and spoke to her nurse immediately after dinner, well before she was taken ill – but her nurse placed the call much later – at around 9.15, by which time there was already one, or possibly two doctors in attendance, and it was this phone call which set in motion the chain of events that would ensure Frances was removed from hospital before the police could interview her the next day.

The police officers and coroner paid surprisingly little attention to the call itself, or to its recipient, even after receiving a letter from someone who was clearly familiar with Frances's household, who intimated that there might be something between Frances and the nurse.

The anonymous letter in question dropped the strongest hints of a possible sexual relationship between the two women, claiming that Nurse Thorne had broken up Frances's first marriage and that she was a 'man-hater'. The investigators may well have dismissed this not least because Frances appeared manifestly interested in members of the opposite sex rather than her own, but in reality the situation could have been much more complex. In the 1920s and '30s, not only was it all but impossible for a woman to openly declare herself a lesbian, it was perfectly possible to remain in complete ignorance of the existence of lesbians. When an attempt was made to make sexual acts between women illegal in 1921, one of the arguments against doing so was that it would advertise the existence of 'such practices' and 'bring it to the notice of women who have never heard of it, never thought of it, never dreamed of it'[2] – a statement which, while it surely exemplified the lack of knowledge and understanding which bedevilled the whole debate, nevertheless contained a particle of truth, for there is no doubt that significant numbers of heterosexual women (and to a lesser extent heterosexual men) were uncertain as to whether or not lesbians really did exist, or what exactly a lesbian might be. At a time when any non-heterosexual relationship was condemned as unnatural, many lesbians chose to marry and bear children. Marriages of social convenience between homosexual and bisexual men and women, to partners who were similarly inclined or else who made no sexual demands upon them, such as that between Cole Porter and his wife Linda Lee Thomas, were commonplace. Those higher up the social scale, or who moved in sufficiently liberal or Bohemian circles (Vita Sackville West and Harold Nicholson are another obvious example) were able to continue extra-marital relationships with members of their own sex either covertly or with the full knowledge of their spouses and immediate social circle, sometimes with friends and social equals and occasionally with another member of the household, whose presence was masked under the guise of employment.

It has been suggested by some students of film and novel that Mrs Danvers, the housekeeper devoted to the memory of her dead mistress in Daphne du Maurier's 1930 novel *Rebecca*, was such an employee. Mrs Danvers was undoubtedly besotted with Rebecca, and claimed that for all her mistress's many love affairs, Rebecca laughed at and despised men, coming home after they had made love to her and laughing with her 'darling Danny' about them.[3] While the suggestion may be considered little short of blasphemy to many of the book's legions of fans, it is strengthened by the fact that du Maurier herself was bisexual, enjoying a long marriage to a frequently absent army officer, while indulging in covert affairs with beautiful women.[4] Whatever the true nature of Mrs Danvers's love of Rebecca, the reader is left in little doubt that she would have done anything for her.

Was Ivy Thorne a kind of Mrs Danvers? Utterly devoted to her mistress and willing to do anything for her? There are plenty of indications that Miss Thorne enjoyed Frances's confidence. Frances told the Chief Constable that Nurse Thorne knew all about her 'peccadilloes' and could be relied on to keep her mouth shut. She was trusted with the children when Frances went down to stay with her husband at Deepcut, trusted to clear out the contents of the bungalow – even when this involved letters of a sensitive nature – and therefore presumably trusted not to reveal their contents.

It can also be adduced that Ivy Thorne's role within Frances's household had altered over time – perhaps because she had proved one of those rare, indispensible women that a busy person needs to run their lives, perhaps because of a growing affection between mistress and servant, maybe a combination of both. Ivy Thorne had arrived as a midwifery nurse, to take care of Frances when she was expecting her son Peter, and she was still with the family almost five years later. There is just one tiny hint in the police files that Frances may have enjoyed sexual liaisons with members of her own sex. It comes in the form of an unsigned, undated list of responses to a set of queries which have not survived. The questions are self-evidently about people involved in the case and it is easy to divine that the response, 'Popular, easy-going officer, easy to please. Engaged to Mrs Jackson before he left for India' relates to some question regarding Hugh Chevis. However, the response: 'With both sexes, not exactly known. Enjoyed a "good time"', cannot be so definitely linked to any of the participants, although the order of its appearance in the list tends to suggest that the person referred to may have been Frances herself.[5]

Nurse Thorne might have been a useful accomplice, but she was not an essential one. Ultimately the death of Hugh Chevis comes down to two alternatives – either the strychnine was in the partridge long before it reached his dinner table thanks to the bird's having ingested the poison in life – or the strychnine was introduced by Frances herself. She had the opportunity and she may have had a motive: but did she do the deed?

CHAPTER TWENTY-FOUR

'SOMEONE MUST HAVE DONE IT'

Lady Amy Chevis, 1931

It is an irrefutable fact that Frances Chevis *could* have murdered her husband. There are even suggestions within the evidence that she might have done so – yet these glimmers of 'proof' are not what they seem. First there is the question of Frances's own illness. Had she actually been poisoned, or was she faking? This issue only arises at all thanks to the incompetence of the analyst associated with case, for had Dr John Ryffel analysed the samples he received separately, as was surely the police's intention, there would have been proof positive one way or the other as to whether Frances had ingested a sufficient quantity of strychnine to account for her symptoms.

We know from Hugh's conversation with Dr Bindloss that Frances had eaten a piece of the suspect partridge and consumed part of the other bird which had been basted in the same fat and therefore, to some degree, contaminated with the poison. It is surely a point in Frances's favour that she was willing to taste the suspect partridge at all. Unaccustomed to cooking, she might not have realised that basting would introduce strychnine into the breast of her own bird, but had she been the guilty party, it seems unlikely that she would have willingly chewed and swallowed some of her husband's partridge – a woman with sufficient guile to plan and execute a murder would presumably have been quick enough on her feet to find an excuse which avoided taking the contaminated bird into her mouth.

It would also require a highly skilled actress to fake the symptoms of strychnine poisoning, acting out dramatic seizures with sufficient conviction that three doctors were taken in. The need for such play acting is in any case questionable. Frances knew that the partridges had both been destroyed – rather than risk her duplicity being detected by faking the symptoms of poisoning, surely it would have made more sense to insist that your own dinner had tasted unpleasant and that you consequently ate very little of it and therefore by inference escaped being poisoned?

There was an additional explanation for the delayed symptoms which no one considered at the time: there is just an outside chance that Frances's symptoms were psychosomatic. Confronted with sudden, unexplained illness, severe anxiety can cause individuals to involuntarily manifest symptoms of the illness, even when they are not suffering from it. 'False' symptoms are most often associated with multiple outbreaks of 'mass hysteria', in which large groups of people in the same school, workplace, or other institution believe themselves at risk from a mysterious condition of some kind, but individual cases of 'false symptoms' have been known. A particular characteristic of such episodes is that the original onset of the illness was sudden, traumatic and initially unexplained, and that the others presenting with symptoms could conceivably have fallen victim to the same illness, because they had been exposed to the same things as the initial complainants. Instances of 'mass hysteria' are statistically more likely to occur among young females, but cases can involve both genders and all age groups, and if Frances was innocent of the crime then the onset of her husband's symptoms must have been terrifying and accompanied by a real fear that she too might have been poisoned, given that both of them had eaten the same things.[1]

One of the obstacles for accepting that Frances was genuinely suffering from strychnine poisoning was the long delay before her symptoms presented. Asked about this at the inquest, the indefatigably inventive Dr Ryffel offered the court some hastily improvised theories about the amount of fat taken with the strychnine and the speed with which individuals 'pass their food'. In fact, while the delayed onset of symptoms was unusual, it was far from unique. Strychnine is a particularly fast acting poison, but individuals react to it in different ways and not everyone will exhibit symptoms within precisely the same time frame.

More significantly in this case, the delay before Frances's symptoms manifested themselves was almost certainly exaggerated. In emergency situations, witnesses are frequently very poor at estimating the amount of time which has passed – examples of this are legion and anyone who has awaited the arrival of an ambulance will recall the way minutes seemed like hours, while conversely someone who has been busy dealing with an emergency in which events have rapidly unfolded, is often surprised to discover how much has happened in a relatively short space of time. Frances herself clearly became confused about the order in which things had taken place around the time when her husband first showed signs of being ill, but we do not have to rely entirely on Frances, because Nicolas Bolger, Ellen Yeomans and two of the doctors also gave statements from which it is possible to estimate the timing of various events.

It is probably the case that neither Frances nor Hugh felt particularly well by the end of their dinner. Both complained of a nasty lingering taste in their mouths and neither had managed to finish their meal. More serious symptoms – an inability to use his legs, followed by a seizure – began to affect Hugh not long after he retired to the drawing room and at this point Frances telephoned for Dr Bindloss. It seems to have been accepted later that Frances's symptoms did not manifest until another whole hour had passed – this is what appears in the police notes on the case – but in reality the time lapse may have been much shorter.

Frances telephoned for Bindloss, who took about fifteen minutes to arrive. At the moment when Dr Bindloss arrived, Hugh Chevis was not suffering from a seizure and the doctor found his patient able to chat quite naturally. Bindloss's statement gives the impression that this state of affairs went on for some considerable time, but that seems most unlikely. In a case of strychnine poisoning, once seizures have commenced they will continue at relatively frequent intervals and Bindloss had probably not been in the house for very long before the Lieutenant suffered a further seizure and the doctor came to appreciate the seriousness of what confronted him. At this point Bindloss decided to call in reinforcements and phoned for Dr Murray, but before Murray arrived, Frances too had been prostrated by the illness.

As a general rule, signs of strychnine poisoning are first observed some fifteen to thirty minutes after ingestion. Therefore if Hugh Chevis ingested strychnine at around 7.50 that evening – which is the earliest possible time he could have done so, assuming that the timings provided by the servants are accurate – then his symptoms were not likely to commence until somewhere between 8.05 and 8.20 at the earliest. Around 8.10-8.15 would be consistent with the fact that in the interval between Hugh's swallowing the partridge and becoming seriously ill, Bolger had to have time to bring in the cheese and salad, then serve coffee and almost finish clearing away; while Frances unsuccessfully attempted to eat the cheese and salad, left the table, telephoned Nurse Thorne and then drank a cup of coffee. Bolger estimated that Dr Bindloss was called at 8.15 and arrived at about 8.30, which is considerably later than the times estimated by other witnesses, but far more consistent with the various events which had taken place prior to the call being made.

Dr Bindloss himself claimed to have arrived at around 8.15 (which scarcely allows time for Hugh Chevis to exhibit symptoms, let alone for the doctor to have arrived) and not to have observed any convulsions until 8.40, at which point he called Dr Murray. As it is most unlikely that Hugh Chevis's convulsions took a twenty-five minute break while he chatted with the doctor, it is fairly safe to assume that Bindloss was mistaken about this. Bindloss may have been right in timing the call to Dr Murray at around 8.40, because this would fit with Bindloss arriving at around 8.30 and Hugh Chevis initially appearing well but then suffering a convulsion after a few minutes. Bindloss and Bolger continued to disagree when it came to the arrival of Dr Murray, with the former believing that Murray turned up at around 9 o'clock and the latter placing this event closer to 9.30. However, both agreed that Frances became ill between the call being made to Murray and his actual arrival.

Irrespective of the definite times when each event occurred, a timeline does emerge from all this confusion. Hugh began to suffer from some alarming symptoms and Frances immediately called the doctor. Everyone agrees that he arrived within about fifteen minutes. After conversing with the patient Dr Bindloss observed symptoms of strychnine poisoning and telephoned Dr Murray, and during the period while they waited for Murray to arrive, Frances too appeared to become ill. The usual progress of strychnine poisoning does not support Dr Bindloss's suggestion that some twenty-five minutes passed between his arrival and the moment when he observed a convulsion and rang for reinforcements and if – as is far more likely – this occurred within five to ten minutes of his arrival, then a mere twenty-five minutes had passed since the Lieutenant's first seizure and no more than forty minutes elapsed between the original onset of Hugh's symptoms and the arrival of Dr Murray. If Frances's symptoms began within a very short time of the call to Murray, then the suspicious time difference between her own illness and Hugh's of 'more than an hour' reduces to perhaps as little as half an hour. In a condition where symptoms appear *on average* with fifteen to thirty minutes, the onset of symptoms some forty to forty-five minutes after ingestion is not particularly exceptional.

The question of Frances's survival in the face of her husband's demise has also been raised. Small doses of strychnine could of course be ingested without ill effects and even where larger doses are involved, the amount of strychnine which proves fatal can vary enormously between one individual and another.[2] There is no great mystery to Frances's survival, for patients do survive, providing their convulsions can be controlled by sedation. According to the attending doctors, Frances's convulsions were markedly less severe than her husband's, and she travelled to the hospital in the car driven by Dr Bindloss, while Dr Murray travelled with her, administering chloroform, so that by the time they reached the hospital Frances was no longer aware of her surroundings. Her husband travelled with Dr Attenborough and had no accompanying medical attendant to help him withstand the movement of the car along uneven roads, which would undoubtedly have exacerbated his condition by stimulating yet more seizures.

There could also have been a significant difference in the amount of poison each had ingested. When asked to recall how much of the contaminated meat had been consumed, Frances estimated that she had only eaten two mouthfuls of her own bird and said she thought that Hugh had eaten about the same amount – but this may have been an underestimate. The servants disagreed about the amount of meat which had gone from each carcass, while Ryffel (admittedly not the most reliable of witnesses) claimed that there had been 'a lot of meat' in the sample of vomit. Frances told the press that her husband had been a big man with a healthy appetite, and when describing the fatal dinner, used the expression: 'he attacked the breast first'[3] which certainly implies the consumption of an initial hearty mouthful or two. She also told reporters that she did not like partridge, and only ate it regularly because her husband had been very fond of it. She herself did not like the strong taste which she particularly associated with foreign partridge, and which she had initially assumed to be the reason for the unpleasant 'musty' taste (coincidentally the precise word chosen by Ryffel to describe the birds he had cooked alongside the contaminated partridges). One can therefore imagine that the bird on her plate was not 'attacked' so enthusiastically, but this also throws up an interesting possibility inasmuch that Frances initially thought the problem to be merely that the game on her plate tasted 'higher' than usual.

Could the strong flavour of the game have initially masked the taste of the strychnine, thereby encouraging Hugh Chevis to plough on until he got a particularly bitter mouthful? This does seem possible, because his initial reaction was not to discard the meat altogether, but to ask Frances to taste it and see if she thought there was something wrong with it. Today it is customary to serve game birds which are young, fresh and tender, but historically it was the custom to hang birds for up to a couple of weeks before cooking, as this was considered to enhance their texture and gave them a very strong flavour – people would eat birds which were practically green – a factor which may have assisted in the game-loving officer's downfall.[4]

There was an abundance of evidence that a bird contaminated with strychnine could end up on a human diner's plate, so it is reasonable to conjecture that in almost every instance when this occurred, the amount of strychnine involved was so small that it had no obvious ill effects. It is just conceivable that Lieutenant Chevis fell victim to a fatal combination of circumstances, in which a partridge with an unusually high concentration of strychnine found its way onto the plate of a man with a particular fondness for strongly flavoured game, an unfortunate susceptibility to strychnine, and a constitution which resisted the doctors' attempts to sedate him. In tragedies it is often a fatal combination of circumstances, rather than one single circumstance, which sets matters in train.

What of Frances's telling Bolger that her husband was suffering from strychnine poisoning before the doctor had mentioned this diagnosis to her? It is of course the classic slip – in a crime novel the murderer often gave himself away by mentioning something which could only have been known by a guilty party. And not just in novels – Ethel Major, who would be convicted of murdering her husband in 1934, babbled to the police about strychnine long before anyone had mentioned to her that this was the medium by which her husband had met his death – a point which undoubtedly did not help her case.[5]

In Frances's situation, however, far from being guilty foreknowledge, there is a perfectly reasonable explanation for her mentioning strychnine poisoning to Bolger and had the coroner asked Frances a direct question on the matter, she could probably have provided it. During his evidence Dr Bindloss stated that when he telephoned to summon the assistance of Dr Murray, he informed his colleague during the call that he believed Lieutenant Chevis was suffering from strychnine poisoning.[6] In such circumstances you do not have to hear a diagnosis direct from the doctor in order to be aware of his professional opinion, for within the confines of the bungalow there is every chance that Frances overheard this call. She told Bolger that the Lieutenant was suffering from strychnine poisoning when she went into the kitchen, to send the batman for some more brandy, after which she returned to the drawing room to help with her husband, and it was at this point that her own legs began to give way. We know that this happened after Bindloss had placed his call to Murray and before Murray arrived.

Then there is the question of the phone call to Nurse Thorne. Frances stated that she phoned the nurse immediately after dinner – a routine call to ask about the children. The call took place after dinner, but before Hugh had been taken ill, whereas Ivy Thorne spoke of a call which took place considerably later and, far from being about the children, was a conversation which led to Mrs Chevis's own doctor travelling down from London and Frances herself being removed back to the capital the next day.

Had Frances been the guilty party, effecting her alibi and getaway after the commission of a perfectly planned and executed murder, we might at the very least have expected her to get her story straight with the nurse. The natural fallibility of the human memory is notorious, particularly in moments of emotional stress, and in any group of people required to give a strictly chronological account of an unexpected death to which they were witnesses there will inevitably be minor discrepancies, with some people laying considerable emphasis on details which others omit from their account altogether – but this does not necessarily make any of these witnesses untruthful. When approaching the question of the phone call from a logical standpoint, it is reasonably clear that the call about the children was actually the first of *two* phone calls Frances made to her flat that night.

The confusion about the telephone calls to Basil Mansions stems from the questions which were never asked of the witnesses concerned. In attempting to make sense of witness statements obtained by the police during this period it is important to bear in mind that the 'statement' is not a coherent monologue, but a series of responses to questions which do not appear in the signed, finished document. Similarly a witness in the coroner's court can only offer responses to the questions asked of them – this can lead to glaring holes in the evidence and false conclusions being drawn from omissions. When Frances was asked for her account of events, she explained in detail what had taken place in the earlier part of the evening, faithfully recalling that she had telephoned her nurse to ask after the children, but saying relatively little about what had transpired later – not mentioning for example that telephone calls had been made to summon both Dr Murray and Dr Attenborough – or indeed her own nurse and practitioner. To Frances these calls would have seemed unimportant in the context of the case – though had the police or coroner specifically asked her, she would no doubt have agreed that there were two calls to Basil Mansions that evening.

Similarly when Ivy Thorne was questioned at the inquest and asked to estimate what time Frances had called her, she answered only in respect of the call which led her to summon Dr Gibson, not mentioning the earlier call about the children, as this was entirely irrelevant to the coroner's question.

Nurse Thorne estimated that the phone call asking her to contact Dr Gibson took place at around 9.15 – an estimate apparently based on nothing in particular, which is not confirmed by any other witness and may have been out by a significant factor. There is nothing on record to indicate at what point Frances became too incapacitated to have made a phone call, but although the usual assumption is that Frances initiated the call because she required the doctor's attendance for herself, it is just as likely that she instructed Nurse Thorne to summon Dr Gibson before she had suffered any seizures, because she wanted to obtain the best possible medical treatment for her spouse.

Again there is nothing sinister or particularly unusual about Frances summoning her own medical attendants, or subsequently discharging herself into their care. In 1931, a patient with a comfortable home would be nursed there, by a medical team funded out of their own pocket. Lieutenant and Mrs Chevis were removed to the cottage hospital solely to enable the doctors to undertake a procedure for which there was no suitable equipment at the bungalow. It was also perfectly normal for a patient who could afford it to be attended by their own personal physician wherever they happened to be. Fashionable London specialists were likely to find themselves summoned to hotels or house parties anywhere in the country if a patient's condition warranted it – a determination which was very much in the hands of the patient and his/her family. When doctors' incomes were solely reliant on the patronage of their better-off clients, a medical man was far more likely to dance to his patients' tune, and a patient far more likely to expect a gold-plated, personal service, at any hour of the day or night, wherever they happened to find themselves.[7]

What at first glance looks like a devious escape from police interrogation would have seemed to Frances Chevis a perfectly normal step to take. With her doctor pronouncing her well enough to travel, Frances would not have waited around in the cottage hospital a minute longer than was necessary. In statements to both the Press and the police, Frances said that she had initially assumed Hugh's death was an accident. If that was the case, it may not have occurred to her that the police would want her to make a statement, or even that there would be an inquest (until forced into dealings with the coroner's office, the vast majority of honest citizens have no idea that any unexpected death will automatically lead to a coroner's inquisition).

In the early days of the inquiry, Frances's lack of availability to make a statement also comes across as the reluctance of a guilty person, but is equally likely to have been a combination of genuine distress at the death of her husband, coupled with a sense that people in her position were not at the beck and call of mere policemen – an attitude shared by various others in the case, which reflected the thinking of her social class at the time.

The most compelling argument for Frances's guilt lies not in any actual evidence against her, so much as an assumption of motive. Her financial independence should have rendered any theory that she had murdered Hugh for money nul and void, but her fortune told against her in another unexpected way, as the Chief Constable noted that she would not have experienced a normal wife's reluctance to murder her breadwinner, because Frances could support herself.[8] With money ruled out, could the new Mrs Chevis have wanted to rid herself of her bridegroom of six months for other reasons? On the face of it, Hugh Chevis's affair with Iris Coates ought to have provoked fierce jealousy, but Frances appeared untroubled by it – just as it is clear from the witness statement provided by John Blair that Hugh had no objection to Frances being squired around London by another man in his absence, both before and after their marriage. This is coincidentally supported by Jack Gwynn-Jones, who tried to warn Hugh off from marrying Frances. Lieutenant Gwynn-Jones had seen Frances out and about with other men and it is a reasonable conjecture that he passed this information on to his friend when trying to discourage the match, but Hugh Chevis was evidently undeterred by the fact that his fiancée had dalliances with other men.

Many people believe that the so-called Permissive Society was invented in the 1960s, but the reality is somewhat different. The 1920s was the decade of the 'Bright Young People', a hedonistic group of monied pleasure seekers and hangers-on, associated in the public mind with 'a compound of cocktails, jazz, licence, abandon and flagrantly improper behaviour' according to D.J. Taylor's study of the era.[9] The term Bright Young People is associated with a particular group and there is no suggestion that Frances or Hugh were directly a part of it, but the lifestyle of parties, cocktails, dances, polo matches and West End nightclubs was common to all the fashionable set who could afford it – principle among them the Prince of Wales, who enjoyed lengthy affairs with at least two other married women, before taking up with Mrs Wallis Simpson. Lady Marguerite Strickland recalls the frisson of being taken out dancing in 1931 London, when: 'we went to nightclubs every night ... it was very romantic ... the idea of the darkness was that you'd be dancing with someone else's husband and your husband was across the room with the other man's wife.'[10] Much to his father King George's disgust, the Prince affected the transatlantic accent which was then a hallmark of the Bright Young People and the fashionable set generally, so it is interesting to note that the Chief Constable (who evidently did not move in these circles) remarked on Frances's 'odd' habit of speaking with something akin to an American accent too.

Marriages in which sexual relationships with outsiders were tolerated have been mentioned in the previous chapter – often known as 'open marriages' – and Frances plainly intended the Chief Constable to understand that she and Hugh Chevis had such an understanding, agreeing that although they were madly in love with one another, they were each also happy to let the other 'go their own way'. While the Chief Constable may have found such frankness disarming, most of Frances's social set would not have done, for similar arrangements and attitudes were commonplace among them.

Even popular culture dared to hint in this direction. In Daphne du Maurier's *Rebecca*, Mrs Van Hopper casually speculates about the infidelity of a visiting duchess to a mere acquaintance, while in Noel Coward's *Private Lives*, principal characters Elliot and Amanda race off to spend the night together with scant consideration to the fact that this entails them both in adultery, while his slightly later play, *Design For Living*, centres on a three-way love triangle between two men and one woman, with much swapping, or assumed swapping of partners.

For the most part the lower classes remained in blissful ignorance that such 'goings-on' were widespread. British newspapers were in general far more reticent than today and although 1930s editors were well aware of the Prince of Wales's private life, the existence of his various mistresses was not revealed to the general public until the impending Abdication Crisis left no alternative but to publicise his relationship with a certain American divorcee.

Unfortunately not every open marriage or adulterous relationship ended in laughter like that of Amanda and Elliot in *Private Lives*, and it was generally when things went wrong that the story broke to a wider audience. In 1941, the permissive elite of Kenya's Happy Valley Set made headlines when the Earl of Erroll was shot dead and the ensuing investigation and trial of the chief suspect (who was acquitted) exposed a world of drink, drugs and extra-marital affairs to the wider public. Perhaps more shocking to many than the murder itself was the fact that Sir Henry (known as Jock) Delves-Broughton and his wife Diana made no secret of the fact that she and the Earl of Erroll had been lovers, or that Sir Henry had been fully aware of it.

In the context of the circles in which she moved, and therefore by Frances's own standards, the fact that she had a 'flave' for another chap within a few months of her husband's death in no way detracted from her affection for him, and was not something she saw any need to conceal from the Chief Constable. For Frances, infidelity was most definitely not an issue which would lead to murder.

Trev Jackson was also described as a philanderer and this may well have been correct, but Frances too was engaged in at least one extra-marital relationship while married to him and it may be that here too was a marriage in which 'peccadilloes' were tolerated until one party actively wished to be free to marry another. The bottom line is that not only did Trev eventually let her go without a fight, he also appeared to remain on reasonably civil terms with the couple afterwards, pausing to chat when he bumped into them and keeping a rendezvous with Frances for 'Auld Lang Syne'.

It was a meeting which Frances had evidently forgotten when interviewed by the police, and the Surrey force's theory that Trev and Frances might have somehow contrived the death of Hugh Chevis together was undoubtedly fuelled by the discrepancies about how often, when and where these two ex-partners had actually seen one another. As well as the meetings mentioned by the two potential 'conspirators' themselves, other witnesses threw more petrol on the fire.

Peter de Havilland, another friend of Hugh Chevis, mentioned in his interview with the police that when he met them at a race meeting at Sandown, Hugh and Frances told him that they had just bumped into Major Jackson,[11] thereby providing yet another encounter between Frances and Trev which neither had mentioned to the police.

The obvious point about this was that Trev and Frances were inevitably liable to 'bump into' one another. Both frequented race meetings, point to points and polo matches. Both moved in overlapping social circles and stayed in the same fashionable hotels. The incestuous nature of their lives is well illustrated by the fact that Jack Gwynn-Jones told the police that he saw Frances with another man at the Metropole Hotel in Brighton – the self same establishment where it was alleged that Trev Jackson had committed adultery with Mrs Tomlins. If Major Jackson was not an habitué of the Savoy Grill Room and the London nightclub, he remained a keen fan of the turf and, like Frances, was drawn to the fashionable seaside towns of the south coast (Frances would eventually return to Eastbourne, buying a house there at some point during the Second World War, which she retained for nearly ten years).[12] Asked to recall how often they had met in recent months, neither could precisely recall off the top of their heads – but a faulty memory is not a hanging offence.

The strong contradiction between the attitude Trev displayed to his ex-wife during the investigation and hers to him may also provide an oblique pointer to Frances's innocence. While the Major was busily describing her as 'the best woman in the world', she was denouncing him to the police as every kind of scoundrel – yet at the same time, she was forced to admit that she had 'no right to accuse him'. It would be easy to dismiss the idea that an amicable relationship had existed between Trev and Frances after their divorce as no more than his bluster to the police and the Press, but this portrait of events does not depend solely on Trev Jackson. Inspector Sawkins of Eastbourne Police made 'discreet enquiries' about the Major at the very outset of the investigation, and learned from his sources that the couple appeared to have continued on good terms. While such enquiries were probably based on little more than gossip, when set alongside the various friendly encounters which had apparently taken place, it becomes apparent that apart from what Frances herself told the police, every other pointer was in favour of this continuing friendship.

The key to this discrepancy may lie in an abrupt change of mind on her part following Hugh Chevis's death, because, after initially believing that the whole thing had been an accident, Frances became convinced that someone had murdered Hugh, but try as she might she could think of no one who had any motive whatsoever apart from her ex-husband. This suspicion – however unjustified – may have transformed what had been until then a reasonably cordial relationship between the couple into something akin to hatred on her part. It is unlikely that there were any more requests to meet for 'Auld Lang Syne'.

The conviction that Hugh Chevis's death was no accident may have stemmed indirectly from the 'Hooray' telegram. Food standards and poison control eighty years ago were nothing like so stringent as today and while accidental deaths from poisoning were not exactly commonplace, they did occur, so that there was every justification for Frances to initially incline toward that theory – but after the arrival of the telegram and the ever increasing outcry, in her own words she was 'forced to believe' that her husband had been murdered. Sir William and Lady Amy were absolutely convinced – thanks to the telegram – that their son had fallen victim to a 'diabolical plot'. The police inquiry also appears to have stepped up with the arrival of the telegram, which briefly elevated the investigation into an international manhunt. It is possible to conjecture that without the telegram, the family might never have become convinced that a murder had been committed – 'Hartigan' undoubtedly had his revenge, inasmuch that his telegram may have had consequences for everyone which he had never foreseen.

Aside from Trev Jackson, the other possible accomplice (though apparently never considered as such by the police) was Ivy Thorne. Hired as a midwife, Nurse Thorne was still with the family several years later, but this was not particularly unusual since many families retained a nurse for the children until the youngest was settled in school, and in 1931 Peter Jackson was only four years old.

If Ivy was on occasion mistaken for a friend, rather than an employee, this may have been because she and Frances enjoyed an entirely platonic friendship. According to family members, Frances maintained a lifelong friendship with her own old governess[13] (who was not a great deal older than herself) and responsible, discreet Nurse Thorne may have provided welcome companionship and intelligent conversation on those occasions when Frances found herself at a loose end. (Ivy Thorne was a mere ten years older than her mistress.)[14]

Whatever the women's fondness or otherwise for each other, by 1939 Nurse Thorne was no longer part of Frances's household. In September that year she appears on the passenger list of the *Nieuw Amsterdam*, travelling with Lady Gladys Garthwaite and her two-year-old son, Michael.[15] According to the records all three were intending to take up permanent residence in Canada, and the ship sailed for New York on 18 September. In all likelihood Lady Garthwaite's intention was to take her son to safety in Canada for the duration of the war, and she did not remain there permanently, eventually maintaining homes in London, Monte Carlo, Paris and Nassau. In Lady Garthwaite, Nurse Thorne may have found another employer who valued discretion. Gladys Galie, formerly Hardy, was the fourth wife of Sir William Garthwaite, a millionaire underwriter and ship owner some twenty years her senior. The couple had married in February 1937, the moment his divorce from wife number three became absolute, and their son was born just five months later. Lady Garthwaite enjoyed a jet-set lifestyle, her activities sometimes featuring in the gossip columns well into the 1960s.[16]

The further career of Nurse Thorne is unknown and the present author has been unable to establish whether she remained in Canada, journeyed on elsewhere, or ultimately returned to Britain. When Ivy Blanche Thorne set sail from Southampton in 1939 she vanishes from the story, her ultimate fate and destination unknown.

Aside from one anonymous letter and one ambiguous note in the police files, there is no real evidence that Frances and Ivy were particularly close, and nothing to say that they enjoyed anything other than a normal employer/employee relationship. Surviving members of the family have no recollection of Miss Thorne, so it appears that Frances did not maintain contact with her – something she might have felt an expedient precaution if her children's nurse had really been complicit in a capital offence.

At one point the Chief Constable noted that he thought Frances Chevis quite clever enough to have committed the murder.[17] As it stands this is a statement with which the present author would have no argument – but was this really such a clever murder at all? The smallest amount of research ought to have suggested to Frances (or any other would-be assassin) that strychnine was hardly the ideal method, given its obvious symptoms and easy traceability. In a domestic case it is inevitable that suspicion will fall on other members of the household. Might not arsenic – easily available and widely believed to be much harder to trace – have served the purpose better?

And were the partridges really the most convenient vehicle for the strychnine – would not coffee, sherry, or gin have served her better and been potentially easier to adulterate? A decision to place strychnine in one of the partridges would have been tremendously risky, since the mistress of the house had no way of knowing in advance that the two partridges she had ordered could be easily differentiated on account of their size. It is also difficult to see why a guilty Frances would have bothered to point this difference out to the investigators – surely it would have served her better to have suggested that it was difficult to tell one bird from another?

Frances also stressed to the police the difficulty any outsider would have had in getting at the birds while they were in the meat safe, mentioning that the dog would surely have given the alarm. Again this hardly seems the best way of detracting suspicion from herself. Her own illness also points to her innocence since even taking a minute amount of poison in order to deflect suspicion was both melodramatic and potentially dangerous. Quite aside from a natural reluctance to put one's self at risk, Frances had a particular reason to eschew poison, because at the time of Hugh Chevis's death she believed herself to be pregnant.[18] Frances informed the police at an early stage in the investigation that she thought she was pregnant, and subsequently that she believed she had suffered a miscarriage. The month of conception was estimated as May – all of which makes it even less likely that she would have chosen to deliberately endanger her health, when there was no need to do so. (Those of a particularly suspicious disposition may doubt the reality of the pregnancy and assume it was just one more lie, intended to elicit sympathy from an otherwise hostile police force, but again there seems no particular reason to disbelieve Frances on the point.)

The case against Frances is that she pulled off a 'perfect murder' with some diabolically clever play acting. Was Frances an extremely clever actress? If so then it was a virtuoso performance, played to extremes and maintained for her entire life. Essentially there is no evidence against her worthy of the name. No evidence that she ever obtained or handled poison, no evidence that she tampered with her husband's food, no evidence that she wanted him dead. Had Ryffel not bungled his tests, a positive result for strychnine in Frances's vomit would have provided powerful evidence in her defence. Had the police or coroner asked for clarification regarding the timings of *both* the telephone calls to Basil Mansions on the evening of the poisoning, an apparent discrepancy would have been resolved. Had Hugh Chevis burned the love letters from his various paramours, there would never have been a 'motive' in the first place.

Strange as it may seem to those whose relationships are more conventional, all the supporting evidence available suggests that Frances spoke the truth when she told the Chief Constable she was 'very much in love' with Hugh, in spite of their both having affairs with other people. The servants were quizzed repeatedly on the subject of relations between their employers and consistently stated that Lieutenant and Mrs Chevis had appeared very happy. This was the opinion of their friends too – even Lieutenant Gwynn-Jones who did not like Frances, did not suggest that the marriage had proved unsuccessful, or that either party would be likely to do the other any injury. Neither the Bowsers, who had called in for cocktails, nor the servants observed any tensions or sharp words on the night of Hugh Chevis's fatal illness, while Dr Bindloss told the police that the couple displayed the greatest affection and concern for one another, even when severely affected by the strychnine, calling each other 'Darling this and Darling That'.[19] Surviving family memories from 1931 are understandably hazy, but Frances's daughters recalled the brief period of their mother's marriage to Hugh Chevis as enormously happy. The young Lieutenant is remembered arriving home to play noisy games in the nursery, setting everything upside down, until he had to be admonished amid much laughter by their Nanny (presumably this was Nurse Thorne).[20]

It is equally interesting to note that while the Chevis family became convinced that Hugh had lost his life to foul play, there is never the slightest suggestion that any of them suspected Frances could have been responsible. Frances Jackson was undoubtedly not the daughter-in-law Sir William and Lady Chevis would have hoped for. She was a woman with a 'past'. There would be no white wedding with full dress uniforms and a photograph appearing in *The Times*, as had been the case when older brother William wed Miss Rita Wilson in 1924.[21] Yet when considering possible suspects, the older Chevises continued to believe in weird conspiracies which emanated from across the Irish Sea and never once breathed a word against their daughter-in-law, which surely suggests that they too thought the marriage a happy one. It was essentially only outsiders, both at the time and afterwards, who pointed a finger at Frances.

The phrase 'Poor Little Rich Girl' came into common parlance before the Great War[22] and it would later be applied to various heiresses whose private (and sometimes public) lives were touched by tragedy – most notably Barbara Hutton, the seven-times married Woolworth heiress. While the life of Frances Rollason Jackson Chevis Braham Bicket Rayson cannot be described as a tragedy, Frances suffered similar tribulations. After an unhappy, unloved childhood she made a series of marriages which, while bringing periods of happiness, were never destined to provide the lifelong love and support she so obviously craved. Finding the right man and marrying him may have become a kind of Holy Grail for Frances. During her interview with the Chief Constable, he noted that having achieved a 'state of bliss' during her marriage to Lieutenant Chevis, Frances's principal desire in life now was to find the right man and settle down with him.[23] More than anything she said, she wanted a happy married life. There is a terrible sadness about her response to the Chief Constable's question in September 1931: 'What is your real outlook at the moment?'

'Anything to be happy,' Frances replied. 'I was happy then.'

It is easy to envy the idle rich their privileged lifestyle of non-stop parties, but throughout the 1920s and '30s a sense of futility and even despair often lurked just below the veneer of glamour. In the midst of the dancing, the laughter, the practical jokes, flirtations and affairs there often lay a sense of pointlessness – what was it all *for*? This duality is brilliantly captured in Noel Coward's popular song of the era, *I Went to a Marvellous Party* (which is said to have been inspired by a series of parties which Coward himself attended on the French Riviera during the 1930s). On the one hand the lyrics hint at sexual shenanigans and unbridled fun of all kinds, but on the other it is clear that there is a wearisome sameliness in everyone drinking too much, behaving outrageously and 'enjoying' the constant frantic pursuit of fun for its own sake. In her interview with the Chief Constable, Frances candidly admitted that while she had found life married to an army officer a little dull at first, particularly while the couple were staying in a Farnborough hotel, that soon wore off and she had been 'glad to have finished with her former life.'

While some escaped unscathed, the rackety lifestyle would claim numerous victims. Marriages contracted by the smartest social set had the highest failure rate, accompanied by consequent levels of distress; others fell victim to different hazards, including financial ruin, court appearances for everything from motoring offences and affray, to drug trafficking, common assault or even murder – as in the cases of Elvira Barney and Sir Henry Delves Broughton – or terminal alcohol (and occasionally drug) addiction.[24] Frances survived the excesses of the era, but during the course of her life she faced widowhood, three divorces and the tragic early loss of her eldest son.[25] At the very end of her life she was still seeking that elusive state of happy matrimony which she believed she had once found with Hugh Chevis. She had been the girl who had everything – wealth, looks, popularity – all of which made it dangerously easy for the outside world to envy her and for that envy to transform into dislike and suspicion.

To the end of her days, Frances always insisted that Hugh Chevis was the love of her life. The present author is inclined to believe her.

NOTES ON THE TEXT

The following frequently used references will be found in abbreviated form in the notes below:

Coroners Papers: 631/1/Box 14 Death of Hubert George Chevis. Surrey History Centre. Files held by Surrey Police respecting the death of Hubert George Chevis.

Chapter 1

1 Statement of Elwin Charles Evered, 12 July 1931 & statement of Arthur Paling Slater, 12 July 1931. 631/1/Box 14.
2 Orwell's essay was first published in *Tribune*, 15 February 1946 and has since been widely reproduced.
3 See Diane Janes, *Poisonous Lies: The Croydon Arsenic Mystery* (The History Press, Stroud, Gloucestershire, 2010).

Chapter 2

1 For supporting information on strychnine poisoning see John Harris Trestrail, *Criminal Poisoning: Investigational guide for law enforcement, toxicologists, forensic scientists & attorneys* (Humana Press, New Jersey, 2007) and R. Sarvesvaran, *Strychnine Poisoning: A Case Report* (University of Malaya, 1992).
2 For an account of the Reilly trial see *The Irish Times*, 6, 7, 8 August 1925 & 19 & 27 March 1926. For the Sandford case see *The Times*, 14 May & 2-4 June 1938.
3 MEPO 3/791 Execution of Mrs Ethel Lillie Major for murder of her husband. National Archives.
4 *The Times*, 5, 6, 7, 8 February & 12 March 1917.
5 *The Times*, 27 October 1925.
6 *The Times*, 24 June & 15 July 1920.
7 This account of the Jones murder derives from the Surrey Police website and *The Times* where the trial and appeal were reported throughout May-August 1924.
8 *The Times*, 21 May 1926 and *Hampstead & Highgate Express*, 10 April, 15 & 22 May 1926.
9 *The Times*, 23 June, 1 & 22 July 1921.

Chapter 3

1   The account of the evening's events which appears in this chapter relies on statement of Philip Randolph Bowser, 12 July 1931, statement of Frances Howard Chevis, 1 July 1931, statement of Ellen Yeomans, 21 June 1931, statement of Edmund Frederick Bindloss, 21 June 1931, statement of Nicholas Bolger, 21 June 1931, statement of Nicholas Bolger, 23 June 1931, statement of Edmund Frederick Bindloss, 23 June 1931, statement of Ellen Yeomans, 23 June 1931, statement of Frances Howard Chevis, 20 July 1931 & undated deposition of Cuthbert Hastings Attenborough. 631/1/Box 14.

2   The military term for installing a new guard and relieving the old one.

3   At the inquest on 11 August 1931 it was established that the 'furnace' was an Ideal Boiler, specifically designed to consume refuse. Statement of Nicholas Bolger, 11 August 1931. 631/1/Box 14.

4   Statement of Frances Howard Chevis, 1 July 1931. 631/1/Box 14.

5   In which the muscles become rigid.

6   'The Hut' was the name of the bungalow, which was very far from being 'a hut' in the accepted sense, since it had a drawing room, dining room, kitchen, separate scullery, larder, two bedrooms, a dressing room, bathroom and a maid's room. A description of the bungalow appears in statement of Nicholas Bolger, 23 June 1931. 631/1/Box 14.

7   Frimley Cottage Hospital is described in *The British Journal of Nursing* 15 July 1916 and photographs of the building in the 1920s can be found on the internet.

8   Statement of Albert William Pharo, 21 June 1931 & deposition of Ivy Blanche Thorne, 11 August 1931. 631/1/Box 14

Chapter 4

1   In 2012, Frances's grandson told the author that his grandmother had been acquainted with Rudolph Valentino. Frances also numbered Clementine Churchill (wife of Prime Minister Sir Winston) and Stella, Lady Reading, founder of the Women's Royal Voluntary Service, among her acquaintances. She is said to have 'known everyone who was anyone'.

2   The information on the Howard family which appears in this chapter has been collated from diverse sources including the General Register Office of England records of Births, Deaths and Marriages; the Calendar of Wills held by the Principal Probate Registry, census records held by the National Archives, David J. Jeremy & Christine Shaw, *Dictionary of Business Biography Vol. 3* (Butterworth, London, 1985), *Walford's County Families of the United Kingdom* (Spottiswoode, Ballantyne & Co. Ltd, London, 1920), *Who Was Who 1897–1915* (AC Black, London, 1920) and *Graces Guide-British Industry* @www.gracesguide.co.uk.

3   The information on the Rollason family which appears in this chapter has been collated from diverse sources including the General Register Office of England records of Births, Deaths and Marriages; the Calendar of Wills held by the Principal Probate Registry, census records held by the National Archives, street and telephone directories, *Kelly's Handbook to the Titled, Landed & Official Classes 1946* (Kelly Directories Ltd, London, 1946) and Stephens W.B.: *A History of the County of Warwick Vol. 7* (Victoria County History, London, 1964).

4   Birmingham did not officially gain city status until 1889, though its population had outstripped those of numerous other British cities well before that date.

5   The Rollason business empire traded under a variety of names as it altered and expanded operations, including Rollason Wire Co. Ltd, and Benjamin Rollason & Sons, etc.

6 The story of Kate and Frank's marriage was told to the author by Charles Jackson, great-grandson of the couple, in 2012.

7 Lawrence Officer & Samuel Williamson, *Five Ways to Compute the Relative Value of the UK Pound 1830 to the Present Day* (www.measuringworth.com)

8 According to widely accepted formulas Frank's estate was worth only £16m if calculated against the Retail Price Index of the day, but up to as much as £150m based on share of Gross Domestic Product – a comparison with average earnings puts the total at around £66m.

9 In 2012, Kate's great-grandson, Charles Jackson, generously shared his own childhood memories of Kate and other family stories about her with the author.

10 Douglas Frederick Howard was awarded the Military Cross for service in the First World War. After the war he joined the Diplomatic Service and rose steadily through the ranks, becoming British Ambassador in Uruguay 1949-53 and Minister to the Holy See 1953-57. He was appointed CMG in 1944 and received a knighthood in 1953.

Chapter 5

1 Information on the Jackson family which appears in this chapter has been collated from diverse sources including the General Register Office of England records of Births, Deaths and Marriages; the Calendar of Wills held by the Principal Probate Registry and census records held by the National Archives.

2 Information on Morecambe has been derived from a variety of Lancashire guides and histories, and images of Morecambe in its heyday are readily available on the internet.

3 Details of George Jackson's professional and military career have been derived from census records held by the National Archives, the Register of Veterinary Surgeons Vols 1900-35, *Journal of the Royal Army Veterinary Corps* Vol. VI no.2, *The Veterinary Record* Vols 1899-1918, *The RAVC Journal* Vol. I, British Army Medal Rolls and the British Army Lists 1899-1919.

4 *The Veterinary Record*, 25 August 1900.

5 Audrey Trevelyan Jackson plays no part in this story and her fate was unknown to the descendants of her stepbrothers and sisters until recently, when it was established that after the deaths of both her parents she emigrated to South Africa, where she married Arthur Leslie Bennett on 1 March 1938.

6 *The Veterinary Record*, 26 October 1918.

7 Register of Veterinary Surgeons 1923.

8 *Kelly's Directory for Eastbourne 1924* (Kelly Directories Ltd, London 1924).

9 Details of the Jackson's separation and divorce cited in this chapter and Mabel Jackson's letter dated 4 February 1922 derive from J77/1878/08675 Jackson v. Jackson. National Archives.

Chapter 6

1 Birth certificate of Elizabeth Boden. General Register Office of England records of Births.

2 As told to the author in 2012.

3 Details of the divorce of George T.T. and Frances H. Jackson which appear in this chapter derive from J77/2551/9375 Jackson v. Jackson. National Archives.

4 *The Times*, 3 December 1949.

5 Aschheim and Zondek produced the first bioassay pregnancy test in 1928.

6 Details of the separation and divorce between George T.T. and Mabel Jackson which appear in this chapter derive from J77/1878/08675 Jackson v. Jackson. National Archives.

7 This was not only recalled by Charles Jackson, Frances's grandson, in 2012, but is also borne out by photographs and interviews in various newspapers at the time of Hugh Chevis's death.

8 Mabel married John B. Anderson in Chelsea between October and December 1923. General Register Office of England records of Marriages.

9 Mabel Anderson's will was administered by Stanley Jackson Rhodes, the son of George Jackson's older sister Annie Rhodes (*née* Jackson). Stanley Rhodes also acted as an executor for his Uncle George.

10 Details of Frances and Major Jackson's life together cited in this chapter have been derived from General Register Office of England records of Births, Deaths and Marriages, J77/2551/9375 Jackson v. Jackson, National Archives, the Register of Veterinary Surgeons Vols 1922–28, *The Royal Army Veterinary Corps Journal* Vols 1 & 6, and various statements made by both Frances Chevis and Major G.T.T. Jackson contained in 631/1/Box 14 and Surrey Police Files.

11 *The Royal Army Veterinary Corps Journal* Vol. VI No.2, p. 82.

12 Statements made by various witnesses including Frances Chevis and Major G.T.T. Jackson all agree that Hugh Chevis initially met the Jacksons 'about five years' before his death in 1931. Major Jackson specifies that their original meeting occurred in 1926 in an undated statement to the police. Surrey Police Files.

Chapter 7

1 Details of the Chevis family cited in this chapter derive from census records held by the National Archives, General Register Office of England records of Births, Deaths and Marriages, parish records of Meerut Bengal, parish registers of Delhi, Christie's Catalogue September 2001, *Who Was Who 1929-40* (AC Black, London, 1941), *Bournemouth Daily Echo*, 22 June 1931 and private family papers in the care of Major William Chevis.

2 This was the unanimous opinion of everyone questioned on the point during the police inquiry. Surrey Police Files.

3 Statement of Dorothy Rose Felicia Heap, 5 August 1931 & statement of George Tweedale Heap, 8 August 1931. Surrey Police Files.

4 Undated statement of George Thompson Trevelyan Jackson. Surrey Police Files.

5 A.P. Herbert, *Holy Deadlock* (Methuen, London, 1934).

6 Unless otherwise stated details of the divorce cited in this chapter derive from J77/2551/9375 Jackson v. Jackson. National Archives.

7 Undated statement of George Thompson Trevelyan Jackson. Surrey Police Files.

8 This is inferred by reference to successive issues of *Mates Bournemouth & Poole Directory & Yearbook* and successive Electoral Rolls for Christchurch Road Bournemouth. It is, however, impossible to be absolutely certain that Miss Bradley actually occupied the flat, because unmarried women who had not attained the age of thirty did not appear on the electoral register before 1929 and only the head of household was listed in the directory.

9 Details of the Granger family which appear in this chapter are derived from General Register Office of England records of Births, Deaths and Marriages, Bournemouth Electoral Roll 1928 and *Bournemouth Echo*, 15 March 1960.

10 Mabel Palmer was also a woman of means. When she died in 1926 she left £38,568 10s 9d. 1926 Calendar of Wills, Principal Probate Registry.

11 A sum worth roughly £80,000 today, based on Lawrence Officer & Samuel Williamson: *Five Ways to Compute the Relative Value of the UK Pound 1830 to the Present Day.* www.measuringworth.com

12 Report of Albert William Pharo, 5 August 1931. Surrey Police Files.

13 *Bournemouth Echo,* 15 March 1960.

14 Bournemouth Electoral Rolls 1928-36.

15 Hugh Chevis's movements are confirmed in various witness statements.

Chapter 8

1 Numerous such references appear in *The Times* and other local and national newspapers.

2 Advertisements for Phyllosan appeared regularly in British daily newspapers. In 1931 they had yet to coin their catchphrase 'Phyllosan Fortifies the Over Forties'.

3 *The Times,* 7 April 1923.

4 *The Times,* 19 February 1918 & 22 June 1918.

5 *The Times,* 17 March 1916.

6 These were the Artle children of Wakefield – all under 5 years old. *The Times,* 4 March 1901 & 7 March 1901, and General Register Office of England record of Deaths.

7 *The Times,* 18-19 May 1922.

8 *The Times,* 8 November 1909.

9 *The Irish Times,* 8 January 1928.

10 *The Times,* 4 March 1921.

11 Two such cases came before the London courts in August 1920 alone and were reported in *The Times,* 10 August 1920 & 16 August 1920, when William Trigg and Charles Slater respectively were jailed. Other instances were numerous.

12 Agatha Christie, *Cards on the Table* (Collins, London, 1936).

13 Among the numerous reports of strychnine being among the drugs taken from doctors' cars in the London area alone, were thefts from Dr Robinson, *The Times,* 27 November 1927, Dr McKenzie, *The Times,* 8 August 1928, Dr Gorsky, *The Times,* 5 January 1929 and Dr Wetherbee, *The Times,* 16 February 1929.

14 Strychnine could be purchased legally over the counter, but the purchaser was required to sign the Poisons Book and inform the chemist of his/her reasons for requiring the drug.

15 *The Times,* 23 July 1953.

16 *The Times,* 1 July 1983.

17 *The Times,* 21 March 1968.

18 Pharo's background and length of service have been confirmed with reference to General Register Office of England records of Births, Deaths and Marriages and the 1911 census.

19 The account of Pharo's actions on 21 June 1931 given in this chapter derives from two reports made by Albert William Pharo, one undated and one dated 21 June 1931. Surrey Police Files.

20 The account of the inquest in this chapter derives from notes of evidence taken on 23 June 1931, 631/1/Box 14, *The Times,* 24 June 1931 and *The Surrey Advertiser & Co. Times,* 27 June 1931. The name of the company which provided the partridges is spelled in a variety of ways throughout the police and coroner's files – I have rendered it throughout as Colebrooks for the sake of consistency.

21 Details of William Chevis's family given in this chapter derive from General Register Office of England records of Births, Deaths and Marriages and statement of William James Christian Chevis, 23 June 1931, 631/1/Box 14.

22 Details regarding Ellen Yeomans given in this chapter derive from General Register Office of England records of Births, Deaths and Marriages, census records and 631/1/Box 14.

23 Captain Chevis's son – Major William Chevis – told the author in 2012 that it was his father who made the funeral arrangements (which appears to be borne out by the coroner's files) and that the gun carriage was drawn by greys. Hugh Chevis lies in plot AG465, Register of Burials Aldershot Garrison. The grave was dug with sufficient room for two internments, although Hugh Chevis remains the only occupant.

24 In many upper and middle-class Victorian families it was accepted that women did not attend funerals, and while this attitude had largely died out during the twentieth century, Lady Chevis may have been observing this protocol.

25 Statement of William James Christian Chevis, 29 June 1931. 631/1/Box 14.

Chapter 9

1 Statement of William James Christian Chevis, 29 June 1931, 631/1/Box 14 and various notes and reports in Surrey Police Files.

2 Undated report of Albert William Pharo. 631/1/Box 14.

3 Statement of Charles John Tyler, 22 June 1931, 631/1/Box 14 & Report of F.R. Seymour, 3 July 1931, Surrey Police Files.

4 Statement of William Frank Noyes, 14 July 1931. 631/1/Box 14.

5 Personal details regarding Superintendent James Stovell derive from General Register Office of England records of Births, Deaths and Marriages and Surrey Police Records.

6 Josephine Tey, *A Shilling for Candles* (Methuen, London, 1937).

7 Juliet Gardiner, *The Thirties: An Intimate History* p. 443 (Harper Collins, London, 2010). The case of Sir Alfred Newton's widow cited in Chapter 8 provides another example – a working-class wife in similar circumstances would certainly have been required to attend the inquest and give evidence.

8 Statement of Frances Howard Chevis, 1 July 1931. 631/1/Box 14.

9 Coroner's annotations to statement of Frances Howard Chevis, 1 July 1931. 631/1/Box 14.

10 Undated report of Albert William Pharo. 631/1/Box 14.

11 *The Irish Times*, 7 August 1925.

12 MEPO 3/791 Execution of Mrs Ethel Lillie Major for murder of her husband. National Archives.

13 Statement of Arthur Paling Slater, 12 July 1931. 631/1/Box 14.

14 Letter from William Million, 12 July 1931. 631/1/Box 14.

15 Letters from W.J. Francis, 16 & 18 July and John Henry Ryffel, 17 July 1931. 631/1/Box 14.

16 According to Gfeller, Roger W. & Messonnier, Shawn P., *Handbook of Small Animal Toxicology* (Mosby Inc., St Louis Missouri, 1998), p. 25 'Seizures remain one of the most common complications resulting from poisoning [in dogs]'. This is confirmed by Peterson, Michael E. & Talcott, Patricia A., *Small Animal Toxicology*, (Elsevier Saunders, St Louis Missouri, 2006) and Poppenga, Robert H. & Gwaltney-Brant, Sharon M., *Small Animal Toxicology Essentials* (Wiley Blackman, Chichester Sussex, 2011). Further information provided in this chapter with regard to the poisoning of the dog is also confirmed in all these publications.

17 Peterson, Michael E. & Talcott, Patricia A., *Small Animal Toxicolgy* (Elsevier Saunders, St Louis Missouri, 2006), p. 1080.

18 Statement of Elwin Charles Evered, 12 July 1931. 631/1/Box 14.

19 Undated, unattributed report (whose contents clearly date it to early July 1931), report of Albert William Pharo, 16 July 931 and statement of Nicholas Bolger, 21 August 1931, Surrey Police Files and General Register Office of England records of Births, Deaths and Marriages.

20 Undated, unattributed report (whose contents clearly date it to early July 1931). Surrey Police Files.

21 Report of Albert William Pharo, 16 July 1931. 631/1/Box 14.

22 Letter from John Henry Ryffel, 7 July 1931. 631/1/Box 14.

23 Letter from W.J. Francis, 9 July 1931 and letter from Cullen Mather, 25 June 1931. 631/1/Box 14.

24 For a more thorough discussion on these issues the reader is recommended to read Diane Janes, *Poisonous Lies: The Croydon Arsenic Mystery* (The History Press, Stroud, Gloucestershire, 2010).

25 One grain is equal to 64.7 milligrams.

26 Letter from John Henry Ryffel, 14 July 1931. 631/1/Box 14.

27 Letter from W.J. Francis, 16 July 1931. 631/1/Box 14.

28 Letter from John Henry Ryffel, 17 July 1931. 631/1/Box 14.

29 Report of John Henry Ryffel, 20 July 1931. 631/1/Box 14.

30 All copies of the police exhibit list use this description, 631/1/Box 14 and Surrey Police Files.

31 A diagram of the meat safe, together with its location and exact dimensions can be found in Surrey Police Files.

32 Report of Albert William Pharo, 18 July 1931. 631/1/Box 14.

33 Letter from the General Post Office of England and Wales, 17 July 1931. 631/1/Box 14.

34 Letter from W.J. Francis, 21 July 1931. 631/1/Box 14.

Chapter 10

1 Details of the inquest which appear in this chapter derive from Notes of Hearing, 20 [*sic*] July 1931, 631/1/Box 14 unless otherwise stated.

2 The nature of this operation and whether it went ahead is unknown, but it can only be assumed that it was something of a very minor nature, as Frances had elected to be elsewhere.

3 *Surrey Advertiser & County Times*, 27 June 1931.

4 The items mentioned all appeared on the front page of the *London Evening News*, 22 June 1931 and are representative of the contents of other newspapers that day.

5 *Bournemouth Daily Echo*, 22 June 1931.

6 The sudden deaths of army officers, whether in a motor accident or a fall from a window, invariably merited a paragraph in the national newspapers at this time.

7 For a classic example of inappropriately close relations between police and press during the period, readers are directed to Diane Janes, *Poisonous Lies: The Croydon Arsenic Mystery* (The History Press, Stroud, Gloucestershire, 2010).

8 *Surrey Advertiser & County Times*, 27 June 1931. The separate forces in Guildford and Reigate were not in fact incorporated into Surrey Police until 1943.

9 *Surrey Advertiser & County Times*, 27 June 1931.

10 *Surrey Advertiser & County Times*, 25 July 1931.

11 Arthur James Faraday Salvage was convicted of the murder and executed.

12 The murder of Louisa Steele in Blackheath in 1930 remains unsolved, but has been linked to Arthur Salvage.

13   Pharo's report dated 18 July 1931 confirms for the benefit of the coroner that only the aforementioned people were aware of the telegram's existence and that they had been warned not to say anything. 631/1/Box 14.

14   Letter from W.J. Francis, 27 July 1931. 631/1/Box 14.

15   Letter from W.J. Francis, 27 July 1931. 631/1/Box 14.

16   Letter from Director of Public Prosecutions, 31 August 1931. 631/1/Box 14.

17   Letter from William James Christian Chevis, 4 August 1931. 631/1/Box 14.

18   Sir Ernley Blackwell was then Legal Under Secretary of State at the Home Office.

19   Letter from W.J. Francis, 5 August 1931. 631/1/Box 14.

20   Letter from Ford, Lloyd, Bartlett & Mitchelmore, 29 July 1931. 631/1/Box 14.

21   Letter from William James Christian Chevis, 6 August 1931. 631/1/Box 14.

22   Letter from Ford, Lloyd, Bartlett & Mitchelmore, 6 August 1931. 631/1/Box 14.

23   The Big Five was the popular nickname for Scotland Yard's top quintet of officers.

24   Letter from W.J. Francis, 7 August 1931. 631/1/Box 14.

25   Letter from Sir William Chevis, 5 August 1931. 631/1/Box 14.

26   Letter from Sir William Chevis, 7 August 1931. 631/1/Box 14.

27   Letter from W.J. Francis, 8 August 1931. 631/1/Box 14.

28   Letter from Sir William Chevis, 10 August 1931. 631/1/Box 14.

29   Letter from William Henry Bird, 13 August 1931. Surrey Police Files.

30   *Surrey Advertiser & County Times*, 11 July 1931.

31   Letter from William Henry Bird, 7 August 1931. Surrey Police Files.

32   Letter from Geoffrey Nicholson, 8 August 1931. Surrey Police Files.

33   Letter from William Henry Bird, 13 August 1931. Surrey Police Files.

34   For a fuller discussion of the phenomena see H. Brown, *The Sahibs* (London 1948), p. 1267.

35   These family memories were shared with the author in 2012.

36   The *Daily Sketch* was among the papers who managed to obtain a quote for their Monday morning edition. *Daily Sketch*, 27 July 1931.

Chapter 11

1   Report of Ernest Sawkins, 21 July 1931. 631/1/Box 14.

2   Mrs Lawrence lived at 5a De Roos Avenue, but listed Willingdon Golf Club as an alternate address in the Eastbourne street directories. She was listed in the 'Court' section, where the names of the towns grandest citizens lived. In July 1931 she took the prize for the Willingdon Golf Club Ladies League Second Division. (*Eastbourne Chronicle*, July 1931.) No Mr Lawrence was listed at 5a De Roos Avenue in any of the years that Mrs Lawrence lived there, which suggests that the couple lived permanently apart, or were divorced – for which 'living abroad' may have been a socially acceptable cover. It would therefore be wrong to automatically assume that Trev Jackson was carrying on with another man's wife.

3   Mabel Anderson died suddenly on 15 May 1926 (after an operation). Calendar of Wills & *The Times*, 17 May 1926.

4   Memo dated 26 July 1931. 631/1/Box 14.

5   Andrew Rose, *Lethal Witness* (Sutton Publishing, Stroud, Gloucestershire, 2007), p. 223. Mrs Barney was charged with the murder of Thomas William Scott Stephen, but the jury accepted Sir Patrick Hastings defence that she had discharged the gun accidentally.

6   Letter from Ernest Sawkins, 27 July 1931. Surrey Police Files.

7   Statement of George Thompson Trevelyan Jackson, 27 July 1931. Surrey Police Files.
8   Kate Rollason had moved to Hove by November 1930, as is evidenced by her
    disappearance from Eastbourne Directories after 1927, the announcement of her
    daughter's marriage in 1930 which listed Kate as 'of Hove' and Ellen Yeomans's
    informing a press reporter in 1931 that Mrs Chevis's mother lived in Hove.
9   Statement of George Thompson Trevelyan Jackson, 27 July 1931 and Memo dated
    26 July 1931. Surrey Police Files.

Chapter 12

1   Report of Albert William Pharo, 21 June 1931. 631/1/Box 14.
2   Letter from W.J. Francis, 9 July 1931. 631/1/Box 14.
3   Letter from W.J. Francis, 4 August 1931. 631/1/Box 14.
4   Diane Janes, *Poisonous Lies: The Croydon Arsenic Mystery* (The History Press, Stroud,
    Gloucestershire, 2010), p. 177.
5   Letter from John Henry Ryffel, 6 August 1931. 631/1/Box 14.
6   Letter from W.J. Francis, 7 August 1931. 631/1/Box 14.
7   An emetic is a means by which the patient will be made to vomit.
8   Letter from W.J. Francis, 9 August 1931. 631/1/Box 14.
9   Presumably this is Harvey Cushing's *Consecratio Medico & other papers*.
10 Letter from John Henry Ryffel, 10 August 1931. 631/1/Box 14.
11 Letter from W.J. Francis, 9 August 1931. 631/1/Box 14.
12 Letter from John Henry Ryffel, 10 August 1931. 631/1/Box 14.
13 This is confirmed in Mr Francis's letter to Ryffel dated 9 August.
14 Letter from Edmund Bindloss, 10 August 1931. 631/1/Box 14.
15 Dr John Ryffel's career coincided with that of Dr Roche Lynch, who having been
    appointed Senior Home Office Analyst, remained in post for more than thirty years.
16 Report of Albert William Pharo, 23 July 1931. Surrey Police Files.
17 The two forces did not merge until 1966.
18 Letter from James Stovell, 28 July 1931 & letter from Northampton Constabulary,
    29 July 1931. Surrey Police Files.
19 Report of G.W. Brumby, 31 July 1931. Surrey Police Files.
20 They played on Mrs Snell's team – it has not been possible to identify Mrs Snell,
    but this was presumably a cricket match organised at someone's country house, with
    teams of friends and guests competing against one another, and enjoying afternoon tea
    together at the end of the match.
21 Letter from James Stovell, 30 July 1931. Surrey Police Files.
22 Letters from James Stovell, 17 & 23 July 1931. Surrey Police Files. In 1931, Ireland had
    not long been an independent nation and as a result many of their regulations, such as
    the procedure for the sale of poisonous substances, were similar or identical to those in
    England.
23 Report of J. Kinsella, report of Superintendent Brennan, report of Malachey Doddy, all
    dated 28 July 1931. Surrey Police Files.
24 Report of Malachey Doddy, 28 July 1931 and letter from W.R.E. Murphy, 8 August
    1931. Surrey Police Files.
25 Report of Malachey Doddy, 28 July 1931. Surrey Police Files.
26 Letter from J.H. Harrington, 5 August 1931, Surrey Police Files and Memo dated
    26 July 1931, 631/1/Box 14.
27 Report of Michael Heraty, 29 July 1931. Surrey Police Files.

28 Undated report of Superintendent Brennan, by inference written 28 July 1931. Surrey Police Files.

29 Statement of E.H. Milmoe, 6 August 1931. Surrey Police Files.

30 For example the lengthy interview which appeared in *The Daily Mail*, 27 July 1931.

31 Letter from W.R.E. Murphy, 13 August 1931. Surrey Police Files.

32 Report of Malachey Doddy, 24 August 1931. Surrey Police Files.

33 Letter from Buckinghamshire Constabulary, 29 July 1931. Surrey Police Files.

34 Details of George and Dorothy Heap's background and family which appear in this chapter derive from General Register Office of England records of Births, Deaths and Marriages, census records, *The London Gazette*, 31 May 1921, and Surrey Police Files.

35 Statement of Dorothy Rose Felicia Heap, 5 August 1931. Surrey Police Files.

36 Statement of George Tweedale Heap, 8 August 1931. Surrey Police Files.

37 Report of Albert William Pharo, 8 August 1931. Surrey Police Files.

38 Undated notes of James Stovell. Surrey Police Files.

39 Details of John Milligan Blair's background which appear in this chapter derive from General Register Office of England records of Births, Deaths and Marriages, J77/2488/7558 Margaret Kirk Blair v. John Milligan Blair and Statement of John Milligan Blair, 7 August 1931. Surrey Police Files.

40 Statement of John Milligan Blair, 7 August 1931. Surrey Police Files.

41 Statement of Jack Llewellyn Gwynn-Jones, 10 August 1931. Surrey Police Files.

42 Report of Albert William Pharo, 10 August 1931. Surrey Police Files.

43 Details of Iris Coates's life, background and relationship with Hugh Chevis which appear in this chapter derive from General Register Office of England records of Births, Deaths and Marriages, *The Oxford Dictionary of National Biography 2004* and statement of Iris Coates, 10 August 1931, Surrey Police Files.

Chapter 13

1 The letter from W.C. Gay and all other correspondence mentioned in this chapter can be found in 631/1/Box 14 or Surrey Police Files.

2 Reports from Scotland Yard, 29 & 24 July 1931. Surrey Police Files.

3 Stovell is thus quoted in *Bournemouth Daily Echo*, 3 August 1931 – from the timing and context of this remark, it is clear with the benefit of hindsight that he was referring to the postcard.

4 *Daily Express*, 24 & 25 July 1931.

5 Letter from Roche Lynch, 10 August 1931. 631/1/Box 14.

6 *Daily Sketch*, 25 July 1931.

7 *Daily Sketch*, 24 July 1931. Similar incidents were appearing regularly in the newspapers e.g. *Dublin Evening Herald*, 31 July 1931.

8 *Daily Sketch*, 25 July 1931.

9 *Daily Mail*, 25 July 1931.

10 *Bournemouth Daily Echo*, 27 July 1931.

11 *Daily Sketch*, 25 & 27 July 1931.

12 *Daily Express*, 27 July 1931

13 *Daily Mirror*, 27 July 1931.

14 F.W. Memory's career is recalled in his memoirs F.W. Memory, *Being the Adventures of a Newspaperman* (Cassel & Co., London, 1932).

15 *Daily Mail*, 25 July 1931.

16 *Evening Herald* (Dublin), 22 June & 27 July 1931.

17 *Daily Express*, 28 July 1931

18 *Daily Sketch*, 28 July 1931.

19 The King's Proctor was an officer of the court whose responsibilities included ensuring that there was no collusion between the divorcing parties.

20 *Daily Sketch*, 30 July 1931.

21 *Daily Mail*, 27 July 1931.

22 *Daily Mail*, 31 July 1931.

23 Percy Savage, *Savage of Scotland Yard* (Hutchinson, London, 1934,) pp 53-8.

24 *Fabian of the Yard* was first broadcast on BBC TV on 13 November 1954 and ran for thirty-six episodes.

25 Peter Deeley & Christopher Walker, *Murder in the Fourth Estate* (Victor Gollancz, London, 1971), p. 113.

26 Robert Bartlet, *Surrey Constabulary* (Open University, 2012)

27 For a full account of this debacle see Laura Thompson, *Agatha Christie: An English Mystery* (Headline Publishing, London, 2007), pp 186-258.

28 An account of the Rougier case can be found on a variety of websites.

29 *The Scotsman*, 10 & 12 January 1931.

30 *Daily Sketch*, 29 July 1931.

31 *Bournemouth Daily Echo,* 29 July 1931.

32 *Bournemouth Daily Echo,* 31 July 1931.

33 *Daily Mail & Daily Sketch*, 29 July 1931.

34 *Bournemouth Daily Echo* and numerous other papers, 28 July 1931.

Chapter 14

1 *Daily Sketch*, 28 July 1931.

2 Letter from Ford, Lloyd, Bartlett & Mitchelmore, 29 July 1931. 631/1/Box 14.

3 *Daily Express*, 28 July 1931.

4 Letter from Ford, Lloyd, Bartlett & Mitchelmore, 29 July 1931. 631/1/Box 14.

5 Letter from Ford, Lloyd, Bartlett & Mitchelmore, 24 July 1931. 631/1/Box 14.

6 Letter from W.J. Francis, 27 July 1931. 631/1/Box 14.

7 Letters from W.J. Francis, 30 July & 4 August 1931. 631/1/Box 14.

8 Notes in Surrey Police Files make it clear that they had been unable to arrange an interview with Frances until 1 July, by which time it was believed that she had already popped down to spend a weekend in Eastbourne.

9 *Bournemouth Daily Echo* and numerous others, 30 July 1931.

10 *Daily Sketch*, 1 August 1931.

11 *Daily Sketch*, 1 August 1931.

12 *Daily Mail*, 1 August 1931.

Chapter 15

1 Although Milmoe's statement was not made until 6 August, it is clear that the Dublin Police had been making efforts to trace him for several days before that, having heard reports that he had told other people about the man he claimed to have seen. The *Daily Express* is among the papers reporting as early as 29 July 1931 that a Dublin man had recognised the description of the sender of the telegram as being a man he had met in the street.

2 Report of Superintendent Strules, 29 July 1931. Surrey Police Files.

3 Report of James Stowell, 29 July 1931. Surrey Police Files.

4 Report of Charles Allum, 31 July 1931. Surrey Police Files.

5   Letter and news clipping dated August 1931. Surrey Police Files.
6   *Daily Sketch*, 1 August 1931.
7   *Daily Sketch*, 29 July 1931.
8   *Daily Sketch*, 31 July 1931.
9   *Bournemouth Daily Echo*, 4 August 1931.
10 *Daily Mail*, 31 July 1931.
11 *Daily Mail*, 1 August 1931.
12 *Bournemouth Daily Echo*, 6 August 1931.

Chapter 16

1   *Bournemouth Daily Echo*, 11 August 1931.
2   The account of proceedings given in this chapter has been compiled drawing
    on reports in *Dublin Evening Herald*, 11 & 12 August 1931, *Daily Express*, 12 & 13
    August 1931, *Daily Sketch*, 13 August 1931, *Daily Mail*, 12 & 13 August 1931, *Surrey
    Advertiser & County Times*, 15 August 1931, *Bournemouth Daily Echo*, 11 & 12 August
    1931, *The Times*, 12 August 1931 and 631/1/Box 14. The order in which the witnesses
    appeared is inferred from the majority viewpoint. It is impossible to state with
    definite certainty in which order the witnesses were called, or exactly when the
    coroner made his various remarks, because neither the notes in the coroner's file, or
    the any of the press reports includes a complete record of what questions were asked
    and what the responses were. Nor does any single account, including the coroner's
    notes, include all the witnesses.
3   Mr W.J. Francis was the Deputy Coroner, but for simplicity he has been referred to
    throughout this book as the coroner.
4   This would not now be the recommended treatment in a case of strychnine poisoning.

Chapter 17

1   *The Times*, 12 August 1931.
2   *Bournemouth Daily Echo*, 12 August 1931.
3   *Evening News*, 12 August 1931.
4   *Evening News*, 12 August 1931.
5   *Daily Sketch*, 13 August 1931.
6   Letter from John Henry Ryffel, 12 August 1931. 631/1/Box 14.
7   Letter from L.J.A. Schulty, 12 August 1931. 631/1/Box 14.
8   Letter from W.J. Francis, 13 August 1931. 631/1/Box 14.
9   Letter from F. Pecks, 13 August 1931. 631/1/Box 14.
10 Undated letter from S. Rickett. 631/1/Box 14.
11 Ethel Peel, *Recollections of Lady Georgianna Peel* (John Lane, Bodley Head, London, 1920),
    pp 61-2.
12 Nova Scotia Department of Education – Information on the Background to Hunting,
    Farming & Market Gardening.
13 This letter, together with the others mentioned in this chapter, can all be found in
    Surrey Police Files.
14 Statement of Nicholas Bolger, 21 August 1931. Surrey Police Files.
15 Report of Superintendent Minter, 20 August 1931. Surrey Police Files.
16 Report of Albert William Pharo, 5 August 1931. Surrey Police Files.
17 Report of Albert William Pharo, 8 August 1931. Surrey Police Files. For some years an
    anomalous situation existed in which numerous Irishmen were fighting in the British

Army, even as their countrymen were waging a campaign for Independence from the British government. The Connaught Rangers Mutiny, which took place in India in 1920, was provoked by the alleged treatment of the servicemen's families by the British during the struggle for Irish independence. The treatment of the Connaught Mutineers was bitterly resented in Ireland – a country which had lost a greater proportion of its population fighting on the British side in the Great War than had the English, Scots, or Welsh. The mutineers were tried in a military court, presided over by Major General Sir G. de St Barrow and the episode had no connection to Sir William Chevis's career. For a full account of the mutiny see Anthony Babington, *The Devil to Pay: The Mutiny of the Connaught Rangers* (Leo Cooper, London, 1991).

18 Report of James Stovell, 6 October 1931. Surrey Police Files.

19 Report of Detective Sergeant Doddy, 8 August 1931. Surrey Police Files.

20 *Evening News*, 22 June 1931.

21 *Bournemouth Daily Echo*, 22 June 1931.

22 According to *Chambers Dictionary of Etymology*.

23 Jilly Cooper, *Class* (Eyre Methuen, London, 1979), p. 79.

24 The programme was *Punt PI – The Case of the Poisoned Partridge* first broadcast 3 September 2011.

25 Undated letter signed 'The Bulldog Detective'. Surrey Police Files.

26 *Daily Mail*, 27 July 1931.

27 Lawrence James, *Raj: The Making and Unmaking of British India* (Little, Brown & Co., London, 1997), p. 426.

28 For more about Ral and Singh see Lawrence James, *Raj: The Making and Unmaking of British India* (Little, Brown & Co., London, 1997). Details of Sir William Chevis's career which appear in this chapter derive from his printed Indian Civil Service records, generously loaned to the author by his grandson, Major William Chevis.

29 Lawrence James, *Raj: The Making and Unmaking of British India* (Little, Brown & Co., London, 1997), pp 473–5.

30 Details of the Punjab Courts and their governance given in this chapter derive from Day Krishna Kapur, *A History of the Development of the Judiciary in the Punjab 1884-1926* (Punjab Government Publications, 1928) unless otherwise stated.

31 Sir Bampfylde Fuller, *Fullers Empire of India* (Sir Isaac Pitman & Sons, London, 1913), pp 375–6.

32 Day Krishna Kapur, *A History of the Development of the Judiciary in the Punjab 1884-1926* (Punjab Government Publications, 1928), p. 19.

33 Day Krishna Kapur, *A History of the Development of the Judiciary in the Punjab 1884-1926* (Punjab Government Publications, 1928), p. 16.

34 Lawrence James, *Raj: The Making and Unmaking of British India* (Little, Brown & Co., London, 1997), p. 436.

35 Day Krishna Kapur, *A History of the Development of the Judiciary in the Punjab 1884-1926* (Punjab Government Publications, 1928), p. 41.

36 Major William Chevis was speaking to the author about his family in 2012.

37 For more information see the official website of Trinity College Dublin.

38 All references for Hartigan's mentioned in this chapter can be found by searching the index of the relevant body, *The Times*, or *The Times of India* for Hartigan.

39 *Daily Sketch*, 31 July 1931.

40 Notes of Geoffrey Nicholson, 9 August 1931. Surrey Police Files.

Chapter 18

1 Report of Albert William Pharo, 5 August 1931. Surrey Police Files.

2 Statement of Peter Hugh de Havilland, 16 August 1931. Surrey Police Files.

3 Statement of Peter Hugh de Havilland, 16 August 1931 and statement of Jack Llewellyn Gwynn-Jones, 10 August 1931. Surrey Police Files.

4 Undated report of an interview between Frances Howard Chevis and Geoffrey Nicholson which took place on 15 September 1931. Surrey Police Files.

5 Undated report of an interview between Frances Howard Chevis and Geoffrey Nicholson which took place on 15 September 1931. Surrey Police Files.

6 Undated letter from Frances Howard Chevis, which by inference from the contents was written on 12 August 1931. Surrey Police Files.

7 *Cadaver in Camberley, Demise in Deepcut* by Ken Clarke is the privately published booklet by a local historian which makes this suggestion.

8 Undated report of an interview between Frances Howard Chevis and Geoffrey Nicholson which took place on 15 September 1931. Surrey Police Files.

9 Statement of Hugh Bruce Campbell, 1 September 1931. Surrey Police Files.

10 Statement of Alfred Bingham, 1 September 1931. Surrey Police Files.

11 Undated notes. Surrey Police Files.

12 List of queries arising from case conference held 24 August 1931. Surrey Police Files. The author has not undertaken the research needed in order to definitely confirm whether or not Benjamin Fieldhouse was a nephew of George T.T. Jackson, although it is certainly possible, as a Kate Jackson married a Henry Fieldhouse in 1894 and one of Trev Jackson's sisters was called Kate.

13 Report of Superintendent Claydon, 16 August 1931. Surrey Police Files.

14 Notes and documents made and received by Bournemouth Police during August 1931. Surrey Police Files.

15 Letter from Amelia Margaret Jackson, 28 August 1931. Surrey Police Files.

16 Statement of Amelia Margaret Jackson, 30 August 1931. Surrey Police Files.

17 Report from Vine Street police station, 12 August 1931 and statement of Herbert Stanley Tosh, 12 August 1931. Surrey Police Files.

18 An infection and inflammation of the fallopian tubes which can be fatal.

19 Report of Superintendent Minter, 20 August 1931. Surrey Police Files.

20 Major Jackson's full service record has not survived. Sections of his service can be pieced together from *The Royal Army Veterinary Corps Journal* and *The Veterinary Record* and these indicate that he returned from a period of duty in India in August 1907, though there is no indication of how long he had been stationed there. The fact of being stationed somewhere in India is very far from identifying him with an officer stationed in Lahore. There were numerous men called Jackson serving in the British Army during this period, including several who served in the RAVC.

21 Statement of Alexander Ewan Fraser, 14 August 1931. Surrey Police Files.

22 Letters from Harry J. Jennings, 26, 27 & 28 August 1931. Surrey Police Files.

23 The Crumbles – a stretch of coastline near Eastbourne – had achieved a degree of notoriety after being associated with two notorious murders: of Irene Munro in 1920 and Emily Kaye in 1924. The perpetrators had been caught and executed in both cases.

24 Report of Superintendent Claydon, 16 August 1931. Surrey Police Files.

25 *Bournemouth Daily Echo*, 30 November 1934.

26 These accounts appear in the *Thames Valley Times*, 24 June 1931 and *Eastbourne Chronicle*, 29 June 1931 and are representative of the kind of stories recounted week after week in regional newspapers of the period.

27 For a particularly comprehensive summary of the dangers on Britain's roads in the early 1930s see Juliet Gardiner, *The Thirties* (Harper Collins, London, 2010) pp 678-685.

28 Though not the highest ever number – the worst year on record being 1941 when there were in excess of 9,000 deaths on Britain's road, partly as a result of accidents occurring during the Blackout.

29 Details of Major Jackson's death have been derived from his death certificate, *Bournemouth Times,* 30 November 1934 and *Bournemouth Daily Echo,* 24 & 27 November 1934. (Those interested in such matters may also wish to note that Aldershot beat Boscombe 4-0 – the attendance was 5,111.)

30 *Journal of the Royal Army Veterinary Corps* Vol.VI No.2, p. 82.

31 *Sunday Graphic,* 6 July 1933.

Chapter 19

1 Statements of Nicholas Bolger and Ellen Yeomans, 23 June 1931 and statement of William Frank Noyes, 11 August 1931. 631/1/Box 14.

2 Conversation between the author and Patricia Beamish in 2012. Mrs Beamish confirmed that Nicholas Bolger continued to serve in the army until demobbed in 1945, by which time he had achieved the rank of sergeant. He had no family left in Ireland and never returned there – eventually even losing all but the faintest trace of his accent.

3 Undated notes of James Stovell. Surrey Police Files.

4 Undated report of an interview between Frances Howard Chevis and Geoffrey Nicholson which took place on 15 September 1931. Surrey Police Files.

5 Notes of Geoffrey Nicholson, 9 August 1931. Surrey Police Files.

6 Fragment of a letter dated 24 April 1931 and undated statement of Evelyn Isobel MacLennan. Surrey Police Files.

7 Queries arising from Chief Constable's conference, 24 August 1931. Surrey Police Files.

8 Undated report of an interview between Frances Howard Chevis and Geoffrey Nicholson which took place on 15 September 1931. Surrey Police Files.

9 Undated report of an interview between Frances Howard Chevis and Geoffrey Nicholson which took place on 15 September 1931 and queries arising from the Chief Constable's conference, 24 August 1931. Surrey Police Files.

10 Details of the surveillance operation given in this chapter derive from reports of George Hector, 26, 27, 28, 29 & 30 August 1931. Surrey Police Files.

11 Anonymous letter, 26 July 1931. Surrey Police Files.

12 Undated notes of an interview with William James Christian Chevis. Surrey Police Files.

13 There are numerous references to this person in the papers which covered the story. That she was a member of Frances's household can be inferred from the fact that she sometimes answered the front door to reporters, which Frances's personal friends would not have been likely to do.

14 Report of Superintendent Minter, 25 August 1931. Surrey Police Files.

15 For a discussion on just how widespread drug taking may have been in Society circles see D.J. Taylor, *Bright Young People, The Rise and Fall of a Generation: 1918-1940.* (Vintage Books, London, 2008), pp 110-12.

Chapter 20

1 See the history of Surrey Police on www.surreypolice.co.uk for details of Geoffrey Nicholson's career.

2 Letter from William Henry Bird, 13 August 1931. Surrey Police Files.

3 Mary Ann Cotton, sometimes referred to as Britain's first serial killer and Herbert Rowse Armstrong, convicted in 1872 and 1922 respectively are cases in point.

4 Undated letter from Frances Howard Chevis. Surrey Police Files.

5 Undated letter from Frances Howard Chevis, by inference written on 12 August 1931. Surrey Police Files.

6 Undated report of James Stovell, by inference written in August 1931. Surrey Police Files.

7 Undated report of an interview between Frances Howard Chevis and Geoffrey Nicholson which took place on 15 September 1931 and queries arising from the Chief Constable's conference, 24 August 1931. Surrey Police Files.

Chapter 21

1 Letter from Cullen Mather, 25 June 1931. 631/1/Box 14.

2 It has been difficult to establish very much about Cullen Mather, whose letter headings and correspondence make it clear that he normally lived and worked in various parts of Asia and was only in England on a visit during the summer of 1931.

3 Letter from Cullen Mather, 25 June 1931. 631/1/Box 14.

4 Report from Scotland Yard, 24 July 1931. Surrey Police Files.

5 Note by Deputy Chief Constable Kenward attached to a report from Scotland Yard dated 24 July 1931. Surrey Police Files.

6 *Bournemouth Daily Echo*, 31 July 1931.

7 Letter from William Henry Bird, 13 August 1931. Surrey Police Files.

8 Note made by Geoffrey Nicholson, 9 August 1931. Surrey Police Files.

9 Letter from John Henry Ryffel, 14 July 1931. 631/1/Box 14.

10 In 2012 first responders are advised against adopting this course of action.

11 Deposition of Frederick Downs, 11 August 1931. 631/1/Box 14.

12 Undated notes by James Stovell. Surrey Police Files.

13 Letter from John Henry Ryffel, 14 July 1931. 631/1 Box 14.

14 Undated report of John Henry Ryffel regarding experiments undertaken on 31 August 1931. Surrey Police Files.

15 Report by John Henry Ryffel, 20 July 1931. 631/1/Box 14.

16 Letter from John Henry Ryffel, 22 September 1931. Surrey Police Files.

17 Report by James Stovell, 6 October 1931. Surrey Police Files.

18 J. McGregor Robertson, *The Household Physician Vol. II* (1900 edition) p. 545. The book went into numerous editions throughout the 1890s and 1900s.

19 *The Times*, 8 June 1935.

20 *The Times*, 26 March 1932.

21 *The Times*, 23 December 1938 & 3 September 1940.

22 Between 1959 and 1969 *The Times* reported strychnine-related deaths among foxhounds in Devon, Dorset, Hampshire, Yorkshire and East Anglia.

23 *The Times*, 22 March 1982, 14 April 1982 & 20 April 1982.

24 *The Times*, 17 February 1919.

25 *The Times*, 1 May 1908 & 30 November 1908.

26 *The Times*, 17 April 1946.

27 *The Times*, 14 April 1914.

28 *The Times*, lo March 1911.

29 *The Times*, 24 February 1911.

30 Letter from Cullen Mather, 27 December 1931. Surrey Police Files.

31   Letter from Arthur de C. Sowerby, December 1931. Surrey Police Files.

32   *China Journal of Science and Arts* Vol. IV 1926 published by *North China Daily News & Herald Inc.* Shanghai.

33   Letter from William Henry Bird, 19 January 1932. Surrey Police Files.

Chapter 22

1   *Daily Express*, 11 January 1932.

2   Hansard 12 April 1932.

3   Report of James Stovell, 6 October 1931. Surrey Police Files.

4   Letter from J.D. La Touche, 21 December 1931. Surrey Police Files.

5   Frances sailed First Class aboard SS *Viceroy of India* on 7 November 1931, Ships' Passenger Lists. National Archives.

6   Letter from Sir William Chevis, 5 December 1931. Surrey Police Files.

7   Letters from William James Christian Chevis, 19 & 21 July 1932 and from James Stovell, 20 July 1932. Surrey Police Files.

8   William and Amy Chevis's death and burial records derive from Bournemouth Cemetaries and General Register Office of England records of Deaths. The garden party is reported in *The Times of India*, 11 April 1922.

9   Information regarding *Isobel's* derives principally from various issues of *The Tatler*. Isobel was accorded the honour of a full page portrait in the 14 October 1925 edition.

10   *Daily Express* & *Daily Mirror*, 1 February 1934.

11   The couple sailed on the SS *Berengaria*. Ships' Passenger Lists, National Archives.

12   *Daily Mirror*, 12 December 1934.

13   Frances's grandson, Charles Jackson, recalled this episode for the benefit of the author in 2012. On hearing the news of the war via the wireless, Frances is said to have remained completely calm – her initial words are recalled as: 'Right. We're going home.'

14   Details of deaths and marriages within this chapter derive from General Register Office of England records of Marriages and Deaths, and various announcements in *The Times*.

Chapter 23

1   It has been conjectured that Evelyn Foster's death was the result of accident or suicide. Julia Wallace was found battered to death.

2   Lord Desart speaking during the 1921 debate in the House of Lords.

3   Daphne du Maurier, *Rebecca* (Victor Gollancz, London, 1938) Chapter 18.

4   For Daphne du Maurier's private life, see Margaret Forster, *Daphne du Maurier* (Chatto & Windus, London, 1993).

5   Unsigned, undated notes. Surrey Police Files.

Chapter 24

1   Although the manifestation of 'false symptoms', 'sympathy pains' etc. is a well attested phenomena, relatively little is know about these conditions even today. The involuntary symptoms are very real to the sufferer and often distressing, but no organic cause can be found. The most widely publicised cases involve large numbers of people, usually associated with the same institution, but individual cases include people who have suffered symptoms of a family member or close friend's illness, while not medically suffering from the condition themselves. Sometimes known as Hysterical Contagion or Mass Psychogenic Illness.

2 The lethal dose is generally accepted as around 32mg, but people have been known to succumb to as little as 5mg.

3 *Daily Sketch*, 28 July 1931.

4 Information provided to the author in 2012 by Cartmel Valley Game Suppliers.

5 MEPO 3/791 Execution of Mrs Ethel Lillie Major for murder of her husband. National Archives.

6 Statement of Edmund Frederick Bindloss, 23 June 1931. 631/1/Box 14.

7 A perfect example of the 1930s doctor's willingness to undertake unnecessary house calls can be found in Arthur Ransome's novel *The Picts & the Martyrs*, when Miss Turner requests a call from the doctor not, as her niece explains to other characters, because the old lady is ill, but because 'she always likes to have the doctor hanging about'. The doctor duly checked his patient over and recommended a lie down after lunch. Arthur Ransome, *The Picts & the Martyrs* (Jonathan Cape, London, 1943), pp 76-86. Doctors were willing to dance attendance on fussy old ladies, providing the old ladies were able to pay.

8 Undated notes by Geoffrey Nicholson. Surrey Police Files.

9 D.J. Taylor, *Bright Young People: The Rise & Fall of a Generation* (Chatto & Windus, London, 2007), p. 4.

10 Juliet Gardner, *The Thirties: An Intimate History* (Harper Press, London, 2010), p. 623.

11 Statement of Peter Hugh de Havilland, 16 August 1931. Surrey Police Files.

12 The house in question was Beaumont, Dittons Road, where Frances is listed as a resident in Eastbourne directories from 1945–51.

13 This information was provided to the author in 2012 by Charles Jackson, grandson of Frances.

14 Ivy Blanche Thorne was born in Secunderbad, India in 1890, according to baptismal records and the 1911 Census for England and Wales.

15 Ships' Passenger Lists. National Archives.

16 Details of the Garthwaite family derive from General Register Office of England records of Births & Marriages, *Burke's Peerage and Baronetage*, *Who Was Who 1951-60*, *Glasgow Herald*, 5 February 1937, *Palm Beach Daily News*, 31 January 1964 and a variety of incidental newspapers.

17 Undated notes by Geoffrey Nicholson. Surrey Police Files.

18 The possibility that Frances was expecting a child is mentioned in various police notes and the month of estimated conception and likelihood of a miscarriage are noted in queries arising from Chief Constable's Conference, 24 August 1931. Surrey Police Files.

19 Report of Albert William Pharo, 25 August 1931. Surrey Police Files.

20 These memories were shared with the author by Charles Jackson, Frances's grandson, in 2012.

21 *The Times*, 22 February 1924.

22 Thanks to the film *The Poor Little Rich Girl* starring Mary Pickford, which was based on a Broadway play of the same name which had premiered in 1913.

23 Undated report of an interview between Frances Howard Chevis and Geoffrey Nicholson which took place on 15 September 1931. Surrey Police Files.

24 Prominent among them was Elizabeth Ponsonby, a contemporary of Frances and leading light of the 1920s and '30s London social scene, who became tragically and ruinously addicted to the party lifestyle. She died from alcohol poisoning in 1940.

25 Peter Hubert Jackson died of natural causes in 1965, leaving a widow and young family.

INDEX

ALSO BY THE SAME AUTHOR

Edwardian Murder: Ightham and the Morpeth Train Robbery

Caroline Luard was shot near Ightham in Kent in 1908. Within weeks her husband, a respectable Major-General, committed suicide. Two years later John Nisbet, a colliery cashier, was robbed and murdered on a train in Northumberland. Police arrested a man called John Dickman, who was subsequently executed. The conviction, however, relied on circumstantial evidence. In 1950 C.H. Norman, who acted as official shorthand writer at Dickman's trial, claimed that Dickman was framed for Nisbet's murder. Is it conceivable that John Dickman was guilty of both murders? Or was he framed, and unjustly executed? These true crimes bear all the hallmarks of traditional English period murder: steam trains, revolvers, an isolated summerhouse, retired army officers, parlour maids, as well as murder and love.

978 0 7524 4945 6

Poisonous Lies: The Croydon Arsenic Mystery

In suburban Croydon over a period of ten months during 1928-9, three members of the same family died suddenly. A complex police investigation followed, but no charges were ever brought and the mystery remains officially unsolved.

In the eighty years which followed, the finger of suspicion has been pointed at one member of the family after another: now, using the original police files and other contemporary documents, Diane Janes meticulously reconstructs these astonishing events and offers a new solution to an old murder mystery.

978 0 7524 5337 8